THE HENRY L.
STIMSON CENTER

THE IMPOSSIBLE MANDATE?
MILITARY PREPAREDNESS,
THE RESPONSIBILITY TO PROTECT
AND MODERN PEACE OPERATIONS

Victoria K. Holt and
Tobias C. Berkman

September 2006

The Henry L. Stimson Center
1111 19th Street, NW   12th Floor   Washington, DC 20036
phone: 202-223-5956   fax: 202-238-9604   www.stimson.org

TABLE OF CONTENTS

ACRONYMS

ACOTA	Africa Contingency Operations Training and Assistance
ACRI	African Crisis Response Initiative
ALNAP	Active Learning Network for Accountability and Performance in Humanitarian Action
AMIB	African Mission in Burundi
AMIS	African Union Mission in the Sudan
AO	Area of Operations
APC	Armored Personnel Carrier
ASEAN	Association of South East Asian Nations
ASF	African Standby Force (AU)
AU	African Union
BMATT	British Military Advisory and Training Team
CIMIC	Civil-Military Cooperation
CMO	Civil-Military Operations
CMTC	Combat Maneuver Training Center
COB	Civilians on the Battlefield
CPKO	Canadian Peacekeeping Operations
CRO	Crisis Response Operation
DDR	Disarmament, Demobilization and Reintegration
DDRRR	Disarmament, Demobilization, Repatriation, Resettlement and Reintegration
DES-PADS	(Office of) Deputy Executive Secretary for Political Affairs, Defense, and Security (ECOWAS)
DEXES	Deployable Exercise Support
DoD	Department of Defense (United States)
DPKO	Department of Peacekeeping Operations (UN)
DRC	Democratic Republic of the Congo
DSRSG	Deputy Special Representative of the Secretary General
EASBRIG	Eastern Africa Standby Brigade
ECOMICI	ECOWAS Mission in Côte d'Ivoire
ECOMIL	ECOWAS Mission in Liberia
ECOMOG	ECOWAS Monitoring Group
ECOWAS	Economic Community of West African States
EDA	European Defense Agency
ESDP	European Security and Defense Policy
ESF	ECOWAS Standby Force
EU	European Union
EUFOR	European Union Force in Bosnia and Herzegovina
FARDC	Forces Armées de la Republic Democratic du Congo
FDLR	Forces Démocratiques de Libération du Rwanda

FEWER	Forum for Early Warning and Early Response
FM	Field Manual
FNI	Forces Nationalistes et Integrationnistes (DRC)
GoS	Government of Sudan
GPOI	Global Peace Operations Initiative
HNP	Haitian National Police
IAPTC	International Association of Peacekeeping Training Centers
IASC	Inter-Agency Standing Committee
ICG	International Crisis Group
ICISS	International Commission on Intervention and State Sovereignty
ICRC	International Committee of the Red Cross
IDP	Internally Displaced Person
IEMF	Interim Emergency Multinational Force
IFOR	Implementation Force (in Bosnia and Herzegovina)
IGAD	Intergovernmental Authority on Development
IRC	International Rescue Committee
IRIN	International Regional Information Network (UN)
ISAF	International Security Assistance Force
ISD	Institute for the Study of Diplomacy
ITS	Integrated Training Service (previously Training and Evaluation Service, or TES)
JMETL	Joint Mission-Essential Task List
JRTC	Joint Readiness Training Center
JTF	Joint Task Force
JWP	Joint Warfare Publication (UK)
KAIPTC	Kofi Annan International Peacekeeping Training Center
KFOR	Kosovo Force
MAGTF	Marine Air Ground Task Force
MCDP	Marine Corps Doctrinal Publication (US)
MIFH	Multinational Interim Force for Haiti
MILOBS	Military Observers
MINURSO	United Nations Mission for the Referendum in Western Sahara (Mission des Nations Unies Pour l'Organisation d'un Référendum au Sahara Occidental)
MINUSTAH	United Nations Stabilization Mission in Haiti (Mission des Nations Unies pour la Stabilisation en Haiti)
MLC	Mouvement pour la Libération du Congo
MNF	Multi-National Force
MONUC	United Nations Organization Mission in the Democratic Republic of the Congo (Mission des Nations Unies en République Démocratique du Congo)
MOOTW	Military Operations Other Than War

MOU	Memorandum of Understanding
MSC	Mediation and Security Council (ECOWAS)
MSF	Médecins sans Frontières (Doctors without Borders)
NATO	North Atlantic Treaty Organization
NEO	Non-Combatant Evacuation Operations
NGO	Non-Governmental Organization
NRF	NATO Response Force
NTC	National Training Center
OAS	Organization of American States
OCHA	Office for the Coordination of Humanitarian Affairs (UN)
OHCHR	Office of the High Commissioner for Human Rights (UN)
ONUB	United Nations Operation in Burundi (Opération des Nations Unies au Burundi)
OSCE	Organization of Security and Cooperation in Europe
PACOM	Pacific Command
PAE	Pacific Architects and Engineers
PKO	Peacekeeping Operation
PO	Peace Operation
POCI	Program of Correspondence Instruction (UN)
POI	Program of Instruction
PRT	Provincial Reconstruction Team
PSC	Peace and Security Council (AU)
PSF	Peace Support Force
PSO	Peace Support Operations
QDR	Quadrennial Defense Review
R2P	Responsibility to Protect
RCD	Rassemblement Congolais pour la Démocratie
RECAMP	Reinforcement of African Peace-keeping Capacities (Renforcement des Capacites Africaines au Maintien la Paix)
RNLA	Royal Netherlands Army
ROE	Rules of Engagement
RPF	Rwandan Patriotic Front
RRF	Rapid Reaction Force
RUF	Revolutionary United Front (Sierra Leone)
SADC	Southern African Development Community
SFOR	Stabilization Force (in Bosnia and Herzegovina)
SG	Secretary General
SGTM	Standard Generic Training Module
SHIRBRIG	Stand-by High Readiness Brigade
SOFA	Status of Forces Agreement
SRSG	Special Representative of the Secretary General
SSTR	Stability, Security, Transition and Reconstruction
STM	Standardized Training Module

TCC	Troop Contributing Country
TEPSO	Training and Education for Peace Support Operations (NATO)
TES	Training and Evaluation Service (now Integrated Training Service, ITS)
TOR	Terms of Reference
TTP	Tactics, Techniques, and Procedures
UJTL	Universal Joint Task List
UK	United Kingdom
UN	United Nations
UNAMA	United Nations Assistance Mission in Afghanistan
UNAMIR	United Nations Assistance Mission for Rwanda
UNAMSIL	United Nations Mission in Sierra Leone
UNFICYP	United Nations Peacekeeping Force in Cyprus
UNHCR	United Nations High Commissioner for Refugees
UNICEF	United Nations Children's Fund
UNITAR	United Nations Institute for Training and Research
UNMEE	United Nations Mission in Ethiopia and Eritrea
UNMIL	United Nations Mission in Liberia
UNMIS	United Nations Mission in Sudan
UNMISET	United Nations Mission of Support in East Timor
UNOCI	United Nations Operation in Côte d'Ivoire
UNPROFOR	United Nations Protection Force
UNSAS	United Nations Stand-by Arrangements System
UNSC	UN Security Council
UNSCR	United Nations Security Council Resolution
UNTAET	United Nations Transitional Administration in East Timor
UPC	Union of Congolese Patriots (Union des Patriotes Congolais)
UPDF	Uganda People's Defense Force
URABATT	Uruguayan Battalion (of MONUC)
US	United States
USAREUR	United States Army Europe

PREFACE

It is with great pleasure that I present a new Stimson Center publication, *The Impossible Mandate? Military Preparedness, the Responsibility to Protect and Modern Peace Operations,* by Victoria Holt and Tobias Berkman. This is an important study that provides new insight and policy ideas on an evolving concept in the peace operations world, the responsibility to protect. R2P, as it is known by the cognescenti, is a phrase that derives from a Canadian-led exercise in 2001, aimed at clarifying the relationship between state sovereignty and the international community's ability to respond to genocide and mass violence against civilians.

The particular focus of Tori Holt and Toby Berkman is moving from the lofty rhetoric of civilian protection to the practical issues for a military role, such as developing doctrine and training for forces deployed in peace operations. They explain why R2P, for all its compelling logic, actually falls through the cracks of planning and doctrine for peacekeeping missions, and offer some concrete suggestions for preventing such lacunae in the international community's responses to conflict. They also provide a useful guide to the range of concepts associated with civilian protection, and important insight into how military culture and practice translate the concept into actionable guidance to troops in the field. This book is a treasure trove of deep research about how peace operations actually work, and the ways national and international actors grapple with the complex and compelling challenge of civilian protection.

This new study is the latest contribution of our *Future of Peace Operations* program. The FOPO team has examined a wide range of topics relating to peace operations, and has been an important facilitator of communication between and among governments, NGOs, and the military and humanitarian communities working to bring peace and stability to post-conflict societies. We hope you will find this book of value, and encourage you to examine the larger body of work, at www.stimson.org/fopo.

This book could not have been produced without the generous support of the Human Security Program, Foreign Affairs and International Trade Canada, which sponsored the original research and work that led to this book.

Sincerely,

Ellen Laipson

Ellen Laipson

ACKNOWLEDGEMENTS

This book benefited from the support of many individuals and organizations. First and foremost, I want to thank the Human Security Program, Foreign Affairs and International Trade Canada, for their generous support to our project and to the development of this study. In particular, I wish to thank Don Hubert, Heidi Hulan, Elissa Golberg, Ingrid Harder and Stephanie Power—they are colleagues of the highest order, rich with insights, expertise and encouragement.

Much of this research is based on interviews and discussion with individuals who gave generously of their time and wisdom. Meetings were usually conducted on a not-for-attribution basis, so I hope that those unnamed here accept my unprinted but sincere thanks. In particular, I appreciate those within the United Nations and its agencies—especially the Department of Peacekeeping Operations and the Office for the Coordination of Humanitarian Affairs, as well as serving in missions in the field—who offered useful information, comments and viewpoints. I would also like to thank those within NATO, the European Union, the African Union and the Economic Community of West African States who contributed to our knowledge of modern operations and concepts. Many within the non-governmental community, research institutes, and civilian and military agencies further provided invaluable wisdom and data.

Special thanks are deserved by a few people who gave substantial time and knowledge, offered criticism and corrections to drafts, or contributed thinking and laughter (as appropriate) to this enterprise: Michael Bailey, Mark Bowden, Roberta Cohen, Timothy Cornett, Anthony Craig, Gareth Derrick, William Flavin, Peter Gantz, Peter Haindl, Stephen Henthorne, Paul Keating, Don Kraus, Iain Levine, Mark Malan, Francesca Marotta, Jim Terrie, John Otte, Richard Roy, Michael Larmas Smith, Pierre Trudel and Taylor Seybolt. Guy Abbate, Karl Farris and Bill Flavin kindly let me try these ideas out on the US and foreign military officers in their peacekeeping courses. Added recognition goes to Victoria Wheeler and Adele Harmer of the Humanitarian Policy Group at the Overseas Development Institute, who offered expertise and assistance in thinking about humanitarian action and concepts of protection. This book includes ideas first published in their HPG Research Report by the Overseas Development Institute in 2005. While this study is stronger for these contributions, I take responsibility for any errors.

My colleagues at The Henry L. Stimson Center enhanced this work substantially. My co-author, former Stimson research associate Toby Berkman, began this project with me in 2004 and contributed richly to its organization and writing. He proved to be a fine colleague with a journalist's talent for finding and deciphering data, as well as a passion for understanding difficult subjects such as Security Council resolutions and the conflict in the Democratic Republic of the Congo. Stimson research associate Joshua Smith skillfully picked up the project after his departure and helped move the study into a final manuscript, doing so with knowledge, humor, and endless persistence, for which I am very grateful.

This book is a project of the *Future of Peace Operations* program at the Center. I thank my co-director, Bill Durch, for his endless insights during a productive and engaging collaboration since 2001, and my Stimson colleagues Ellen Laipson and Cheryl Ramp, for their abiding interest in this work. Thanks also go to research staff Katherine Andrews and Alix Boucher, who offered insightful comments and editing. Research, fact-checking and proof-reading were also provided by Daniel Levine, Michael Broache, and Brandon Hunt. Jane Dorsey made the production possible, with patience that is appreciated.

Finally, I would like to thank Sean Marrett, for his ever-lively mind and enduring support.

Victoria K. Holt
Washington, DC

—1—
INTRODUCTION

In June 2004 the African Union (AU) announced plans to deploy 60 to 80 military observers to monitor a ceasefire agreement in Darfur, Sudan, accompanied by a 300-man protection force. Worldwide, many welcomed this news, especially those who thought the AU Mission in Sudan (AMIS) would help to protect civilians.

Days before Rwandan troops were to arrive in Darfur in August 2004, a BBC journalist interviewed the Rwandan Foreign Minister Charles Murigande about the mission. "If [troops] come across militias attacking civilians...wouldn't they have a moral duty to protect the civilians under attack?" the journalist asked.

"Yes, they would have a moral duty," Murigande responded. The journalist pressed, asking if they would protect the civilians and fire on the militia. "I am not sure... Let's allow them to go there to play out their mission," Murigande said, given "their mandate."[1]

The mandate for AMIS initially authorized the force to protect only the monitors of the ceasefire—not the Sudanese civilians. By late 2004, however, the AU mandate was expanded to include the protection of civilians whom AMIS forces "encounter under imminent threat and in the immediate vicinity, within resources and capability, it being understood that the protection of the civilian population is the responsibility of the government of Sudan."[2]

This broader language provided little clarity to the AU forces, however. How much protection could a small, fledgling military deployment offer "within resources and capability" in a region the size of France?[3] How could it offer meaningful protection to the population at large when it was instructed to focus only on those "under imminent threat" and "in the immediate vicinity?" A more fundamental challenge for AMIS was that the Government of Sudan (GoS) remained "responsible" for "the protection of the civilian population," despite the government's role in aiding and abetting the

---

[1] Rwandan Foreign Minister Charles Murigande, interview with the BBC World Service Newshour News, broadcast over WAMU Radio, 13 August 2004, Washington, DC.

[2] AU Peace and Security Council (PSC), Communiqué, PSC/PR/Comm. (XVII), 20 October 2004, para. 2.

[3] AMIS's authorized force level expanded from an initial deployment of 300 to 7,731 personnel by March 2006.

ongoing violence. In short, the AU was not supposed to pick a fight with the Sudanese authorities.

In light of these difficulties, it is perhaps understandable that the Rwandan Foreign Minister was not "sure" about the role of his nation's troops in quelling the crisis. His hedge reveals the difficult nature of such military interventions: well-intentioned or not, the deploying troops may not have a clear understanding of how their mission intends to provide, or may be unprepared to provide, physical protection to civilians facing egregious abuses. The crisis in Darfur—in which nearly two million people have been displaced and 400,000 killed—places certain questions for the international community in stark relief: What should be done? What can be done? How, exactly, can military forces best be used to protect civilians from extreme violence?

*   *   *

This inquiry builds on the work of the International Commission on Intervention and State Sovereignty (ICISS) and its December 2001 report, *The Responsibility to Protect.*[4] The ICISS report sought to square international concern for the victims of egregious violence, such as genocide, ethnic cleansing, and mass killing, with the long-standing norm of non-intervention in the internal affairs of sovereign states. The basic argument of the ICISS report was both elegant and groundbreaking: sovereignty, by definition, implies responsibility for the welfare of one's own citizens.[5] When a state abrogates this responsibility by failing to prevent genocide, ethnic cleansing, or mass killing, the responsibility falls on the international community. The basis for action by the international community, therefore, should not be understood as a *"right* of humanitarian intervention," but rather as a *"responsibility* to protect" civilians facing mass violence.

The Commission report successfully introduced a broad audience to the idea of civilian protection, which has grown in acceptance and parlance in the nearly five years since the report's publication. Indeed, adoption of the "responsibility to protect" as a framework for intervention is being considered by governments and international organizations, and was met with general endorsement at the United Nations (UN) World Summit in September 2005.

---

[4] International Commission on Intervention and State Sovereignty, *The Responsibility to Protect* (Ottawa: International Development Research Centre, December 2001).
[5] The Commission drew in part upon the work of others who had begun to articulate the notion of "sovereignty as responsibility" throughout the 1990s. Prominent examples include: Francis M. Deng, *Protecting the Dispossessed: A Challenge for the International Community* (Washington, DC: The Brookings Institution, 1993); Roberta Cohen and Francis M. Deng, *Masses in Flight:The Global Crisis of Internal Displacement* (Washington, DC: The Brookings Institution, 1998).

The goal of this study is to stimulate discussion on how to "operationalize" the "responsibility to protect" and on how to make UN mandates requiring peacekeepers to "protect civilians" more achievable. If there is, indeed, an international "responsibility to protect," then identifying *when* this responsibility should be upheld is only part of the question. As this idea moves forward in policy circles, is capacity being developed to keep up? How are military forces preparing to uphold a "responsibility to protect" civilians from mass violence and killing?

PEACE OPERATIONS AND CIVILIAN PROTECTION

A premise of this study is that a military intervention designed expressly to protect civilians from mass killing is fundamentally different from a peace operation mandated to protect civilians from much lesser risks. Such peace operations typically balance their civilian protection tasks with numerous other goals, such as establishing long-term peace and security. While much in the *Responsibility to Protect* report addresses conflict prevention, peace operations, and peacebuilding efforts, the report's clear call for intervention in specific cases of mass violence sets such interventions apart from traditional peacekeeping missions.

> *A military intervention designed to protect civilians from mass killing is fundamentally different from a peace operation mandated to protect civilians from much lesser risks.*

Thus, this study distinguishes between missions designed to halt mass killing and peace operations with civilian protection mandates. The former type of mission crosses the sovereignty threshold identified by *The Responsibility to Protect*, where a desire for consent, impartiality, and limited use of force take a back seat to the immediate goal of saving lives. Such missions are unlikely to be led by the United Nations. The latter type of mission exists today in numerous incarnations, including UN operations in Haiti and the Democratic Republic of the Congo (DRC), and the AU operation in Darfur.

The two types of missions are similar, of course—both aim to save lives. Civilian protection, however, has historically been an *implied* goal of a peace operation; the primary goals have usually been political in nature. UN peacekeeping missions traditionally have deployed to support negotiated ceasefires and to prevent a return to interstate warfare, for example. The protection of civilians was thus a likely and important result of such activities rather than their direct or immediate goal. More recently, multidimensional peace operations have sought to support stability in countries emerging from civil war, so that political reconciliation can take place and governance reform efforts can proceed safely. Even robust "peace enforcement" missions that deploy during ongoing conflict, such as the NATO-led forces and international coalitions in Bosnia-Herzegovina and the US-led multinational force in Haiti, have been more about "compelling compliance" with political agreements than protecting people.[6]

Inevitably, the presence of internationally mandated forces in conflict zones has led to calls for their safeguarding civilian lives and supporting humanitarian efforts directly. Such calls often compete with political imperatives, however. While peace operations' overarching goals have typically related to negotiations, peace agreements, ceasefires between opposing armies, governance, and statecraft, they have never been able to wholly ignore the security and well-being of the populations in their midst. Peace operations have thus straddled a troublesome and sometimes unstable divide between their protection- and political-oriented goals.

Box 1.1

WHAT IS PEACEKEEPING?

Peacekeeping is designed primarily to help support and sustain the end of wars, rather than to intervene directly to save civilian lives. The UN Department of Peacekeeping Operations' definition of peacekeeping, for example, demonstrates this approach:

> Peacekeeping is a way to help countries torn by conflict create conditions for sustainable peace. UN peacekeepers—soldiers and military officers, police and civilian personnel from many countries—monitor and observe peace processes that emerge in post-conflict situations and assist conflicting parties to implement the peace agreement they have signed. Such assistance comes in many forms, including promoting human security, confidence-building measures, power-sharing arrangements, electoral support, strengthening the rule of law, and economic and social development.

Source: UN Department of Peacekeeping Operations website, "Questions and Answers," 11 July 2006, www.un.org/depts/dpko/dpko/faq/q1.htm.

THE UNITED NATIONS ROLE

Beginning in 1999, the UN Security Council began to mention "the protection of civilians" in peacekeeping mandates, making explicit that which had long been

---

[6] Thomas G. Weiss, "The Humanitarian Impulse," in David M. Malone, ed., *The UN Security Council: From the Cold War to the 21st Century* (Boulder: Lynn Rienner, 2004), 46. NATO refers to the North Atlantic Treaty Organization.

expected of peacekeepers by the public at large. Since then, the Council has regularly referenced the protection of civilians "under imminent threat of physical violence" in mandates for UN-led peace operations authorized under Chapter VII of the UN Charter and used such language in authorizing missions led by other multinational organizations or coalitions.[7]

Despite this new mandate language, the peacekeeper's job in "protection" is often vague and undefined, particularly in the more challenging, non-permissive environments where mass killing is likely to occur.[8] Just as the international community has provided little guidance on how military forces should implement the "responsibility to protect," it has also offered little guidance to peacekeepers in violent, unstable regions on the "civilian protection" tasks expected of them.

COERCIVE PROTECTION OPERATIONS

If peace operations are not primarily designed to protect civilians, a different name is needed for missions that deploy in non-permissive environments with the *immediate goal* of saving civilians who are being killed *en masse*. Certainly, it is possible to imagine such a military intervention that looks very little like "peacekeeping." Halting violent actors in their tracks might require operations more akin to combat and entail coercion to prevent harm to civilians. Analysts have offered hypothetical intervention forces to combat killers and *génocidaires* in Darfur and Rwanda, for example, involving rapidly deployable, high-tech special operations forces and combat-ready support.[9] While often called humanitarian interventions, the ICISS Panel suggested that such missions be termed "human protection operations," or "military intervention for human protection purposes."[10] As discussed later, "coercive protection" is a more apt

---

[7] Chapter VI of the UN Charter refers to the organization's role in the pacific settlement of disputes that threaten international peace and security and was the authority for most UN peacekeeping missions before 1990. Chapter VII is invoked for operations with more robust mandates and where peacekeepers may use force beyond self-defense. The majority of UN-led peace operations since 1999 have had Chapter VII mandates, including missions in East Timor, Kosovo, Sierra Leone, the DRC, Liberia, Côte d'Ivoire, Haiti, Burundi, and Sudan.

[8] The US military has defined non-permissive environments – and most recently "hostile environment" – as areas where "hostile forces have control as well as the intent and capability to effectively oppose or react to the operations a unit intends to conduct." Department of Defense, *Department of Defense Dictionary of Military and Associated Terms*, Joint Publication 1-02, as amended through 14 April 2006, 390.

[9] David C. Gompert, Courtney Richardson, Richard L. Kugler, and Clifford H. Bernath, *Learning from Darfur: Building a Net-Capable African Force to Stop Mass Killing*, Defense and Technology Paper 15 (Center for Technology and National Security Policy, National Defense University, July 2005); Micah Zenko, "Saving Lives With Speed: Using Rapidly Deployable Forces for Genocide Prevention," *Defense and Security Analysis* 20, no. 1 (March 2004), 3-19.

[10] ICISS, *The Responsibility to Protect*, 8. The term "humanitarian intervention" is also used widely to refer to a range of missions, including US interventions in Iraq and Afghanistan, and can lack a clear meaning.

name for the approach to protection needed to provide physical safety in non-permissive environments, as noted in the supplement to the ICISS report.[11] "Coercive protection" describes the specific strategy of using or threatening force for the purpose of protecting civilians, as suggested by *The Responsibility to Protect* for military interventions or for some robust, Chapter VII peacekeeping operations with protection mandates.[12] These types of missions exist somewhere between traditional peace operations, which impartially uphold political mandates, and warfighting, where the goal is to defeat a designated enemy.

THE PROBLEM OF PROTECTION: ENACTING THE RESPONSIBILITY TO PROTECT

To many observers, the question of how best to protect civilians using military force seems straightforward. "I don't see what the problem is," said one. "Troops either protect civilians or they don't. They either stop militia that are raping and killing, or they stand aside and let it happen."[13]

> *Missions exist somewhere between traditional peace operations, which impartially uphold political mandates, and warfighting, where the goal is to defeat a designated enemy.*

For a number of reasons, however, protecting civilians can be a significant challenge in military operational terms. First, deployed forces may have limited or unclear *authority* to act, even in situations of mass killing and genocide. Troops sent to regions where civilians face violence usually operate with the presumed consent of the parties on the ground and with the understanding that the sovereign nation is responsible for the protection of its citizens. Such an arrangement is flawed in situations such as Darfur or the DRC, for example, where government forces ignore abuses against civilians, are incapable of halting them, or even take part in the abuses themselves. Nevertheless, few peacekeepers today have the authority of the Security Council to use *all means necessary* to protect civilians.

Second, some states lack *willingness* to offer peacekeepers for operations that use force to protect civilians. Troop contributing countries (TCCs) are not eager to send their troops into harm's way to engage with armed groups or to challenge a sovereign authority.

---

[11] Thomas G. Weiss and Don Hubert, *The Responsibility to Protect: Research, Bibliography, and Background* (Ottawa: International Development Research Centre, December 2001), 178-203.
[12] Ibid., 179-180.
[13] Amnesty International activist, interview with author, Washington, DC, 7 November 2005.

Box 1.2

HUMAN PROTECTION VS. WARFIGHTING AND PEACEKEEPING

The International Commission on Intervention and State Sovereignty argued that neither traditional peace operations nor traditional warfighting may be wholly appropriate for protecting civilians from genocide, ethnic cleansing, or mass killing. According to the ICISS report:

7.1 Military interventions for human protection purposes have different objectives than both traditional warfighting and traditional peacekeeping operations. Such interventions therefore raise a number of new, different and unique operational challenges. Because the objective of military intervention is to protect populations and not to defeat or destroy an enemy militarily, it differs from traditional warfighting. While military intervention operations require the use of as much force as is necessary, which may on occasion be a great deal, to protect the population at risk, their basic objective is always to achieve quick success with as little cost as possible in civilian lives and inflicting as little damage as possible so as to enhance recovery prospects in the post-conflict phase. In warfighting, by contrast, the neutralization of an opponent's military or industrial capabilities is often the instrument to force surrender.

7.2 On the other hand, military intervention operations – which have to do whatever it takes to meet their responsibility to protect – will have to be able and willing to engage in much more robust action than is permitted by traditional peacekeeping, where the core task is the monitoring, supervision and verification of ceasefires and peace agreements, and where the emphasis has always been on consent, neutrality and the non-use of force. The *Panel on United Nations Peace Operations* compiled in 2000 a thorough review of the operational challenges facing United Nations military missions, but for the most part that panel focused on traditional peacekeeping and its variations, not the more robust use of military force – not least because there is not within UN headquarters the kind of logistic planning and support, and command and control capacity, that would make possible either warfighting or military interventions of any significant size. Their report confirmed that "the United Nations does not wage war. Where enforcement action is required, it has consistently been entrusted to coalitions of willing states."

7.3 The context in which intervention operations take place also has important operational significance. Military intervention to protect endangered human lives should and will occur only as a last resort, after the failure of other measures to achieve satisfactory results. Inevitably, it will be part of a broader political strategy directed towards persuading the targeted state to cooperate with international efforts. The consequences for such operations suggest that the specific nature of the task to protect may over time lead to the evolution of a new type of military operation, carried out in new ways.

Source: International Commission on Intervention and State Sovereignty, *The Responsibility to Protect* (Ottawa: International Development Research Centre, December 2001), 57.

Third, peacekeeping missions may lack sufficient *capacity* to act. If AMIS had a new mandate to protect civilians fully throughout Darfur, without caveats, its capacity would restrict its ability to create a secure environment for the region's seven million civilians. AMIS lacks the size, equipment, mobility, funding, and coordination for such an operation. Even for deployments in smaller regions with less violence, capacity shortfalls are common in modern peace operations.

Finally, troops may lack the *operational guidance* and *military preparation* for specific kinds of missions. If authorized to intervene to protect civilians, forces must be prepared to make tactical and strategic judgments about how to react to threats of abuse against civilians groups. Choices will include whether to strive for the pacification or defeat of the abusive groups, whether to establish broad security or to provide a show of force in a specific area, and how to ensure long-term stability and security once mass killing is brought to a halt. Given limited resources, most missions must decide which civilians to protect and which to leave vulnerable, and how to allocate resources for programs with long-term and short-term benefits. They must also balance operating in as large an area as possible—and protect the maximum number of civilians—with sustaining the protection of the force itself.

These certainly are not easy choices. Troops in such situations must walk a tightrope between using too much and too little force. The balancing act has real consequences, as seen in the UN Mission in the DRC (MONUC) today, where UN peacekeepers in the eastern Ituri region of the country are using robust levels of force for a UN operation, and face both praise and criticism as a result. Praise and criticism also met earlier missions such as the Economic Community of West African States (ECOWAS) mission in Liberia in the early 1990s, which attempted to stabilize the country but used excessive force and committed human rights abuses. Other operations have used too little force and failed to challenge egregious human rights abusers. The UN Protection Force in Bosnia-Herzegovina (UNPROFOR), the UN Assistance Mission for Rwanda (UNAMIR), and the UN Mission in Sierra Leone (UNAMSIL) all tried to support weak peace agreements despite ongoing warfare and failed terribly in protecting civilians. In the words of Lt. Gen. Romeo Dallaire, force commander of UNAMIR at the time of the genocide, his efforts to pursue negotiations in the face of unmistakable evil, rather than use force, caused him to "shake hands with the devil."[14]

---

[14] Roméo A. Dallaire with Brent Beardsley, *Shake Hands With the Devil: The Failure of Humanity in Rwanda* (Toronto: Random House, 2003).

Given such challenges, it is *not enough* to deploy forces and hope they figure out an effective protection strategy once they arrive. Civilian protection requires an operational concept to guide troops in facing questions on the ground and a strategic framework for addressing these questions quickly and effectively. It requires, in short, that we "operationalize" the "responsibility to protect" by addressing how both types of missions (peace operations with protection mandates and full-scale "responsibility to protect" military interventions) should be conducted. There are two immediate questions for us today. First, are military forces preparing to lead missions to respond to genocide, ethnic cleansing, or mass killing, where civilian protection is *the* immediate and essential goal of the mission? Second, are forces in peace operations deployed in regions of instability prepared to protect civilians, while simultaneously carrying out their other tasks to achieve the mission's goals? This study will address how militaries have begun to address such questions and point out the gaps in their operational guidance and preparation.

> *Civilian protection requires an operational concept to guide troops on the ground and a strategic framework for addressing these questions quickly and effectively. It requires, in short, that we "operationalize" the "responsibility to protect."*

METHODOLOGY

The Henry L. Stimson Center began to investigate these issues in 2004. The Center hosted a small workshop with military and civilian experts in December 2004 to discuss military efforts at "civilian protection" and identify some of the concepts involved.[15] In January 2005, the Center published an initial report on its findings, geared toward an expert audience.[16] The present study expands on the initial report and seeks to introduce a broader audience to the issues involved.

Findings are based on dozens of interviews with military and civilian experts on peace and stability operations within governments, international organizations,

---

[15] Workshop, *Operational Capacities for Civilian Protection Missions*, The Henry L. Stimson Center, Washington, DC, 8 December 2004. Participants, many with military experience, came from the United Nations, the United States, the United Kingdom, Canada, NATO, South Africa, and international NGOs.

[16] Victoria K. Holt, *The Responsibility to Protect: Considering the Operational Capacity for Civilian Protection* (Washington, DC: The Henry L. Stimson Center, January 2005), www.stimson.org/fopo/?SN=FP20040831715.

non-governmental organizations (NGOs), and research centers. Interviewees were asked a series of interrelated and seemingly straightforward questions. First, which international organizations have declared a willingness and authority to use military force to halt genocide, ethnic cleansing, or mass killing? Second, what tools do these organizations and their member states typically use to prepare their military forces? Third, have such means been employed to prepare forces for a military mission to protect civilians from genocide, ethnic cleansing, or mass killing in a non-permissive environment? Fourth, have these tools been used to prepare forces in peace operations to implement their "civilian protection" mandates in regions of large-scale violence and/or mass killing?[17]

Answers to the first two questions were relatively easy to find. The UN, NATO, the European Union (EU), the AU, and ECOWAS have authority to conduct military interventions. Such interventions might also be led by coalitions of the willing, endorsed by the UN or by another organization. The typical tools these organizations use to prepare their forces include concepts of operation, doctrine, training, simulations, and gaming. As for the third and fourth questions, the response was surprising and nearly universal: *"I don't believe there is much that addresses that type of mission or mandate."*[18]

The full story is not that simple, however. Forces often receive guidance on protecting civilians in more traditional, permissive, and low-threat post-conflict environments, with a focus on the requirements of international humanitarian law. They have become increasingly adept at working with humanitarian organizations, promoting civil order, offering security to internally displaced person (IDP) camps, conducting preventive patrols, and other such tasks vital for the safety and security of civilians.

What is missing is explicit guidance for contingencies that approach or cross the threshold identified by the ICISS—namely genocide, ethnic cleansing, and mass killing. Current situations in Darfur and the DRC highlight this need, where such

---

[17] Additional specific questions included: What would a mission to protect civilians from mass killings, ethnic cleansing or genocide in non-permissive, Chapter VII environment look like? Who is willing and able to conduct such missions? What are the operational challenges that need to be met for such missions? Does current doctrine address the conduct of such missions? Do training, simulations, and gaming exercises deal with such missions? Do rules of engagement for such operations address civilian protection scenarios? Where are the gaps, and how can they be addressed?

[18] Many people generously offered insights and leads, however, on the components of capacity that do exist, which serve as the basis for this study. To encourage candor, interviews were mostly conducted on a not-for-attribution basis. For a list of individuals and organizations interviewed, please contact the authors.

violence is taking place today while guidance to forces on how to act remains in development.

Varied definitions also muddle the understanding of what protection means in practice. Few militaries or international organizations have developed concepts, doctrine, and training for missions designed to protect vulnerable civilians from genocide, ethnic cleansing, or mass killing. Even fewer have identified the specific tasks for such missions. Although Security Council resolutions began to call for peace operations to "protect civilians" in insecure environments more than six years ago, the UN is just starting to develop guidance on how to interpret or prepare for this directive. In practical military terms, therefore, there is little evident preparedness for missions to carry out the "responsibility to protect."[19]

STRUCTURE

This study is structured to guide the reader through the origins of the "responsibility to protect" concept and UN civilian protection mandates, an analysis of what civilian protection means in a military context, and the preparation of forces towards making it a reality. Chapter 2 addresses *why* the discussion about protecting civilians is timely and important, including background on civilian protection and the evolution of the "responsibility to protect" concept, the emergence of UN civilian protection mandates, and the protection debate today. Chapter 3 identifies the concepts of civilian protection most commonly used by militaries, humanitarian groups, and international organizations, which inform current thinking on the subject. The overlap of concepts and the need for clarity in operationalizing the protection of civilians by forces on the ground is analyzed.

Chapter 4 identifies areas of military preparedness for operationalizing the "responsibility to protect," including which actors have the *authority* to intervene in genocide and mass killing, and their broad level of *capacity* to undertake such actions. Chapter 5 looks at the significance of mandates and rules of engagement. Chapter 6 then reviews military doctrine in relation to the protection of civilians and Chapter 7 considers training programs in search of relevant guidance on civilian protection. Chapter 8 looks at civilian protection in practice, evaluating the recent approach to protection by peacekeepers in the challenging DRC. Finally, Chapter 9 takes a step back, summarizes key findings, and offers areas for further investigation.

---

[19] There may well be more capacity for and understanding of civilian protection in a military context than identified in this study, reflective of a gap between military thinking and an external understanding of that preparedness. Terminology also affects these findings. The definition of civilian protection is still being worked out and language varies across and within civilian and military communities.

This study is *not* a comprehensive analysis of specific military capacities or the literature on humanitarian intervention, although both are considered briefly. Scholars and practitioners have addressed these subjects in thoughtful and important detail elsewhere.[20] Instead, this study assumes a level of current military capacity and looks at the nuts and bolts of military preparation for the specific goal of protecting civilians, particularly in hostile environments. It attempts to draw a clearer picture of what the protection of civilians in peace operations and the "responsibility to protect" might mean in military operational terms—and to narrow what is now a wide debate over capacity to a more specific question of how to conduct certain operations. The goal is to make the policy options clearer to decision makers, in part to spur military thinking on the subject, and in part to take stock of how far, exactly, the world has come towards realizing new interventionist norms.

THE IMPOSSIBLE MANDATE?

The title of this study is purposely provocative. The topic is controversial too. Some observers argue that militaries should not overly involve themselves in "saving strangers."[21] They worry that humanitarian interventions lead to mission creep, with an open ended task of protecting civilians that is too hard for military forces—or a waste of their time—and best left to police forces. To these critics, a mandate for military forces to "protect civilians" is naïve and ignores operational realities. Others present equally sharp arguments in support of using military forces for "good," and suggest that stopping genocide would be easy if the international community could muster sufficient political will, that the military's capacity for warfighting does not prevent it from offering needed humanitarian support, or that an obsession with force protection has prevented military forces from taking sufficient action against abusive armed groups.

> *If the international community expects military forces to protect civilians, current peace operations with protection mandates badly need more guidance.*

Is the protection of civilians "the impossible mandate?" Because so few militaries have considered the operational implications of such a mandate in detail, or outlined the necessary steps for making it a reality, this remains an open question. The answer depends on who is being asked to do what. Asking lightly armed peacekeepers to protect civilians in violent regions without a clear

---

[20] For sources on global capacity for peace operations and humanitarian intervention, see Chapter 3.

[21] This term, though not the argument, is borrowed from Nicholas J. Wheeler, *Saving Strangers: Humanitarian Intervention in International Society* (New York: Oxford University Press, 2000).

strategy or sufficient capacity to achieve their aims may be nearly impossible. Asking nations to support a robust military intervention to protect civilians without the consent of the host nation, as suggested by *The Responsibility to Protect,* is also difficult. Both missions face added challenges if they lack sufficient capacity and political leadership to act. Yet much is known about how to structure forces to prepare them to achieve their goals. The chances of success are further improved if the challenges involved in a future mission are considered in advance, and the tools used to prepare armed forces and their leaders are put into practice.

Thus, if the international community expects military forces to effectively protect civilians, forces currently deployed to peace operations with protection mandates badly need more operational guidance. Those leaders who may conduct military interventions to support the "responsibility to protect" also need to prepare for what those missions could entail. Until this takes place, the "responsibility to protect" may remain a mandate that is impossible to execute until the vision aligns with the preparedness of the world's military forces. The time has come to translate the "responsibility to protect" into terms that militaries can understand and implement—such as concepts of operation, doctrine, training, rules of engagement, and mandates—to move lofty ideals into concrete actions on the ground.

— 2 —
THE PROTECTION DEBATE:
ORIGINS AND MOMENTUM

Fresh attention is focused on the issue of civilian protection by military forces. This trend deserves examining, as it points to a growing interest in civilian protection more broadly. Why are UN troops now being asked to "protect civilians under imminent threat?" How did the notion of an international "responsibility to protect" come about? Are these ideas taking hold? This chapter considers these questions, outlines the development of contemporary calls for civilian protection by military forces, and suggests where such appeals may head in the future.

CIVILIANS IN CONFLICT

The notion of an international "responsibility to protect" emerged both from hard experience and from political debate about international affairs and "humanitarian intervention" in the 1990s.[22] The post-Cold War period witnessed calls for such interventions in Somalia, Bosnia-Herzegovina, Haiti, Rwanda, Kosovo, Sierra Leone, and elsewhere. In some cases, troops sent to mitigate human suffering met with only limited success. High profile failures to protect civilians catalyzed calls for a reassessment of the use of force and effective

---

[22] The justification of warfare on "humanitarian" grounds is as old as the state itself — only the terminology is new. Sources abound on humanitarian intervention and debates regarding its legality, history, and efficacy. See, for example, David Chandler, *From Kosovo to Kabul: Human Rights and International Intervention* (London: Pluto Press, 2002); Deen K. Chatterjee and Don E. Scheid, eds., *Ethics and Foreign Intervention* (Cambridge: Cambridge University Press, 2003); Simon Chesterman, *Just War or Just Peace? Humanitarian Intervention and International Law* (Oxford: Oxford University Press, 2001); Neta Crawford, *Argument and Change in World Politics: Ethics, Decolonization and Humanitarian Intervention* (Cambridge: Cambridge University Press, 2002); Richard Falk, Mary Kaldor, Carl Tham, Samantha Power, Mahmood Mamdani, David Rieff, Eric Rouleau, Zia Mian, Ronald Steel, Stephen Holmes, Ramesh Thakur, Stephen Zunes, "Humanitarian Intervention: A Forum," *The Nation* 277, No. 2, 14 July 2003; J. L. Holzgrefe and Robert O. Keohane, eds., *Humanitarian Intervention: Ethical, Legal and Political Dilemmas* (Cambridge: Cambridge University Press, 2003); Anthony F. Lang, *Agency and Ethics: The Politics of Military Intervention* (New York: State University of New York Press, 2002); David Rieff, *At the Point of a Gun: Democratic Dreams and Armed Intervention* (New York: Simon & Schuster, 2005); Taylor B. Seybolt, *Humanitarian Military Intervention: The Conditions for Success and Failure* (Oxford: Oxford University Press, forthcoming 2007); Jennifer M. Welsh, *Humanitarian Intervention and International Relations* (Oxford: Oxford University Press, 2004); Wheeler, *Saving Strangers*; Weiss and Hubert, *The Responsibility to Protect: Research, Bibliography and Background*; Victoria Wheeler and Adele Harmer, eds., *Resetting the rules of engagement: trends and issues in military–humanitarian relations*, HPG Report 21 (London: Overseas Development Institute, 2006).

international responses. Concern for vulnerable civilians deepened within and beyond the human rights and relief communities, emerging as a political and normative force among international leaders, policymakers and NGOs.

Why did the 1990s witness such interest in "humanitarian intervention?" Much of the story is well-known: The end of the Cold War brought optimism about cooperation through a newly activist UN Security Council no longer constrained by the superpower tensions.[23] The Council authorized a powerful US-led coalition to expel Iraq from Kuwait, for example, gaining new stature. In Africa, the Balkans, Central America, and elsewhere, conflicts suppressed by the US-Soviet dynamic burst forth, leading to vicious civil wars. Buoyed by a sense of common purpose, the international community agreed—prematurely, in some cases—that these conflicts could be resolved through a combination of international negotiations, sanctions, peace operations, and enforcement. Many citizens saw images of these crises—and the efforts to remedy them—on television, as news reports brought pictures of famine, ethnic cleansing, and mass killing into their homes. The so-called "CNN effect" increased pressure on leaders to respond or, when interventions went awry, to get out.[24]

During these "uncivil wars" of the 1990s,[25] civilians bore the brunt of the violence.[26] Wars between distinguishable, uniformed armies facing off over national boundaries were the exception rather than the rule. Most warfare, instead, took place *within* states, often among armed groups that operated beyond the control of governments. Conflicts spilled across borders to impact entire regions. Non-combatants faced displacement, crossfire, and even direct targeting by fighters.[27]

---

[23] The Security Council approved roughly as many resolutions in the 1990s as in the period from 1946 to 1989. Peter Wallensteen and Patrik Johansson, "Security Council Decisions in Perspective," in Malone, ed., *The UN Security Council*, 18.

[24] A senior military advisor in the George H. W. Bush administration argued that the US intervention in Somalia was offered to the President as a means to get the conflict in the Balkans off American television screens. Lecture, Naval War College class, Washington, DC, 1994.

[25] William J. Durch, *UN Peacekeeping, American Politics, and the Uncivil Wars of the 1990s* (Washington, DC: The Henry L. Stimson Center, 1996).

[26] Precise data on civilian deaths in conflict is difficult to collect. The percentage of civilian casualties in modern wars is disputed, but all agree it is far too high. See Debarati Guha-Sapir and Olivier Degomme with Mark Phelan, *Darfur: Counting the Deaths, Mortality Estimates for Multiple Survey Data* (Brussels: Centre for Research on the Epidemiology of Disasters, University of Louvain, School of Public Health, 2005); Médecins sans Frontières, *Nothing New in Ituri: The Violence Continues* (Médecins sans Frontières, August 2005); Lisa Schlein, "UN: 25 Million Civilians Displaced by War are Unprotected," *Voice of America News*, 6 March 2005; Fred Kaplan, "What Peace Epidemic?" *Slate*, 25 January 2006; Ronald Waldman, "Public Health in War, Pursuing the Impossible," *Harvard International Review* 27, Is. 1, Spring 2005.

[27] Some argue that limited interventions contribute to more mass violence, or spur the need for greater intervention. Alan Kuperman has argued that there is a "moral hazard to humanitarian intervention" when rebellious actors are encouraged to stand up to their stronger opponents in the (mistaken) belief that the international community will back them, e.g., the Kurds in Iraq, the

In addition to deaths caused directly by violence, an enormous number of civilians perished due to the social disruption, disease, and malnutrition that accompany warfare, especially in developing states. There are relatively few systematic analyses of *total civilian* deaths caused by conflict, including those due to disease and famine. The International Rescue Committee (IRC) has estimated that nearly four million people have died from the war in the DRC since August 1998; less than two percent of the fatalities stem from direct violence.[28]

Policymakers in the 1990s wrestled with the nature of intervention, conscious of their failures to halt egregious human rights violations. In Rwanda, 800,000 Tutsis and moderate Hutus died despite the presence of a UN peacekeeping mission. In Srebrenica, Serb forces massacred roughly 7,000 Muslims in a UN "safe area" as Dutch peacekeepers looked on, even though NATO close air support was nearby.[29] Individuals directly involved in both missions believed that only a modest use of military firepower could have saved thousands of lives.[30] Sobered by these failures, the international community let the number of UN peacekeeping missions dwindle by the mid-1990s.

Toward the end of the decade, however, with chances for peace after brutal conflicts in Sierra Leone, the DRC, Kosovo, East Timor, and elsewhere, international support shifted again towards military interventions, peace operations, and efforts to protect civilians. With the onset of NATO bombing in Kosovo in June 1999, US President Bill Clinton declared, "If the world community has the power to stop it, we ought to stop genocide and ethnic cleansing."[31]

Kosovo Liberation Army in Kosovo, and secessionists in Bosnia-Herzegovina. Alan J. Kuperman, "Humanitarian Hazard," *Harvard International Review* 26, Is. 1, Spring 2004, 64-68.

[28] The IRC studies of mortality are groundbreaking. Benjamin Coghlan, Richard J. Brennan, Pascal Ngoy, David Dofara, Brad Otto, Mark Clements, and Tony Stewart, "Mortality in the Democratic Republic of Congo: a nationwide survey," *Lancet* 367, 7 January 2006, 44-51; International Rescue Committee, "The Lancet Publishes IRC Mortality Study from DR Congo; 3.9 Million Have Died: 38,000 Die per Month," International Rescue Committee, 6 January 2006, www.theirc.org/news/page.jsp?itemID=27819067.

[29] The International Committee of the Red Cross estimates 7,079 were killed in Srebrenica. Paul Watson, "Bosnia's 1995 Massacres Still Cloaked in Denial," *Los Angeles Times*, 6 July 2000.

[30] Dallaire, *Shake Hands With the Devil*; UN General Assembly, A/54/549, *Report of the Secretary-General pursuant to General Assembly resolution 53/35: The fall of Srebrenica*, 15 November 1999; S/1999/1257, *Letter dated 15 December 1999 from the members of the Independent Inquiry into the actions of the United Nations during the 1994 genocide in Rwanda addressed to the Secretary-General*, 16 December 1999.

[31] G-8 Summit: Interview of President Clinton by Wolf Blitzer *CNN Late Edition*, 20 June 1999, www.state.gov/www/issues/economic/summit/990620_clinton_cnn.html. Even for humanitarian purposes, any intervention by one state into another is highly controversial and there is a major argument about its legality under the UN Charter except when based on authorization of the Council. "Editorial Comments: NATO's Kosovo Intervention," *The American Journal of International Law*

INSUFFICIENT RESPONSE

The 1990s revealed where traditional humanitarian action and traditional peacekeeping *could not* effectively protect civilians. The principles of traditional humanitarian action—neutrality, impartiality, and consent—proved difficult to uphold in situations of severe insecurity.[32] In dozens of situations, humanitarians delivered assistance, often heroically, only to witness the beneficiaries face injury or death at the hands of armies, militia groups, or thugs. A painful phrase emerged to describe the victims of such violence: "the well-fed dead."[33] Humanitarians thought hard about ways to reduce and eliminate such violence against civilians, and began to call for the more effective provision of security.[34]

Traditional peacekeeping—where third-party military forces deploy to support a political peace—also failed to protect civilians effectively in renewed or ongoing conflicts. The Geneva Conventions aimed to shield civilian populations, but belligerents often ignored such laws of war in modern conflicts, whether in Haiti, Sierra Leone, El Salvador, Chechnya, Angola, Cambodia, or Bosnia. Peacekeeping operations and other military interventions that followed the signing of peace accords were usually poorly designed to address the reemergence of large-scale violence or the meddling of "spoilers" in the peace process.[35] Unarmed or lightly armed peacekeepers mandated to use minimal force faced tough choices when civilians came under threat. In many situations, peacekeepers tried to carry out their missions without clear political direction and faced threats they could not counter. For example, peacekeepers in UNPROFOR in the Balkans had an implicit mission to protect civilians in UN-designated "safe areas," but were not authorized to intercede when those civilians came under attack. Nor did other, stronger military forces from NATO back them up. In its report on Srebrenica, the UN harshly criticized the strategy of establishing safe areas and then failing to defend them forcefully:

> Protected zones and safe areas can have a role in protecting civilians in armed conflict, but it is clear that either they must be demilitarized and established by

---

93, no. 4, October 1999; Louis Henkin, "Kosovo and the Law of 'Humanitarian Intervention,'" *The American Journal of International Law* 93, no. 4, October 1999, 824.

[32] Humanitarian impartiality was further challenged by situations such as the aftermath of the Rwandan genocide, when refugees streamed into camps in the eastern DRC. Relief groups could not distinguish the *génocidaires* and distributed food and shelter to victim and killer alike. The *génocidaires* proceeded to spread discord and instability in the DRC.

[33] The term "well-fed dead" emerged out of the carnage of Bosnia in the early 1990s. Roberta Cohen and Francis M. Deng, "Exodus Within Borders: The Uprooted Who Never Left Home," *Foreign Affairs* 77, no. 4 (July/August 1998), 15.

[34] This view has migrated into policy circles today. Stewart Patrick, "The Role of the US Government in Humanitarian Intervention," US Department of State, 5 April 2004, address at Lewis and Clark College.

[35] Stephen John Stedman, "Spoiler Problems in Peace Processes," *International Security* 22, no. 2, January 1997.

the agreement of the belligerents, as in the case of the "protected zones" and "safe havens" recognized by international humanitarian law, or they must be truly safe areas, fully defended by a credible military deterrent.[36]

The Srebrenica report made an eloquent call for a more robust response to future humanitarian tragedies:

> The cardinal lesson of Srebrenica is that a deliberate and systematic attempt to terrorize, expel or murder an entire people must be met decisively with all necessary means, and with the political will to carry the policy through to its logical conclusion. In the Balkans, in this decade, this lesson has had to be learned not once, but twice. In both instances, in Bosnia and in Kosovo, the international community tried to reach a negotiated settlement with an unscrupulous and murderous regime. In both instances it required the use of force to bring a halt to the planned and systematic killing and expulsion of civilians.[37]

Thus, a new consensus developed: the rules needed to change.

Humanitarian Literature on "Protection"

Humanitarian organizations realized that they could not simply deliver food, shelter, and healthcare without also attempting to reduce civilian vulnerability to violence. The result is a significant body of literature laying out a humanitarian framework for the protection of civilians. The International Committee of the Red Cross (ICRC), for example, began a workshop series in 1996 to identify the legal, policy, and operational issues of protection. In 1999, the ICRC produced a broad and influential definition of "protection" as:

> [A]ll activities aimed at ensuring full respect for the rights of the individual in accordance with the letter and the spirit of the relevant bodies of law (i.e., human rights law, international humanitarian law and refugee law)...[38]

The ICRC also created a multilayered "egg" model of protection, involving three categories of activity to support protection: *responsive action, remedial action,* and *environment building.* These layers reflect the non-chronological use of broad-to-specific actions to create "an environment conducive to respect for human beings, preventing and/or alleviating the immediate effects of a specific pattern of abuse, and restoring dignified conditions of life through reparation,

---

[36] UN General Assembly, *Report of the Secretary-General Pursuant to General Assembly Resolution 53/35: The Fall of Srebrenica,* A/54/549, 15 November 1999, para. 499.

[37] Ibid., para. 502.

[38] Sylvie Giossi Caverzaslo, *Strengthening Protection in War – A Search for Professional Standards: Summary of Discussions Among Human Rights and Humanitarian Organizations* (Geneva: International Committee of the Red Cross, 2001); cited in Roger Williamson, *Protection of Civilians: Bridging the Protection Gap, Report on Wilton Park Conference 766* (West Sussex, UK: Wilton Park, 2005).

restitution and rehabilitation."[39] Intergovernmental processes, such as the multinational Good Humanitarian Donorship Initiative, sought to develop consensus around an international obligation to protect civilians when their governments were unwilling or incapable of doing so, to agree on criteria that would trigger a response, and to establish the operational parameters of that response for donors, the military and humanitarian and human rights agencies.[40]

In 2002 the Inter-Agency Standing Committee (IASC), made up of UN agencies, the ICRC, and NGOs, published field strategies used to protect or promote rights through humanitarian practices. The report demonstrated the sheer diversity of activities under the umbrella of human rights, humanitarian action, and the "protection" agenda, covering topics from protection against forced marriage to planning shelter, from dissemination of international humanitarian law to sanitation. The IASC also recognized the basic tension between the provision of humanitarian assistance and the prevention of violations of humanitarian law: assistance does *not* "always consciously aim" to stop violations of international humanitarian, human rights and refugee law. The report suggested that the agenda to protect civilians links the two concepts:

> Programmes may not be strategically designed to enhance the protection of civilians. The inextricable link of protection and assistance must be recognized if humanitarians are to play a significant role protecting the rights of those participating in their programmes. This collection of field practices demonstrates some of the ways humanitarian assistance programmes have moved beyond the provision of material assistance in an effort to enhance protection.[41]

The IASC report focused on the protection of civilians by promoting protection through law, including international humanitarian and human rights law. It made virtually no mention of working with military or peacekeeping forces to enhance the physical protection of civilians, however.

Yet the humanitarian community increasingly recognized the challenge of physical protection. A 2005 guide for humanitarian agencies from the Active Learning Network for Accountability and Performance in Humanitarian Action

---

[39] Carlo Von Flue and Jacques de Maio, *Third Workshop on Protection for Human Rights and Humanitarian Organizations: A Report of the Workshop Held at the International Committee of the Red Cross, 18-20 January 1999* (Geneva: International Committee of the Red Cross, 1999), 21.

[40] Under the Initiative, the objectives of humanitarian action are "to save lives, alleviate suffering and maintain human dignity during and in the aftermath of man-made crises and natural disasters, as well as to prevent and strengthen preparedness for the occurrence of such situations." Another objective is "the protection of civilians and those no longer taking part in hostilities," as part of the provision of traditional assistance (e.g., food, water and sanitation, shelter, health services and other items of assistance).

[41] Inter-Agency Standing Committee, *Growing the Sheltering Tree: Protecting Rights Through Humanitarian Action* (UNICEF, 2005), 5.

(ALNAP) described this shift since 2001. The first ALNAP *Review of Humanitarian Action* analyzed the Kosovo crisis and found that humanitarian agencies "did not give enough attention to people's protection."[42] In particular, the report found:

> Many agencies focused on the provision of material assistance, leaving protection to mandated agencies such as UNHCR and ICRC. The Review concluded that the humanitarian community was at last waking up to the fact that all humanitarian agencies have a role to play in people's protection in war and disaster. Agencies realized that they have an obligation to work with communities, mandated agencies and responsible authorities to ensure people's safety as well as providing assistance to those in need.[43]

ALNAP has since published additional guidance for humanitarian protection, aimed at helping practitioners "get to grips" with both the conceptual and operational elements of protection.[44] A 2004 field-based study of international protection for IDPs also examined UN protection strategies, and cited the problems faced when peacekeepers do not see their role as providing protection or offering a preventive presence.[45]

Overall, this humanitarian approach to civilian protection has moved to include a wide range of aims, concepts, strategies and operational parameters. "Protection" can entail, for example: encouraging peace and economic development; preventing conflict; promoting compliance with international law; addressing the special needs of women, children and the displaced; stopping small-arms proliferation; ensuring the safety of humanitarian-relief workers and their access to vulnerable populations; disarming, demobilizing, reintegrating and rehabilitating ex-combatants; and tackling "hate media." Where the military's role lies in relation to these aims remains the subject of ongoing debate.

Improving Peace Operations

Nations and their military leaders also began to consider their responsibilities in areas of extreme violence, refining the mandates and doctrine for peace operations, and expanding peacekeeping capacity at the UN and elsewhere. The US experience in Somalia, which resulted in a broad US distaste for

---

[42] John Mitchell, preface to Hugo Slim and Andrew Bonwick, *Protection: An ALNAP Guide for Humanitarian Agencies* (London: Overseas Development Institute, August 2005), 3.

[43] Ibid. UNHCR refers to the United Nations High Commissioner for Refugees.

[44] Ibid.

[45] Simon Bagshaw and Diane Paul, *Protect or Neglect? Toward a More Effective United Nations Approach to the Protection of Internally Displaced Persons* (Washington, DC: The Brookings-SAIS Project on Internal Displacement and the UN Office for the Coordination of Humanitarian Affairs, November 2004).

"humanitarian intervention," also led to more realistic appraisals of what was needed for effective peace operations, ranging from better planning and coordination to mission design and increased firepower. Countries recognized that doctrine and training for peace operations needed to prepare troops better for more robust missions, to manage "spoilers" to a peace process, to engage with civilian actors, and to promote the rule of law.

UN peacekeeping mandates grew to include new tasks. The UN Security Council began to authorize operations to "protect civilians under imminent threat" under Chapter VII of the UN Charter, as seen for the first time with UNAMSIL in 1999. The following UN mandates for operations in the DRC, Liberia, Haiti, Burundi, Côte d'Ivoire, and Sudan contained similar language. Mandates also included directives to protect or facilitate the return of IDPs and to create "necessary security conditions" for the provision of humanitarian assistance. In addition, the UN increasingly authorized operations led by individual nations and regional organizations to protect civilians and IDPs, including the European Union's *Operation Artemis* in the DRC in the summer of 2003, the French-led *Operation Licorne* in Côte d'Ivoire beginning in 2003, the ECOWAS operation in Côte d'Ivoire in 2003—2004, and the AU mission in Darfur, Sudan since 2004. [For a full list of UN authorizations, see *Annex I: UN Security Council Resolutions for Missions Involving Aspects of Civilian Protection*].

In 2000, UN Secretary-General Kofi Annan appointed an international group, the Panel on United Nations Peace Operations, to assess the challenges of peacekeeping operations and offer recommendations to improve their conduct. The Panel's "Brahimi Report," named after Panel chairman UN Under-Secretary-General Lakhdar Brahimi, called for greater UN planning and management capacity, more effective and rapid deployment, and clearer mandates, doctrine, and strategy. The Panel recognized the fundamental challenges faced by peacekeepers operating without the full consent of local parties. It argued:

> [P]eacekeepers may not only be operationally justified in using force but morally compelled to so. Genocide in Rwanda went as far as it did in part because the international community failed to use or to reinforce the operation then on the ground in that country to oppose obvious evil.[46]

The Panel also offered clear limits as to the scope of UN-led interventions. "The United Nations does not wage war," it stated. "Where enforcement action is required, it has consistently been entrusted to coalitions of willing States, with

---

[46] UN General Assembly and Security Council, *Report of the Panel on United Nations Peace Operations* A/55/305-S/2000/809, 21 August 2000, para. 50.

the authorization of the Security Council, acting under Chapter VII of the Charter."[47] Despite the report's acknowledgement of the UN failure during the Rwandan genocide, it offered a roadmap for improving operations that were not responses to genocide. As a result, the UN baseline capacity for missions was greatly improved, but the UN role in protecting civilians from large-scale violence remained unclear.[48]

In 1999, the Security Council also began to increasingly invoke Chapter VII authority for UN-led missions. This authority reflected less a call for "enforcement action" than recognition of UN authority and its potential intrusiveness in leading efforts to improve local governance. Nevertheless, the use of Chapter VII indicated that a line was being crossed in many missions and that the Council expected peacekeepers to use force to uphold their mandates.

Reports of the Secretary-General and Security Council Resolutions on Civilian Protection

Just as the humanitarian and peacekeeping communities responded to the disasters in Rwanda, Srebrenica and elsewhere with an emphasis on protecting civilians, so too did the UN Secretary-General and Security Council. The Secretary-General began publishing a series of reports on "the protection of civilians in armed conflict" in 1999. The Security Council also looked at the question, approving three resolutions and six presidential statements under the same title and holding semi-annual open briefings on the subject.

The UN Office for the Coordination of Humanitarian Affairs (OCHA) has been particularly focused and active on the protection agenda. OCHA has seen protection as a core element of its role, and worked to focus the attention of the Security Council and key Secretariat departments on protection issues. It has developed reports, online resources, a glossary of relevant "humanitarian terms," and other materials on the subject.[49] These include an *Aide Mémoire*, which outlined various keys to effective civilian protection to assist the Security Council in its deliberations over peacekeeping missions; a ten-point "Plan of Action" on the protection of civilians for the Security Council; and a "Roadmap" for implementing the UN's protection responsibilities. OCHA also hosted a series of regional workshops on the topic.

---

[47] Ibid., paras. 52-53.

[48] For details on progress in implementing the Brahimi Report recommendations, see William J. Durch, Victoria K. Holt, Caroline R. Earle and Moira K. Shanahan, *The Brahimi Report and the Future of Peace Operations* (Washington, DC: The Henry L. Stimson Center, December 2003).

[49] OCHA maintains an active website, http://ochaonline.un.org/webpage.asp?Site=civilians.

Box 2.1

MODERN PEACE OPERATIONS:
THE BRAHIMI REPORT & CIVILIAN PROTECTION

The Brahimi Report famously detailed the challenges facing modern UN peacekeeping missions – and the new call for peacekeepers to protect civilians. Throughout the report, the Panel is conscious of the implications of this responsibility and called for the UN Secretariat to "tell the Security Council what it needs to know, not what it wants to hear" about the requirements for successful operations and necessary commitments from member states. The Report also acknowledged the new trend in UN mandates to identify the protection of civilians as a key component of peacekeeping operations:

62. Finally, the desire on the part of the Secretary-General to extend additional protection to civilians in armed conflicts and the actions of the Security Council to give United Nations peacekeepers explicit authority to protect civilians in conflict situations are positive developments. Indeed, peacekeepers – troops or police – who witness violence against civilians should be presumed to be authorized to stop it, within their means, in support of basic United Nations principles and, as stated in the report of the Independent Inquiry on Rwanda, consistent with "the perception and the expectation of protection created by [an operation's] very presence" (see S/1999/1257, p. 57).

63. However, the Panel is concerned about the credibility and achievability of a blanket mandate in this area. There are hundreds of thousands of civilians in current United Nations mission areas who are exposed to potential risk of violence, and United Nations forces currently deployed could not protect more than a small fraction of them even if directed to do so. Promising to extend such protection establishes a very high threshold of expectation. The potentially large mismatch between desired objective and resources available to meet it raises the prospect of continuing disappointment with United Nations follow-through in this area. If an operation is given a mandate to protect civilians, therefore, it also must be given the specific resources needed to carry out that mandate.

Source: UN General Assembly and Security Council, *Report of the Panel on United Nations Peace Operations*, A/55/305-S/2000/809, 21 August 2000, 11.

The Security Council first passed a resolution in September 1999 on "the protection of civilians." In it, the Council expresses "its willingness to respond to situations of armed conflict where civilians are being targeted or humanitarian assistance to civilians is being deliberately obstructed, including through the consideration of appropriate measures at the Council's disposal."[50] The precise nature of "appropriate measures" was not elaborated. The Council offered a few

---

[50] S/Res/1265, 17 September 1999, para. 10.

more details in April 2000. A new resolution indicated the Council's intention to provide peacekeeping missions with appropriate mandates and resources to protect civilians. It also called on peacekeepers to consider the use of "temporary security zones for the protection of civilians and the delivery of assistance in situations characterized by the threat of genocide, crimes against humanity, and war crimes against the civilian population."[51] The resolution established "the deliberate targeting of civilian populations or other protected persons and the committing of systematic, flagrant and widespread violations of international humanitarian and human rights law in situations of armed conflict" as a "threat to international peace and security"—the legal trigger for a UN response.[52] Thus, the Council approach to protection of civilians began to shift.

A SHIFT IN NORMATIVE LANGUAGE

The international community's struggle with the mass killing in the 1990s also led to redefining the terms of intervention. In 2000, reflecting on the UN's devastating reports on international inaction in Rwanda and Srebrenica, Annan challenged Member States to "forge unity" on the matter of humanitarian intervention and to identify a basis for preventing future catastrophes:

> ...[I]f humanitarian intervention is, indeed, an unacceptable assault on sovereignty, how should we respond to a Rwanda, to a Srebrenica—to gross and systematic violations of human rights that affect every precept of our common humanity?[53]

The International Commission on Intervention and State Sovereignty, designed as an independent international body with distinguished leaders from 11 countries, was organized by the government of Canada to take up Annan's challenge. In December 2001, the ICISS published its landmark report, *The Responsibility to Protect*. The Commission's central conclusion was that there are limits to the general non-intervention rule for certain kinds of emergencies, namely:

> **[L]arge scale loss of life**, actual or apprehended, with genocidal intent or not, which is the product either of deliberate state action, or state neglect or inability to act, or a failed state situation; or **large scale 'ethnic cleansing'**, actual or apprehended, whether carried out by killing, forced expulsion, acts of terror or rape.[54]

---

[51] S/Res/1296, 19 April 2000, para. 15.

[52] Ibid., para. 5.

[53] UN General Assembly, *"We the Peoples": The Role of the United Nations in the 21st Century*, A/54/2000, Millennium Report of the Secretary-General, 27 March 2000, 48.

[54] ICISS, *The Responsibility to Protect*, xii. Note: bold is in original text.

The Commission also suggested doing away with the term "humanitarian intervention," and replacing it with simply "intervention," "military intervention for human protection purposes," or "human protection operation."[55] The ICISS duly noted that humanitarian relief organizations chafe at the use of the term "humanitarian" to describe violent military activities, such as dropping a bomb, for example, although such displays of force might be needed to save lives. Moreover, the phrase "human protection" put the emphasis on potential victims of violence rather than on the "rights" of prospective interveners.

Borrowing from just-war theory, ICISS specified six criteria for military intervention for human protection purposes: *right authority; just cause; right intention; last resort; proportional means;* and *reasonable prospects.* The preferred "right authority" was the Security Council, although ICISS recognized other routes if the Council deadlocked, including the General Assembly's "Uniting For Peace Procedures," and regional organizations acting within their "defining boundaries."[56] ICISS added that any intervention must be both "defensible in principle" and "workable and acceptable in practice."[57]

The report emphasized that there is a "continuum" of responsibilities to reduce the likelihood of abuses before, during, and after conflict. The "responsibility to protect" includes a "responsibility to *prevent*" mass killing and ethnic cleansing before they occur, a "responsibility to *react*" when these abuses are taking place, and a "responsibility to *rebuild*" in the wake of conflict. In line with these priorities, the report advocated the increased use of preventive deployments and follow-on peacebuilding missions. In the case of ongoing abuses, the Commission stated that the "responsibility to react" should involve "appropriate measures, which may include coercive measures like sanctions and international prosecution, and in extreme cases military intervention."[58]

A New View of Humanitarian Intervention? Cycling Back

The timing of the ICISS report—coming shortly after September 11, 2001—initially blunted its impact. In December 2001, few in the international community were thinking seriously about humanitarian intervention. The earlier debates about such missions—which many observers felt culminated with the 1999 bombing of Belgrade and the subsequent NATO peace operation in Kosovo—waned with the advent of the US-led "Global War on Terror," at least temporarily.[59] Many observers believed the wars in Afghanistan and Iraq,

---

[55] Ibid., 8.

[56] Ibid., 53.

[57] Ibid., 29.

[58] Ibid., xi, viii.

[59] As Weiss points out, articles on humanitarian intervention represented roughly half of those

undertaken for defensive and/or strategic reasons yet justified *ex post facto* as a kind of active humanitarianism, further undermined efforts to establish an international consensus on the legitimacy of "saving lives with force."[60] By 2004 some analysts even went so far as to wonder, "Is anyone interested in humanitarian intervention?"[61]

The ICISS had hit a nerve, however, and demonstrated enduring relevance. In the US the growing concern that "failed states" could become terrorist havens further aligned American strategic interests with "humanitarian" issues and support for international peace operations. The 2006 US *National Security Strategy* called for an increase in the number of troops available worldwide for "conflict intervention," for example. It also concluded, "Where perpetrators of mass killing defy all attempts at peaceful intervention, armed intervention may be required."[62]

> *While billions of dollars fund operations in Iraq and Afghanistan, the Bush Administration has expanded its funding for international peacekeeping training programs, as well as offered support to UN and regionally-led peace operations.*

While billions of dollars fund operations in Iraq and Afghanistan, the Bush Administration has expanded its funding for international peacekeeping training programs, as well as offered support to UN and regionally-led peace operations. New US efforts aim to create capacities for dealing with failed states and mounting post-conflict operations, as evidenced by the creation of a US State Department office to coordinate reconstruction and stabilization operations, and a Department of Defense (DoD) directive in November 2005 giving standing to stability operations equivalent to warfighting in its plans and policies.

---

published in the scholarly journal *Ethics & International Affairs* by the end of the 1990s, but fell precipitously after September 11, 2001. Thomas G. Weiss, "The Sunset of Humanitarian Intervention? The Responsibility to Protect in a Unipolar Era," *Security Dialogue* 35, no. 2, June 2004, 136.

[60] This phrase, though not the argument, is borrowed from Michael O'Hanlon, *Saving Lives With Force: Military Criteria for Humanitarian Intervention* (Washington, DC: Brookings Institution Press, 1997).

[61] Neil S. Macfarlane, Carolin J. Thielking and Thomas G. Weiss, "The Responsibility to Protect: Is anyone interested in humanitarian intervention?" *Third World Quarterly* 25, no. 5, 2004, 977-992.

[62] *The National Security Strategy of the United States of America*, March 2006, Chapter 4, "Working with Others to Defuse Regional Conflicts," 16-17. See also *The National Security Strategy of the United States of America*, September 2002, Chapter 4, "Working with Others to Defuse Regional Conflicts."

Motivation for capacity building reflects the sustained surge in peace operations around the world. More personnel are deployed in international peace and stability operations today than ever before. Assorted security providers lead missions—including the UN, NATO, EU, AU, ECOWAS, and coalitions of the willing. In addition to US-led counterinsurgency/stability operations in Iraq and Afghanistan, NATO has substantial operations in Afghanistan, Iraq, and Kosovo, and the EU heads a major mission in Bosnia-Herzegovina. The UN leads 15 peacekeeping operations with more than 70,000 uniformed personnel from 107 countries, plus additional peacebuilding missions. Many of its operations are in countries where civilians face severe insecurity, such as the DRC, Haiti, Côte d'Ivoire, and Burundi, testing the limits of UN willingness and capacity to use force in defense of civilian life.

> *This dynamic time offers opportunities to identify gaps in capacity and to suggest ways for national and multinational organizations to prepare for and conduct operations.*

In response to this increase in peace operations, multinational organizations have authorized more missions to use force and are developing greater capacities to intervene. Military organizations are reconsidering the doctrine, scenarios, and training programs for peace and stability operations. This dynamic time offers opportunities to identify gaps in capacity and to suggest ways for national and multinational organizations to prepare for and conduct operations.

In addition, the American public may be less wary of humanitarian intervention than a decade ago.[63] Many decry the lack of stronger action or media attention on the crisis in Darfur, for example, displaying an outpouring of concern for the victims there. The crisis has spawned innumerable US student groups, NGO coalitions, and even the arrest of political leaders and others protesting in front of the Sudanese Embassy.[64]

---

[63] In a 2003 poll, fifty-five percent of Americans expressed the belief that "the US and other Western powers have a moral obligation to use military force in Africa, if necessary, to prevent one group of people from committing genocide against another." Seventy-four percent responded that the US had such an obligation in Europe. Program on International Policy Attitudes, Humanitarian Military Intervention in Africa, Americans and the World website, www.americans-world.org/digest/regional_issues/africa/africa4.cfm. Cited in Macfarlane, Thielking and Weiss, "Is anyone interested in humanitarian intervention?" 986.

[64] "Rep. Rangel Arrested in Sudan Embassy Protest," *Democracy Now!* 14 July 2004, www.democracynow.org/article.pl?sid=04/07/14/1411202.

Box 2.2

HUMANITARIAN INTERVENTION: BASIC ARGUMENTS

Arguments over the legitimacy of humanitarian intervention were particularly pointed in the 1990s. Opponents of intervention worried that it could be used as a proxy for neo-colonialist impulses, or that human rights were a "Western" concept that should not be imposed on others. They argued that powerful rich countries dominated the institutions responsible for adjudicating decisions to intervene, such as the UN Security Council. Moreover, these same countries had endured centuries of violent rebellions, and peace had taken hold only after they exhausted such disputes. Decisions about when and where to intervene were therefore viewed with suspicion, and many believed that such decisions had more to do with self-interest than genuine concern for civilian well being.

Observers in developed countries also questioned the utility of humanitarian interventions and decried the resource expenses that they entailed. Not only were such interventions wrong in *practice* – as interveners inevitably arrived too late, with insufficient understanding of local grievances and history – they were also wrong in *principle*, as the "realist" theory of international relations holds that foreign policy should be based on the pursuit of states' self-interest. Humanitarian intervention was an oxymoron in that it sapped resources from more worthy endeavors, and often caused more harm than good. Some analysts also questioned the grounds for humanitarian intervention under international law.

The arguments on the other side of this debate were straightforward and emotionally appealing: if we can save innocent lives or protect populations, we should do so. Because the most troubling crimes against humanity in the post-Cold War era were connected to fighting within states rather than among them, states could no longer simply be left to conduct their internal business as they pleased. International legal theorists thus sought justification for humanitarian interventions in new readings of international law (much of which supports state sovereignty, due to its origins in the post-World War II era) or, as in Resolution 1296, through expanding the definition of threats to "international peace and security" (specified under Chapter VII of the UN Charter as one of two legal justifications of war, the other being self-defense) to include human rights concerns. Some analysts also argued that intervention was not nearly as difficult or as risky as many people supposed. Others pointed out that militaries have served humanitarian purposes for centuries, so that humanitarian intervention was just a new shine on an old problem. Some cast humanitarian goals as a component of national security interests. Finally, practical voices argued that it is better to support Council-authorized humanitarian interventions than to leave such adventures to coalitions of the willing to define their missions as they wish. Many further noted that, like it or not, the dramatic increase in the speed of news worldwide increased both knowledge of crises and the calls to do something, making it likely that interventions were here to stay.

Sources: Mohammed Ayoob, "Humanitarian Intervention and International Society," *Global Governance* 7, no. 3 (July—September 2001), 225-230; Michael Walzer, "The Argument about Humanitarian Intervention," *Dissent* (Winter 2002), 30; See Henry Kissinger, *Does America Need a Foreign Policy? Toward a Diplomacy for the 21st Century* (New York: Simon & Schuster, 2001); Chesterman, *Just War or Just Peace?*

Real Impact

The ICISS report itself has made a substantial impact, receiving high-level attention and endorsement of its framework by governments, non-governmental organizations, and scholars worldwide. Five years after the Commission's report, there is growing acceptance of the "responsibility to protect" concept and increasing use of its terminology.[65] Human Rights Watch, the International Crisis Group, Refugees International, Oxfam and other groups frequently reference the "responsibility to protect" in their statements and reports on the crisis in Darfur and elsewhere.[66] Among others, Human Rights Watch and International Crisis Group have called for UN peacekeepers to directly "protect civilians" in conflict zones such as the DRC; likewise, many NGOs call for AU forces to protect civilians in Darfur. For example, the United Kingdom House of Commons International Development Committee published a strong endorsement of the "responsibility to protect" framework in its 2005 report, *Darfur, Sudan: The responsibility to protect*. The report condemns inaction on Darfur and suggests that political pressure on the Government of Sudan should be combined with humanitarian relief, "protection," and support for rebuilding efforts.[67] Amnesty International, after years of maintaining a policy of relative neutrality on the use of force and military intervention, decided in 2005 to develop guidelines for when it will call for military intervention to end widespread and grave human rights abuses.[68]

In the United States, a 2005 bipartisan task force directed by Congress to evaluate US interests with the United Nations cited and strongly endorsed the "responsibility to protect" framework as grounds for considering intervention:

> The United States government should affirm that every sovereign government has a 'responsibility to protect' its citizens and those within its jurisdiction from genocide, mass killing, and massive and sustained human rights violations.... Sovereignty belongs to the people of a country, and governments have a responsibility to protect their people. If a government fails to protect the lives

---

[65] *Responsibility to Protect* project of the World Federalist Movement, www.responsibilitytoprotect.org/.
[66] Amnesty International, "Sudan: UN Security Council must meet 'responsibility to protect' civilians," Amnesty International Press Release, 25 May 2006; International Crisis Group, *Darfur: The Failure to Protect*, Africa Report No. 89 (Washington, DC: International Crisis Group, 8 March 2005); Michael Clough, "Darfur: Whose Responsibility to Protect," in Human Rights Watch, *World Report 2005* (Human Rights Watch, 2005); Oxfam International, "Ugandan government must fulfill its responsibility to protect civilians in war-torn north," Oxfam Press Release, 27 October 2005; Sally Chin and Jonathan Morgenstein, *No Power to Protect: The African Union Mission in Sudan* (Refugees International, November 2005); Cheryl O. Igiri and Princeton N. Lyman, *Giving Meaning to "Never Again": Seeking an Effective Response to the Crisis in Darfur and Beyond*, Council Special Report No. 5 (Washington, DC: Council on Foreign Relations, September 2004).
[67] House of Commons International Development Committee, *Darfur, Sudan: The responsibility to protect*, Fifth Report of Session 2004-05, Volume 1 (London: March 2005), 30.
[68] Amnesty International representative, interview with author, 13 February 2006, Washington, DC.

of those living within its jurisdiction from genocide, mass killing, and massive and sustained human rights violations, it forfeits claims to immunity from intervention (based on the principle of nonintervention in a state's internal affairs) if such intervention is designed to protect the at-risk population... Those engaged in mass murder must understand that they will be identified and held accountable.[69]

The task force further recommended that if the Security Council failed to act in such cases, "The United States should insist that states asserting an absolutist doctrine of nonintervention explain why they are preventing action against the world's *génocidaires*."[70]

Adding real weight to the endorsements of the "responsibility to protect," the United Nations has begun to embrace the framework. In its December 2004 report, *A More Secure World: Our Shared Responsibility*, the UN High-level Panel on Threats, Challenges, and Change endorsed "the emerging norm that there is a collective international responsibility to protect...in the event of genocide and other large-scale killing, ethnic cleansing or serious violations of international humanitarian law."[71] Secretary-General Annan's 2005 report *In Larger Freedom* referenced the "responsibility to protect" concept as grounds for action, arguing that, "[I]f national authorities are unable or unwilling to protect their citizens, then the responsibility shifts to the international community." Moreover, if "diplomatic, humanitarian and other methods...appear insufficient, the Security Council may out of necessity decide to take action under the Charter of the United Nations, including enforcement action, if so required."[72]

After tumultuous negotiations, the 2005 UN World Summit made a strong statement for collective enforcement action to halt serious crimes against humanity. Member States agreed:

Each individual State has the responsibility to protect its populations from genocide, war crimes, ethnic cleansing and crimes against humanity.... [W]e are prepared to take collective action, in a timely and decisive manner, through the Security Council, in accordance with the Charter, including Chapter VII, on a case-by-case basis and in cooperation with relevant regional organizations as appropriate, should peaceful means be inadequate and national authorities are

---

[69] Task Force on the United Nations, *American Interests and UN Reform* (Washington, DC: United States Institute of Peace, 2005), 29.

[70] Ibid.

[71] The High-level Panel designated the Security Council as the legitimate authorizing body for such interventions, where the ICISS left open other possibilities. UN General Assembly, *A More Secure World: Our Shared Responsibility, Report of the Secretary-General's High-level Panel on Threats, Challenges and Change*, A/59/565, 2 December 2004, 66, para. 203.

[72] UN General Assembly, *In Larger Freedom: Toward Development, Security and Human Rights for All, Report of the Secretary-General*, A/59/2005, 21 March 2005, para. 135.

manifestly failing to protect their populations from genocide, war crimes, ethnic cleansing and crimes against humanity.[73]

Saying or Acting?

Even with such broad endorsement by UN member states, NGOs, and others, the concept of a "responsibility to protect" is far from achieving universal acceptance. Fundamental to the question of how far it will go is the ICISS argument that—in cases where the appropriate thresholds and criteria for intervention are met—states should feel, indeed are, *compelled* to act. A "responsibility" is therefore more than an *option* to protect.

> *A "responsibility" is therefore more than an option to protect.*

As the "responsibility to protect" language is tracked through these documents—from the initial ICISS report to the recommendations of the US task force on UN reform, the High-level Panel, the Secretary-General's *In Larger Freedom* and, finally, the Summit Outcome Document—analysis reveals that qualifiers dilute the stronger language of the ICISS report. *In Larger Freedom* argues that the Security Council "*may* out of necessity" authorize intervention, while the Summit Outcome promised only to act on "a case by case basis." These endorsements thus support action, but do not suggest it is a requirement.

Many states at the 2005 World Summit, particularly countries within the Non-Aligned Movement and the G-77, initially opposed the inclusion of language on "responsibility to protect" in the final outcome document. The US rejected language from an early draft that indicated an *obligation* among states to respond to a certain scale of atrocities, while states such as Zimbabwe, China, and Egypt expressed opposition to the concept as a whole.[74] Nevertheless, the Summit produced a clearer statement than many expected: the international community has the responsibility to act when nations "are manifestly failing to protect their populations" from these categories of violence.[75] Even if some

---

[73] UN General Assembly, *2005 World Summit Outcome*, A/Res/60/1, 24 October 2005, para. 139. That the "responsibility to protect" concept gained support was surprising given that other substantive proposals at the Summit did not.

[74] John Bolton, "Dear Colleague" letter from US Ambassador John Bolton, 30 August 2005, ReformtheUN.org, www.reformtheun.org/index.php?module=uploads&func=download&fileId=813; ReformtheUN.org, *Overview Chart of State-by-State Positions on the Responsibility to Protect*, World Federalist Movement – Institute for Global Policy, 12 August 2005, www.reformtheun.org/index.php?module=uploads&func=download&fileId=797. The US reportedly shifted its position to support inclusion of the "responsibility to protect" language in the final document.

[75] A/Res/60/1, 2005 World Summit Outcome, as adopted by the UN General Assembly, 24 October 2005, 30.

arms were twisted along the way, UN Member States officially recognized an international "responsibility to protect" civilians.

The Security Council reaffirmed this Summit position on the "responsibility to protect" with its third resolution on "the protection of civilians" in April 2006. The United Kingdom spearheaded this effort and won Council approval unanimously despite initial opposition from Russia and China.[76] Unlike earlier resolutions, Resolution 1674 provides some specific guidance to peacekeepers. It calls on peacekeepers to ensure the security of refugee camps, to associate the UN Emergency Relief coordinator in the early stages of mission planning, and to prevent sexual violence. The resolution also reaffirms the Council's practice of including provisions for the protection of civilians in peacekeeping mandates. It proposes that "such mandates include clear guidelines as to what missions can and should do to achieve those goals," and that measures to protect civilians be "given priority in decisions about the use of available capacity and resources, including information and intelligence resources, in the implementation of the mandates."[77]

Thus, on the heels of the 2005 World Summit, the UN Security Council further embraced the "responsibility to protect" and recognized a role for peacekeeping forces in making it a reality. This is big news.

---

[76] Security Council Report, "Update Report No. 7, Protection of Civilians in Armed Conflict," 20 April 2006, www.securitycouncilreport.org/site/c.glKWLeMTIsG/b.1563699/k.B611/Update_report_No_7brprotection_of_civilians_in_armed_conflictbr20_April_2006.htm.
[77] S/Res/1674, 28 April 2006, paras. 4, 11, and 14-19.

— 3 —
MEANINGS OF "PROTECTION": TOWARDS A UNIFIED CONCEPT

Ideas about protecting civilians in the humanitarian, legal, and peacekeeping communities run deep and broad. These ideas, however, are not translated easily to those serving in peace operations. Certainly the meaning of "protection" is not the same for everyone. When talking about protecting civilians, a humanitarian worker with Oxfam is likely to have a separate understanding than a Brazilian peacekeeper in Haiti or a staffer with the UN High Commissioner for Refugees (UNHCR). Imagine the different views of civilian protection for a protection officer in the UN Mission in Sudan (UNMIS), for a colonel in the US Marine Corps, for a UN contingent commander, and for a human rights expert from Amnesty International. Are these actors speaking the same language and working towards the same ends?

In short, no, they are not. Military leaders, NGOs, and international organizations offer numerous and varied understandings of the meaning of civilian protection. These divergent views cut across legal, political, operational, and moral realms in peace operations today.

Six distinct concepts of civilian protection are commonly employed in the field, each with implications for a military role. First, protecting civilians can be conceived of as a legal obligation of military actors to abide by international humanitarian and human rights law during the conduct of war. Second, protection may be seen as the natural outcome of traditional warfighting through the defeat of a defined enemy. Third, it may be viewed as a job for humanitarian organizations aided through the provision of broad security and "humanitarian space" by military forces. Fourth, it may be considered the result of the operational design of assistance by relief agencies to reduce the vulnerability of civilians to physical risk. Fifth, it may be viewed as a set of tasks for those deployed in peace operations or other interventions, potentially involving the use of force to deter or respond to belligerent attacks on vulnerable populations. Sixth, and finally, protecting civilians may be the primary mission goal, where the operation is designed specifically to halt mass killing in the immediate term, as stipulated in *The Responsibility to Protect*.

With these varied approaches to the protection of civilians, it may be difficult to sort out the role for military forces, especially in peace operations. To establish a mission, military planners rely on clear concepts of operation, distinct operational goals, a definable end-state, and realistic means to measure the effectiveness of their efforts along the way. "Just tell me what my mission is, and I'll go accomplish it," said one military officer.[78] Innumerable activities in war zones could be construed as civilian protection if viewed in the right light. Military forces may thus be pulled in multiple directions.

> *With varied approaches to the protection of civilians, it may be difficult to sort out the role for military forces, especially in peace operations.*

Even political and civilian leaders involved in peace operations may be challenged by the idea. "I just can't get my head around it," said one official in the UN Department of Peacekeeping Operations (DPKO) when asked about the meaning of civilian protection for UN peacekeepers.[79] Moreover, successful protection according to one definition may, in fact, conflict with success according to another. If civilian protection is broadened to mean everything, it may very quickly come to mean nothing at all.

A key question for militaries and political leaders is whether civilian protection should be construed primarily as a set of military tasks within a mission, or as the primary goal of the mission. In military parlance, tasks are specific activities that can be mixed and matched to accomplish the operation's goals. For example, peacekeeping operations traditionally involve the tasks of monitoring and patrolling to achieve its mission goals.

Until now, civilian protection has largely been addressed as a task or set of tasks that militaries pursue in the service of other goals, and thus, the hopeful result of military action in collaboration with various actors on the ground. In UN peacekeeping mandates, the direction "to protect civilians under imminent threat" appears as one requirement—albeit a particularly important requirement—amidst many others. The military's role in facilitating humanitarian space or in promoting and enforcing human rights law likewise represents but a few of its responsibilities—often of relatively low priority. This approach to protection may work in post-conflict environments where long-term issues of governance and state building are paramount, or where civilians face

---

[78] Workshop, *Operational Capacities for Civilian Protection Missions*, The Henry L. Stimson Center, Washington, DC, 8 December 2004.

[79] DPKO official, interview with author, 29 November 2005.

malnutrition and disease but remain relatively secure. Elsewhere, particularly in cases of immediate physical threat to civilians, or more extreme violence such as genocide, ethnic cleansing, and mass killing, this approach alone is inadequate. Thus, there is a need to develop the concept of civilian protection as the primary mission goal. For operations with this approach, saving civilian lives is the central purpose and organizing principle of the mission.

This chapter briefly analyzes the meanings of protection listed above and discusses their military implications. It then analyzes how they have been considered by the UN Secretary-General and more broadly. Finally, the focus turns to the concepts most applicable to peace support operations and military interventions to protect civilians, especially coercive protection as it parallels the ideas in *The Responsibility to Protect* for preventing mass violence against vulnerable populations.

DISTINCT CONCEPTS OF PROTECTION

The following six concepts of civilian protection fall into three general categories: civilian protection as perceived in traditional military thinking; civilian protection as understood in humanitarian thinking; and civilian protection in relation to modern peace operations and military interventions. This section briefly outlines each of these categories and explains the differing understandings of civilian protection within them.

Civilian Protection and Traditional Military Approaches

There are two familiar views of a military role in the protection of civilians. Both are based on traditional assumptions of military operations involving clearly defined warring parties. Neither view suggests a central role for military actors in offering protection.

Concept 1: Protecting Civilians as an Obligation of Military Actors during the Conduct of War (the Geneva Conventions Concept)

In this formation, the protection of civilians is viewed as an obligation of militaries during the conduct of war. This obligation, based in international law (such as the Geneva Conventions and Additional Protocols I and II), originated in a time when uniformed militaries faced each other over clear boundaries. It requires combatants to minimize death and injury to civilians during times of war—to do the least harm possible. The obligation includes not targeting civilians, providing space for humanitarian action, and allowing for the treatment of prisoners of war, the sick and the wounded. It also includes the responsibilities of occupying powers. In short, this concept puts constraints on the use of military force as a way to limit harm and better protect civilians. It is best understood as a form of negative or passive protection—militaries protect civilians through what they *do not* do (i.e., directly target non-combatants), while pursuing other goals.

This formulation is frequently invoked during military interventions and bombing campaigns, such as those by coalitions in Iraq, Afghanistan, or the Balkans. The leadership and personnel in these operations are called upon to "protect civilians" by minimizing "collateral damage."

Concept 2: Protecting Civilians as the Result of Using Force Traditionally (the Warfighting Concept)

Traditional warfighting concepts address the defeat of one's enemy as part of achieving a nation's political goal. Although such concepts do not explicitly address the protection of civilians, the use of force to achieve an end state may directly or indirectly result in better physical safety for civilians. Some military thinkers therefore point out that *the result* of traditional military action may be that people are safer and more protected after force is used to stop an enemy's actions. As stated by one retired US Marine Corps officer: "If you want to protect civilians, go kill the bad guys."[80] In other words, where traditional military action is used to achieve a political aim or to prevent actions by others, the end result—political stability, wider security, restoration of government, disbanded fighters—may most easily reduce the threats faced by civilians. Some military leaders offer this approach as a means of preventing violence against civilians in a conflict.[81]

Civilian Protection and Humanitarian Thinking

Generally speaking, the humanitarian, human rights, and legal communities are ahead of most militaries in developing a conceptual framework for protection. The humanitarian community, in particular, has an extensive protection agenda focused broadly on reducing risks to vulnerable populations. The tremendous body of work in this area cited in Chapter 2, from Oxfam guidelines on designing refugee camps to the ALNAP handbook on advocacy for internally

---

[80] US Marine Corps officer, interview with author, October 2004.

[81] There is a similarity between the thinking of such military leaders and those who advocate humanitarian intervention: both are driven to use the necessary means to meet their objective. The clear difference is that warfighting does not have as its central aim the protection of civilians. Some even suggest that there is a closer link between the goals of military counter-insurgency missions and the goals of humanitarian efforts than many NGOs would like to recognize. See Hugo Slim, *With or Against? Humanitarian Agencies and Coalition Counter-Insurgency* (Geneva: Center for Humanitarian Dialogue, July 2004).

displaced persons, has helped to elucidate a protection agenda. There is also a substantial body of scholarly work on the subject.[82]

Non-governmental organizations hold divergent views on the appropriate military role in providing support to their protection efforts.[83] One reason is that humanitarian and relief agencies strive to remain politically neutral in conflict settings, while peace operations deploy in support of a particular political aim.

> *The humanitarian, human rights, and legal communities are ahead of most militaries in developing a conceptual framework for protection.*

For humanitarian staff, neutrality means providing food to all members of a needy population, regardless of the population's previous actions or political allegiances. Ensuring that their operations are perceived as neutral by combatant parties is often essential for maintaining access to vulnerable populations in hostile territory and ensuring the safety of humanitarian staff.

Military forces within a peace operation, on the other hand, will forgo such neutrality to support their mandate and may use force against spoilers whose actions undermine security or threaten the mission. Humanitarian organizations that work closely with peacekeeping troops therefore risk being targeted by groups that perceive them as aligned against their interests, especially since relief agencies may remain in a country long after peacekeepers or other military forces depart. NGOs thus have varying levels of tolerance for civil-military cooperation. The *Handbook on United Nations Multidimensional Peacekeeping Operations*, guidelines for peacekeepers published by DPKO in 2003, recognizes the competing priorities that impact cooperation between civilian and military actors:

---

[82] Deng, *Protecting the Dispossessed*; Cohen and Deng, *Masses in Flight*; Mark Frohardt, Diane Paul, and Larry Minear, *Protecting Human Rights: The Challenge to Humanitarian Organizations*, Occasional Papers 35 (Providence, RI: The Watson Institute, 1999); Hugo Slim, "Military Intervention to Protect Human Rights: The Humanitarian Agency Perspective," *Journal of Humanitarian Assistance*, March 2002; Wheeler and Harmer, eds., *Resetting the Rules of Engagement*; James Darcy, *Human Rights and International Legal Standards: What Relief Workers Need to Know*, Network Paper 19 (Humanitarian Practice Network, February 1997).

[83] NGOs have mixed views, for example, on the provincial reconstruction teams (PRTs) in Afghanistan that combine military civilian affairs units with special operations forces working on local reconstruction projects. PRTs have implied back-up forces if conflict erupts. Some NGOs see PRTs as providing useful services and security through their presence in insecure regions. Others view them as dangerously blurring the lines between military and humanitarian workers, endangering the ability of NGOs to work as neutral actors. "CARE says ISAF Expansion Must Meet Security Challenges in Afghanistan," 31 October 2003, posted by InterAction, www.interaction.org/newswire/detail.php?id=2300.

On one hand is the need for a coherent UN response, one that assists in finding a lasting solution to a crisis, and on the other hand is the need to ensure that however long a conflict lasts, civilians are provided basic protection, including humanitarian aid.[84]

Relief and development groups debate whether forces should provide *broad* security to support peacebuilding in a post-conflict environment—by expanding the International Security Assistance Force (ISAF) beyond Kabul, Afghanistan, for example—or provide *direct* security, by escorting convoys and securing major transit routes used by NGOs, for instance. Even in the effort to assure security, the basic issue remains how closely the military and humanitarian groups work together.[85]

Concept 3: Civilian Protection as the Provision of Broad Security (the "Humanitarian Space" Concept)

Most NGOs and humanitarian agencies agree that an appropriate military role is to help support "humanitarian space" through the provision of security. Creating "humanitarian space" can mean both space in a definable, physical sense (e.g., providing security for a relief convoy) and space in terms of a policy outcome (e.g., maintaining a clear distinction between military and humanitarian activities so as to promote the perception of humanitarian independence and neutrality).[86] The military itself need not provide direct protection to civilians, or even interact with the civilian population much at all—it facilitates such activity by others.[87] Uniformed personnel may be asked to be present in IDP camps as a deterrent to abusive armed groups, for example.[88]

Alternatively, the military might actively collaborate with humanitarian organizations in protection efforts. Although many groups vehemently oppose

---

[84] Peacekeeping Best Practices Unit, Department of Peacekeeping Operations, *Handbook on United Nations Multidimensional Peacekeeping Operations* (United Nations, December 2003), 168.

[85] This relationship is particularly difficult during war. Guidance to UN personnel in Iraq in March 2003 stated that they "may not directly assist or participate in the delivery of humanitarian assistance by military forces." UN Office for the Coordination of Humanitarian Affairs, "General Guidance for Interaction Between United Nations Personnel and Military and Other Representatives of the Belligerent Parties in the Context of the Crisis in Iraq," United Nations, white paper 2.0, updated version, 9 April 2003.

[86] Wheeler and Harmer, *Resetting the Rules of Engagement*, 8.

[87] Workshop, *Operational Capacities for Civilian Protection Missions*, The Henry L. Stimson Center, Washington, DC, 8 December 2004. For discussion of civilian protection for IDPs in peace operations, see William G. O'Neill, *A New Challenge for Peacekeepers: The Internally Displaced* (Washington, DC: The Brookings Institution-John Hopkins School of Advanced International Studies Project on Internal Displacement, April 2004).

[88] Oxfam International, *Protection into Practice* (Oxford, United Kingdom: Oxfam, 2005). Oxfam has a broad definition of protection that goes beyond the design of humanitarian assistance to advocacy efforts and support for policies that lead to the deployment of peacekeeping forces and military actions.

military involvement in the provision of relief assistance, it is a reality on the ground in many conflict regions today. Militaries typically enjoy better logistical and transportation resources than NGOs, and often have capacity to spare. They can help NGOs reach otherwise inaccessible regions, serve as force multipliers for humanitarian action, and offer them physical protection as well. Groups would not be able to reach many of the DRC's most vulnerable civilians if MONUC helicopters did not fly them to remote or hard to access areas, for example. In situations of extreme violence, military forces may be the only outsiders able to safely access particular areas, and will often deliver humanitarian goods on their own.

Concept 4: Protecting Civilians through the Operational Design of Assistance (the Relief Agency Concept)

Relief agencies try to assure protection to civilians by minimizing threats of violence and coercion to vulnerable populations being offered humanitarian support. The design of relief and humanitarian efforts maximizes civilian security, thus achieving protection. The placement of refugee camps and means of access to water supplies, fuel, and latrines, for example, should be designed to reduce threats to civilians under the care of others. Camps should be laid out so that no one is attacked within or near the facility, or on the way to collect firewood or draw water. Civilian protection, therefore, can be strengthened by the design of assistance programs, the architecture of a refugee camp, and by understanding the impact of how aid is delivered.

Civilian Protection and Coercive Protection Operations

A direct military role in protecting civilians has developed in two ways. These operational approaches treat protection as either a set of tasks or the central goal of forces in an operation.

Concept 5: Civilian Protection as a Set of Tasks in Peace Operations (the UN Peacekeeping Task Concept)

Civilian protection has been addressed in UN peacekeeping operations as a substantive component of, or set of tasks within, the larger mission mandate. As discussed, UN-led missions increasingly have been organized under mandates that direct the mission to "protect civilians under imminent threat." In this view, peacekeepers are tasked with civilian protection as one of many potential roles within a Chapter VII mission. Protection, then, is a component of achieving the goals of a multidimensional peace operation, not its singular aim. This concept reflects the way that most UN missions with complex mandates operate.

Peacekeeping tasks that broadly protect civilians, however, are numerous and encompass a range of actions. Tasks can include providing support to law and order, escorting convoys, protecting camps, establishing safe havens, breaking up militias, demilitarizing refugee/IDP camps, organizing disarmament, and intervening on behalf of an individual or community under threat. Many in the military consider protection first and foremost a role for military police or civil affairs units, however, bound closely to the functions of the rule of law.[89] Others see it as a question of using force to deter would-be killers from attacking vulnerable populations.

Concept 6: Protecting Civilians through a Military Intervention to Prevent Mass Killings (the "Responsibility to Protect" Concept)

The protection of civilians can be the primary goal of an operation, where the central purpose is to stop or prevent mass killings, ethnic cleansing, crimes against humanity, or genocide, as laid out by the ICISS Commission. Such interventions are likely to be located in non-permissive environments where conflict continues and coercive action is required.[90] The concept presumes that military force is used under specific conditions in which high levels of violence are threatened (for example, Rwanda before and during its 1994 genocide).

The above concepts are broad categories that reflect protection approaches within the international community that contain clear implications for military actions. This brief survey demonstrates clear, but operationally distinct, views offered to guide the work of actors in the field.

More Approaches to Protection

Before turning to focus on these concepts, it is important to note additional views that are less directly related to military roles but which shape policies on protection. Protection has been identified, for example, with traditional "civil defense," the shielding of civilians from weapons of mass destruction and natural disasters,[91] and as a domestic law and order function, since protection is what society normally provides for its citizens. Protection is also viewed as the result of the establishment of individual human and political rights. From this

---

[89] Military police are like infantry forces with arrest powers; they can escort convoys, operate in non-permissive environments, and carry weapons. What differs, perhaps, is that military police more regularly define their mission as restoring and maintaining civil order than do traditional military forces.

[90] Given the coordination, speed, and coherence required, such operations are unlikely to be UN-led.

[91] This view is suggested by the European Union's civil protection policies. European Union, "The Community Mechanism for Civil Protection," http://ec.europa.eu/environment/civil/prote/mechanism.htm.

perspective, protection is construed as a legal issue, accomplished through the enforcement of international law concerning asylum and refugee-resettlement issues or human rights, for example. This rights-based perspective has received substantial consideration by NGOs and within UN agencies such as UNHCR. In peace operations, the activities of civilians can reflect this concept, as they may take actions such as denouncing the denial of political rights and advocating for legal protections of civilians.[92]

Box 3.1

WHAT KIND OF TASKS?

The Stimson Center hosted a workshop on operationalizing *The Responsibility to Protect* to look at the preparedness of military and peacekeeping forces to protect civilians from major violence. During the workshop, participants agreed that there was no joint concept of operation for missions involving the protection of civilians. To help sort out a military role, participants drafted a list of potential tasks that forces might use to support protection. They identified:

- Securing safe corridors and the passage of convoys
- Establishing safe havens
- Separating armed elements (especially in relation to border control, IDP camps, and roads)
- Military observation and surveillance
- Preventing mob violence and crowd control
- Disarmament, Demobilization and Reintegration (DDR)
- Coercive disarmament
- Seizing arms caches
- Demining
- Facilitating humanitarian access to conflict areas
- Securing key facilities and cultural properties
- Enforcing curfews
- Ensuring freedom of movement
- Supporting police presence and patrols
- Protecting VIPs
- Providing backup for high-risk arrests
- Eliminating special threats
- Handling detainees
- Preventing looting and pilfering
- Supporting the prosecution of human rights abuses
- Transmitting information about human rights abuses to monitoring groups
- Training local security forces
- Providing intelligence support focused on civilian protection
- Stopping hate media
- Direct use of force against killers

Source: Workshop, *Operational Capacities for Civilian Protection Missions*, The Henry L. Stimson Center, Washington, DC, 8 December 2004.

---

[92] A potential military role within this concept could involve the detention or arrest of those accused of war crimes, or the provision of security to protection officers and human rights observers.

Definitions of protection also extend deeply into non-physical needs. For example, the 2005 ALNAP guide for humanitarian agencies argues: "The inner emotional experience of an individual is as important as their outward physical needs."[93] The guide suggests that self-respect can help a person survive physical suffering, and thus, "Protection...is as much about preserving the dignity of the human person as it is about the safety of that person."[94] Finally, protection is sometimes cast as the result of political strategies. Some suggest that international mediators protect civilians by promoting political agreement between warring parties.[95]

THE UN'S UMBRELLA APPROACH

These varied and diverse meanings of protection have, to a certain extent, been codified in UN publications on the protection of civilians, beginning in 1999. Since such UN publications often reflect the general consensus of the international community about particular issues, it is worth examining in some detail how civilian protection is conceived of at the United Nations—in particular for peacekeepers.

To what extent does the wealth of UN literature on civilian protection offer a concrete vision of the operational responsibilities of peacekeepers and other internationally mandated forces? With OCHA as a motor behind the civilian protection concept, the treatment of civilian protection in UN Secretary-General reports and other UN documents has far more detail about non-coercive forms of protection—legal, humanitarian, and otherwise—than coercive military protection. OCHA describes civilian protection as an "umbrella concept of humanitarian policies that brings together protection elements from a number of fields, including international humanitarian and human rights law, military and security sectors, and humanitarian assistance."[96] UN documents on the protection of civilians have therefore included recommendations from a wide array of disciplines, but without specific, meaningful guidance to military forces. Recent UN publications are somewhat more direct in describing a military role in protection.

In April 1998, the Secretary-General mentioned "civilian protection" in the context of conflict and deemed it a "humanitarian imperative" in a report

---

[93] Slim and Bonwick, *Protection: An ALNAP Guide for Humanitarians*, 31.
[94] Ibid.
[95] Workshop, *Operational Capacities for Civilian Protection Missions*, The Henry L. Stimson Center, Washington, DC, 8 December 2004.
[96] UN Office for the Coordination of Humanitarian Affairs, "Institutional History of Protection of Civilians in Armed Conflict," OCHA Online, http://ochaonline.un.org/webpage.asp?Page=780.

focused on Africa and the erosion of humanitarian norms in armed conflict.[97] He provided some limited guidance for protecting civilians with military force, however, in his first in-depth report on the subject in September 1999. That report argued that civilian protection can be provided by international legal mechanisms, parties to conflict, and humanitarian action, and hinted at a larger international military role should these measures fail. It recommended that military forces receive better training in "soft security" areas such as humanitarian and human rights law and civil-military coordination, but also recognized the potential need for "hard security" tasks such as forcible disarmament.[98]

In a section on "physical protection," the report affirmed the UN's authority to mandate military interventions to protect civilians at risk: "[T]he Security Council can promote the protection of civilians in conflict...by peacekeeping or enforcement measures under Chapters VI, VII or VIII of the Charter."[99] The report also outlined a series of tasks for peacekeepers.[100] These include:

> Discouraging abuses of civilian populations; providing stability and fostering a political process of reconciliation, supporting institution-building efforts, including in such areas as human rights and law enforcement; protecting humanitarian workers and delivering humanitarian assistance; maintaining the security and neutrality of refugee camps, including separation of combatants and non-combatants; maintaining "safe zones" for the protection of civilian populations; deterring and addressing abuses including through the arrest of war criminals.[101]

The report recognized that certain types of civilian protection, such as forcibly disarming combatants, were beyond the UN's capacity to perform, and might require regional or international military forces.[102] The creation of "humanitarian zones, security zones and safe corridors" could protect civilians as a "last resort," provided the zones were demilitarized and there was a safe-exit option.[103] Finally, the report addressed the potential need for enforcement action in language that foreshadowed *The Responsibility to Protect*:

---

[97] UN Security Council, *The Causes of Conflict and the Promotion of Durable Peace and Sustainable Development in Africa*, S/1998/318, 13 April 1998, 11.

[98] UN Security Council, *Report of the Secretary-General on the Protection of Civilians in Armed Conflict*, S/1999/957, 8 September 1999, rec. 28 and 29, para. 58. In addition, "credible deterrent capacity" and "enforcement action" may be necessary in some cases to fulfil specific mandated tasks.

[99] Ibid., para. 44.

[100] Ibid., rec. 12.

[101] Ibid., para. 57.

[102] Ibid., rec. 35.

[103] Ibid., para. 66 and rec. 39.

> In situations where the parties to the conflict commit systematic and widespread breaches of international humanitarian and human rights law, causing threats of genocide, crimes against humanity and war crimes, the Security Council should be prepared to intervene under Chapter VII of the Charter.... I recommend that the Security Council... [i]n the face of massive and ongoing abuses, consider the imposition of appropriate enforcement action.... The protection of civilians...is fundamental to the central mandate of the Organization. The responsibility for the protection of civilians cannot be transferred to others.[104]

In comparison to this strong 1999 report, two following reports on the protection of civilians provided less guidance for internationally-mandated forces. In March 2001, the Secretary-General did not even include UN peacekeepers in his list of "entities providing protection," focusing instead on governments, armed groups, civil society, and regional groups.[105] The report offered four broad measures to protect civilians—prosecution under international law, humanitarian access to civilians at risk, separation of civilians from armed elements, and media and information in conflict situations—but no role for international forces.

The Secretary-General's third report on civilian protection in November 2002 also focused on key humanitarian and peacebuilding tasks: securing humanitarian access to vulnerable populations; separating civilians from combatants; and re-establishing the rule of law, justice, and reconciliation. While a number of these tasks could—and, in situations of extreme violence, probably should—be performed by military forces, the report focused on non-coercive, consent based strategies. It did not mention what to do if these strategies failed.

It is not clear why the Secretary-General shifted away from delineating a protection role for international forces after 1999. Much UN work on protection came from OCHA, so it is understandable, perhaps, that the resulting reports would focus on non-coercive strategies for protection, and keep the military at arms length. OCHA's *Aide Mémoire* on civilian protection, first published in March 2002, detailed numerous humanitarian strategies for protection. The role for military peacekeepers was to help humanitarians to achieve access and provide security in camps, but there was no further role.

In May 2004, the Secretary-General re-established a military role in protection in his fourth report. His report noted that UN mandates had begun to allow for troops to "physically protect" civilians under imminent threat. It called for the

---

[104] Ibid., para. 67, rec. 40 and para. 68.
[105] UN Security Council, *Report of the Secretary-General on the Protection of Civilians in Armed Conflict*, S/2001/331, 30 March 2001, 10.

physical protection of refugees and IDPs "during transit as well as after return" and from sexual and gender-based violence.[106] A sequence of actions for the Security Council was laid out to uphold the international community's "responsibility to respond" to "large-scale or systematic international crimes," with the use of military force within this sequence:

> A series of gradated measures to be carried out by the Security Council, the broader United Nations system and the international community as a whole *are required* to respond to evidence of widespread crimes against civilians. Measures that the Council could consider include better monitoring and evaluating crisis situations...forceful demands that the parties cease their attacks on civilians and comply with their obligations under international law, the threat and imposition of sanctions when obligations continue to be breached, referrals to the Prosecutor of the International Criminal Court...and *the rapid deployment of an appropriate force with an explicit mandate and adequate means to protect civilian lives* [italics added].[107]

This more explicit reference to a military role continued in the fifth report on civilian protection in November 2005, which called on peacekeepers to provide physical protection to civilians in camps, during population movements, and in their places of origin. The report also described a peacekeeping role in restoring law and order, ensuring the civilian character of IDP camps, and securing humanitarian access. Importantly, it recommended improving the design of peacekeeping operations to better protect civilians.[108]

Under-Secretary-General for Humanitarian Affairs Jan Egeland has also emphasized the need for physical protection by military peacekeepers in recent statements. In a refreshingly bold statement to the Security Council in June 2005, Egeland argued:

> We must provide better physical security. Humanitarian presence is not enough. The creation of a secure environment for displaced populations should be a primary objective of peace-keeping operations. We need strategic deployment around camps to provide area security for the displaced, we need it in areas of unrest to prevent new displacement, and in areas of origin to facilitate voluntary and safe return. Both peace-keeping missions and regional organizations have an important role to play.... The provision of protection against violence needs to be incorporated into the concept of peace-keeping operations and clear guidance developed.[109]

---

[106] UN Security Council, *Report of the Secretary-General on the Protection of Civilians in Armed Conflict*, S/2004/431, 28 May 2004, paras. 25, 29.

[107] Ibid., para. 39.

[108] UN Security Council, *Report of the Secretary-General on the Protection of Civilians in Armed Conflict*, S/2005/740, 28 November 2005.

[109] Jan Egeland, "Statement by Under-Secretary-General Jan Egeland to the Security Council on the protection of civilians in armed conflict," UN Department of Public Information, 21 June 2005.

Egeland's call for better physical security to protect vulnerable populations, combined with the Secretary-General's increasing support, represented a potential shift in approaches within the UN, a sign of room to bring humanitarian concerns and peace operations into better alignment over the operational aspects of protecting civilians.

EVALUATING CIVILIAN PROTECTION CONCEPTS

Continuum or Confusion?

Problems can arise from so many alternate coercive and non-coercive approaches to civilian protection. Different views can engender confusion or contradiction, or result in strategies that operate at cross-purposes or render each other meaningless. At the same time, protecting civilians is a complex, multifaceted goal engaging varied and diverse actors. Some argue, therefore, that having a range of activities labeled under "protection" is wise, particularly if they can be viewed as a *continuum* of responses toward the same goal. But this continuum can also become a kitchen sink approach if the meanings of and priorities of protection are not clarified.

Within the UN, the "protection of civilians" agenda impacts those within its peacekeeping offices and humanitarian programs. MONUC Deputy Special Representative of the Secretary-General (DSRSG) Ross Mountain, for example, has worked to bring together these varied actors within MONUC and to develop clearer operational approaches to civilian protection. He has suggested that multiple approaches can be fruitful as long as groups work to build a house rather than merely lay bricks: who needs a field of bricks?[110] The result may be that learning to work together can demonstrate real results.

One challenge, therefore, is to clarify how the different types of protection work can be harmonized and situations identified in which only specific approaches should be utilized. Sometimes a particular type of protection strategy is inappropriate or irrelevant, such as the use of unarmed military observers in the midst of a large-scale genocide. In other cases, one actor should temporarily take a backseat to another, or even withdraw altogether. Some robust military activities to target or compel the disarmament of murderous militia, for example, might make the delivery of humanitarian assistance impossible in the short term. In other situations, cooperation between actors may enable them to accomplish more than on their own. Peacekeepers and civilian agencies may create a useful strategy to identify vulnerable populations that lack food and security.

---

[110] Ross Mountain, interview by author, Washington, DC, 27 October 2005.

Military actors can balance some concepts of protection simultaneously, such as living within the Geneva Conventions, providing support to humanitarian space, and helping reduce vulnerabilities at refugee camps. There is also a range of actions that can support civilian protection within either a peace operation or for a mission whose central goal is the protection of civilians. These include working at a strategic level to prevent attacks against civilians, using force on a limited tactical level within an operation, or acting as a deterrent presence broadly. Actions along this scale could involve the direct use of preventive force to counter and/or eliminate abusive armed groups, the use of reactive or defensive force to physically protect civilian population centers, the threat or use of force to protect humanitarian activities and/or expand humanitarian access, deterrence through a particular military stance, the use of low-level force in individual circumstances to promote the rule of law, and the provision of logistics and/or operational support to humanitarian organizations without using force. The use of force involves trade-offs, and thus needs to be appropriately calibrated to the situation at hand.

> *The multitude of military tasks implied by civilian protection mandates is pulling peacekeepers in opposing directions.*

Military Role: A Tug of War?

The multitude of military tasks implied by civilian protection mandates is pulling peacekeepers in two opposing directions. In UN operations, forces are already being asked to engage in more "soft security" issues—tasks relating to development, reconstruction, and long-term peacebuilding. These are not typically activities for which militaries train and some argue that civilian actors are better suited to perform them. At the same time, many peace operations have Chapter VII authority and are now expected to use robust force. Troops might be called on to dissuade armed groups from targeting innocents through coercive or punitive tactics, to conduct robust cordon and search operations, to serve as an interpositional force, or to forcibly disarm belligerents.

Peacekeepers thus are being pulled toward more engagement in questions of governance, humanitarian action, and human rights, *and* pushed towards using more force in conflict zones. In both cases, the need to protect civilians is invoked as justification. Although all these activities are important and legitimate, given limited resources, there are tradeoffs within the continuum: doing everything may result in few things being done well and effectively; doing a few central tasks may be effective but insufficient to meet a mission's objectives. In some situations, peacekeepers will need to choose between supporting humanitarian space and offering direct physical protection to a population in need, for example.

The language of protection in peace operations may also mask a political problem, where outside observers interpret peacekeeping missions as protecting vulnerable populations from physical threats when their real work is support to a political process, the development of local governance, and assisting humanitarian activities. Deploying peacekeepers without either a clear vision of how to protect civilians or the means and authority to do so may result in a tragic shortfall. AU contingents in Darfur have a limited ability to use coercive methods to protect civilians, for example. AMIS cooperates with the Sudanese police force to inculcate human rights norms, but it does not prevent raids by the Janjaweed militia on villages.[111] With roughly 7,000 personnel in a hostile environment the size of France, AMIS activities to protect civilians are limited and not equal to coercive protection operations. Using protection language to describe non-coercive activities in situations of genocide, ethnic cleansing, or mass killing virtually strips it of its meaning.

TOWARDS A MILITARY CONCEPT FOR COERCIVE PROTECTION

In more stable environments with less, or localized, ongoing violence against civilians, a complex peace operation with civilian protection as a mandated task might be appropriate. Such a mission would deploy with a primary goal of promoting long-term stability and security by building up local governance capacity. The peace operation would protect civilians through local interventions and the calibrated use of force where civilians remain under threat. But the mission would approach this work as a set of tasks toward achieving goals such as peacebuilding, the provision of security for humanitarian assistance, and support for the rule of law.

When a peace operation is conducted in an environment where civilians face immediate physical threats and insecurity, however, a decision to use force to provide for their protection may shift the operation to a coercive protection mission. This approach, which can be consistent with a UN Chapter VII mandate, requires protection to be a major objective of the operation and to operate as such. In doing so, it will come close to crossing a line into the intervention approach suggested by *The Responsibility to Protect*. Modifying traditional peacekeeping operations is an inadequate answer for upholding protection mandates in extreme circumstances such as large-scale violence or

---

[111] William G. O'Neill and Violette Cassis, *Protecting Two Million Internally Displaced: The Successes and Shortcomings of the African Union in Darfur*, An Occasional Paper (Brookings Institution – University of Bern Project on Internal Displacement, November 2005).

genocide, however. In those circumstances, forces need to have a central goal of protecting civilians, with that objective driving their strategy and tactics.

Thus, stopping harm to civilians through coercive protection needs to be operationalized *both* as a mission type and as a series of tasks within peace operations. Clarifying the mandate and mission goal is therefore crucial, a point obvious to most military thinkers and planners. They argue that a military mission must be defined first and that the strategy, tactics, and procedures fall in place to accomplish it. Thus, by identifying protection of civilians as the goal of the mission, military leaders will design a strategy to achieve it, just like any other mission assigned to

> *Stopping harm to civilians through coercive protection can both apply as a mission type and as a series of tasks within peace operations.*

them. Importantly, full-scale interventions to protect civilians should take place only in extreme circumstances and for a limited amount of time. By necessity, they could involve significant use of force and war-like tactics to eliminate the capacity of the killers to conduct mass-murder, and would respond rapidly to halt the killing as quickly as possible.

A New Mission?

If coercive protection is re-conceptualized as a mission, would it represent something wholly new for military forces? The answer largely depends on the nature of the environment and the tasks involved. Of course, many existing skills in the military toolkit can be utilized to protect civilians. The specific and easily identifiable tasks for protecting civilians—such as guard duty, protecting convoys, manning checkpoints, conducting patrols, or engaging in crowd control—are familiar to militaries and are already part of training packages used to prepare forces. Preparing to protect civilians would then be a matter of identifying the right tasks and making sure the troops deploying to protect civilians are prepared to carry them out. There is not much difference between protecting a military convoy and a civilian convoy, for example. Likewise, providing security to a clearly defined area is a similar task whether for a camp of IDPs or a compound of military personnel.

One UN official suggested that the question is less about preparing troops for something new and different, and more about how contingents appreciate the task when they get on the ground, and how they see the scope of their area of responsibility. Likewise, one US Army officer suggested he uses the same operational principles wherever he deploys; the rules of engagement are the difference.[112]

A concept of operations for civilian protection as a military mission would likely build off existing concepts of counterinsurgency, peace operations, and strict adherence to the laws of war, which have been around for decades. The 1940 US Marine Corps *Small Wars Manual*, for example, instructed its readers on the difference between traditional warfighting and operations aimed at other ends:

> Instead of employing force, one strives to accomplish the purpose by diplomacy. A Force Commander who gains his objective in a small war without firing a shot has attained far greater success than one who resorted to the use of arms. While endeavoring to avoid the infliction of physical harm to any native, there is always the necessity of preventing, as far as possible, any casualties among our own troops.... The motive in small wars is not material destruction. It is usually a project dealing with the social, economic, and political development of the people.[113]

The manual further emphasized that small wars are a "different order" than usual military duties. In traditional roles, military personnel "simply strive to attain a method of producing the maximum physical effect with the force at their disposal. In small wars, caution must be exercised...the goal is to gain decisive results with the least application of force and the consequent minimum loss of life."[114]

On the other hand, certain aspects of a mission under the "responsibility to protect" concept could represent new challenges for militaries. As suggested by Thomas Weiss, these "coercive protection" missions must define their objectives in relation to civilians rather than other military forces.[115] Provision of coercive protection does not necessarily involve defeating traditional military forces or conducting traditional peacekeeping tasks. Rather, it requires forces to come between potential attackers and civilians, and carry out tasks that are "not favored by militaries" such as forcible disarmament, maintaining safe areas, and protecting humanitarian efforts and staff.[116]

Providing security to an undefined location, such as a group of civilians dispersed over an area, can be extremely difficult, and may require a broad

---

[112] For example, he cited the principles of mass, synchronization, command and control, traditional components for soldiers in operations. US Army Major, interview with author, Washington, DC, 14 October 2004.

[113] United States Marine Corps, *Small Wars Manual, 1940* (Washington, DC: US Government Printing Office, declassified 1972; Manhattan, Kansas: Sunflower University Press, 1996).

[114] Ibid., 31-32.

[115] Weiss, "The Humanitarian Impulse," 47-48.

[116] Ibid.

strategic vision of its own. Defending a population is more challenging than defending a specific convoy, building, or area with a perimeter, especially if abusive armed groups are interspersed in the area, difficult to identify, and free to move around. New military thinking on the matter may be necessary.

Key Issues with Coercive Protection

There are a number of key issues that emerge when considering the military role in providing protection: when and how to use force, proactive or reactive tactics in coercive protection, concerns over consent of local parties, the question of whom to protect where, and the potential challenge of transferring from a robust protection mission to a more traditional peacekeeping operation. Each of these issues poses potential dilemmas for troops in the field and should, therefore, be incorporated into the strategic planning and preparation for such missions prior to deployment.

Use of Force

A 2004 workshop on the use of force in UN peace operations with the DPKO and former UN force commanders found that Council mandates do not authorize force robustly enough.[117] Force commanders reported that protection often requires pre-emptive or preventive actions, yet they are often prohibited from acting except in response to opposing forces' actions. In many cases, by the time they could respond, it was already too late to be effective. Troop contributing countries often had a mindset that reflected a "one bullet for one bullet" mentality, meaning that they would not act unless responding to attacks by a belligerent. While there was strong interest in the workshop topic, no consensus emerged on the way forward on use of force in UN peace operations.[118]

The use of force to achieve a humanitarian end can involve causing physical damage to people and property, and may include loss of life. In a human protection operation, one must harm fewer people than one saves, one must injure fewer than one protects, and one must not destroy an area to save it. Regardless, those on the receiving end of such violence will inevitably see any use of force as a warlike attack. Controlling the continuum of violence and the reaction of those engaged (as well as the perception of those who are to be "saved") is difficult, heightening the importance of political leadership and public information.

---

[117] They also suggested that, legally, the question of Chapter VI or VII authorization does not matter. Kirsti Samuels (rapporteur), *Use of Force in UN Peacekeeping Operations*, Report, IPA/UNDPKO workshop (International Peace Academy, 6 February 2004).

[118] Kirsti Samuels, interview with author, October 2004. The report recommended increased general training for peacekeepers, as well as specific training in rules of engagement and human rights. It also called for better equipment for troops.

Protecting in Advance or in Response?

Another difficulty relates to the nature of protection itself. Protection may include, for example, escorting individuals and protecting camps, safe areas, and key roads. If a force charged with protection reacts to an attack on civilians after the fact, however, it will already have failed in its goal of providing protection. As a result, success will often require taking aggressive action prior to the use of violence. This requirement shifts the burden from reacting to a defined state (e.g., an attack) to reacting to a threat for which there may not be a clear trigger or definition. It could require direct action targeting bad actors or preventing such actors from operating in the first place.

Consent & Escalation

If mass killing or genocide is ongoing, should an intervention force strive for pacification or the outright defeat of the killers? What if a militia responds to efforts to protect civilians in one area by killing even more civilians elsewhere? What if the force engages a militia, incurs casualties, and troop contributing countries respond by withdrawing their forces? When forces employ a more aggressive approach, they may spawn an increase in violence against themselves, against international workers, or even against civilians in the short term. This may be anticipated in usual warfighting, but it is the opposite of the premise of traditional peacekeeping, where consent is sought for the actions of the international forces. As seen in the DRC and Haiti, these questions are not theoretical.

> *As seen in the DRC and Haiti, these questions are not theoretical.*

Protect Whom, Where?

In a complex peace operation with a mandate to protect, which civilians should the mission strive to protect, given limited capacity? Is it better to focus resources on programs with long-term benefits, such as the reintegration of former combatants, or on creating a rapid reaction capacity to halt abuses as they occur? How should the force respond to attacks occurring three blocks from its area of control? What about three miles? Human protection operations, by definition, will take place in complex, unpredictable environments, often with extremely limited resources. With few exceptions, they cannot hope to *protect every civilian all the time from everything*. The EU-authorized *Operation Artemis* in the DRC in 2003, for example, brought security to civilians in the town of Bunia, but not beyond. In such circumstances, strategy and priorities are paramount: Protect who, from what, in what area, with what means, to what ends, with what goal?

Transition to Peace Operations

One serious question with such missions is what to do *after* the intervention completes its work and the killers are incapacitated—to whom do they hand the reins? A forceful military intervention could result in a deeply traumatized populace, with some portions of society ambivalent or hostile to the intervention force. If not managed carefully, such a mission could leave civilians worse off in the long run. A rapid transition to peacekeeping and peacebuilding activities is likely to be necessary. Even military interventions that are not coercive protection operations face this issue, such as the 2003 intervention into Iraq, which serves as a caution against failing to prepare adequately for such transitions.

In an ideal world, military interventions to protect civilians would transition neatly to peace operations that include civilian protection as a mandated set of central tasks. Because of the complex nature of post-war environments, however, the transition from a "coercive protection mission" to a peace operation may not be linear. In some extremely violent regions, the protection of local civilians could remain the most important, overriding task of the force, or even its primary mission. Other, more secure areas might offer the luxury (and difficulty) of focusing on state-building. Moreover, the situation in any specific region could change rapidly over the course of weeks, days, or even hours. The operation must therefore be prepared to operate at different tempos and to utilize different degrees of force depending on the local situation on the ground.

The above challenges represent but a sampling of those that any coercive protection operation would likely face. The first step, however, is simply recognizing that such a military mission needs to be conceived in the first place. Troops need a clear understanding of and preparation for using coercive force to physically protect those in need.

Looking Forward

Awareness of the protection concepts from varied communities benefits everyone who seeks to protect civilians. Gaining a clearer understanding of what protecting civilians means and what it requires in the field is a first step.

Even as policy debates over the "responsibility to protect" continue, military personnel today are already deployed worldwide in peace and stability operations with mandates to protect civilians, sometimes in horrific circumstances. These forces need clear guidance on their role to support the physical protection of civilians and, if called upon to do so, how they should intervene directly to save lives. What is known then about the capacity and authority of organizations to lead such coercive protection operations and about how they employ traditional methods such as rules of engagement, doctrine, and training to ensure that these missions succeed? Halting the slaughter of non-combatants requires not just a working concept of operation, but capable organizations willing to employ these known tools to prepare forces for current and future missions.

—4—
INDICATORS OF CAPACITY:
WILLING ACTORS AND
OPERATIONAL CAPABILITIES

The effective deployment of forces—a prerequisite to providing protection to civilians in hostile environments—is one of many challenges facing traditional military and peacekeeping missions. Only a few multinational organizations can mount interventions with military forces to protect civilians from mass killings, genocide, or ethnic cleansing under their own authority. This section first considers which organizations are willing and able to authorize and lead such forces. It then looks at their capacity to conduct operations in non-permissive environments. Finally, the general operational challenges that affect all peace operations are reviewed, in the context of missions involving the protection of civilians.

WILLING ACTORS

The willingness to act usually depends on the authority to act. Five multinational organizations have authority to organize peace operations to intervene and employ force for more than self-defense: the UN, NATO, the European Union, the African Union, and the Economic Community of West African States.[119] Other groups may assist these missions, such as the Multinational Stand-by High Readiness Brigade for UN Operations (SHIRBRIG), which is designed to deploy rapidly to help set up UN peace operations.[120] Each of these organizations has a unique structure and capacity that affects its willingness and ability to intervene.

---

[119] Numerous multinational groups can intervene diplomatically or politically. The Organization of American States (OAS) and the Organization of Security and Cooperation in Europe can provide observers for a peace operation; the Intergovernmental Authority on Development has supported political missions to negotiate peace in the Sudan and Somalia. The Association of South East Asian Nations (ASEAN) operates under a non-interventionist framework, without the capacity for peace operations, although Indonesia has called for creating a regional ASEAN peacekeeping force.

[120] SHIRBRIG provides support for the establishment of UN operations with Chapter VI mandates, such as UNMEE in Ethiopia/Eritrea. SHIRBRIG has also supported mission planning for operations under Chapter VII, including the transition from the ECOWAS-led mission in Liberia (ECOMIL) to a UN operation (UNMIL).

The United Nations

The United Nations has a broad mandate to act against threats to international peace and security. The UN authorizes and leads peace operations and authorizes actions led by individual countries, coalitions as multinational forces (MNFs), and regional bodies in response to threats to international peace and security. Traditionally when the Security Council cited Chapter VII of the UN Charter and authorized a mission to use "all necessary means" to implement its mandate, the resulting operations were referred to as "peace enforcement" missions, reflecting the charter's language. The UN typically has not led these kinds of missions. By early 2006, the UN had increasingly taken on the leadership of many complex operations, however—most with Chapter VII mandates.

The North Atlantic Treaty Organization

As a collective defense organization, NATO is designed to intervene and can do so at the direction of its Member States. It has the capacity to organize and lead military interventions. NATO prefers, but does not require, a UN Security Council mandate to operate. This issue was raised regarding NATO's actions during the conflict in the former Yugoslavia; the Alliance responded with air strikes after UN forces were attacked beginning in the fall of 1994. NATO members argued that such actions were within the authorization provided by UN resolutions on sanctions[121] and resolutions establishing safe areas and a no-fly zone.[122] NATO then deployed forces under the Stabilization Force in Bosnia and Herzegovina (SFOR), as part of the follow-on to the peace agreement reached at Dayton in 1995. NATO's action in Kosovo in 1999, however, was taken without Council authorization, and remains controversial for that reason. NATO has since led operations in Afghanistan, where it assumed leadership of ISAF in 2003. It additionally provided training assistance to Iraqi forces and airlift and planning support to the AU mission in Darfur.

In April 1999, the NATO Strategic Concept was updated and approved to commit members of the Alliance to defend not just other members, but peace and stability in NATO's region and periphery. Thus, the Strategic Concept provided for NATO to undertake military operations as "non-Article 5 Crisis Response Operations (CROs)." Peace support operations are within the CRO category and are intended to deal with complex emergencies. Such operations usually support the United Nations or the Organization for Security and Cooperation in Europe (OSCE). The range of operations NATO will undertake

---

[121] S/Res/713, 25 September 1991; S/Res/757, 30 May 1992; and S/Res/787, 16 November 1992.
[122] S/Res/816, 31 March 1993; S/Res/836; 4 June 1993.

in this category includes peace enforcement, peacekeeping, conflict prevention, peacemaking, peacebuilding, and humanitarian relief.

The European Union

The EU has attempted to increase its military crisis response capacity, particularly since the establishment of the European Security and Defense Policy (ESDP) in 1999. According to the "Petersburg tasks" from the 1992 Western European Union Petersburg Declaration, the EU has authority to pursue a limited range of military tasks, including "humanitarian and rescue tasks, peacekeeping tasks and tasks of combat forces in crisis management, including peacemaking."[123] The 2003 European Security Strategy detailed a few more possible missions: "joint disarmament operations, support for third countries in combating terrorism, and security sector reform."[124]

The final Petersburg task, "crisis management, including peacemaking," appears to give the EU broad authority to intervene using force. The language of this task, however, is vague and has been an item of considerable contention. Does "crisis management" include interventions to halt genocide or mass killing? The EU has no detailed strategy documents or official doctrine to answer this question. Given the difficulty of achieving agreement among EU Member States on the nature of future military activities, actions in the field may well precede an articulated military strategy. The EU may choose to improve its capacities before it identifies specific missions, including missions that view the protection of civilians as either an operational task or a specific goal. Continent-wide capacity building efforts are well underway, as dictated in a number of documents, such as the 1999 *EU Headline Goal* and 2004 *Headline Goal 2010*.

The African Union

While the AU Constitutive Act affirms the principle of non-interference by Member States in the internal affairs of others and bans the use or threat of force against other Member States, it makes a major exception for intervention "in a Member State pursuant to a decision of the Assembly in respect of grave circumstances, namely: war crimes, genocide and crimes against humanity."[125] The AU Peace and Security Council (PSC) is to have "an operational structure"

---

[123] Western European Union Council of Ministers, *Petersburg Declaration* (Bonn: Western European Union Council of Ministers, 19 June 1992), 4, para. 2.

[124] Javier Solana, *A Secure Europe in a Better World: European Security Strategy* (Brussels: European Union, 12 December 2003), http://ue.eu.int/uedocs/cmsUpload/78367.pdf. The *Strategy* is an important declaration of the EU's broad strategic intent, but makes no mention of genocide, does not attempt to explain the Petersburg tasks, and does not indicate the nature of the missions towards which EU military capacity will be directed.

[125] African Union, *The Constitutive Act of the African Union*, Article 4, Principles (Lomé: African Union, 11 July 2000).

to implement its "decisions taken in the areas of conflict prevention, peacemaking, peace support operations and intervention, as well as peacebuilding and post-conflict reconstruction..."[126] It shall "anticipate and prevent disputes and conflicts, as well as policies that may lead to genocide and crimes against humanity" and "recommend to the Assembly, pursuant to Article 4(h) of the Constitutive Act, intervention, on behalf of the Union, in a Member State in respect of grave circumstances, namely war crimes, genocide, and crimes against humanity, as defined in relevant international conventions and instruments." The PSC will also support and facilitate humanitarian action in situations of armed conflicts or major natural disasters.

The AU Policy Framework for establishing the African Standby Force (ASF), adopted by the African Chiefs of Defense Staff in May 2003, sets forth six potential conflict scenarios of escalating intensity: *Scenario 1* (military advice to a political mission); *Scenario 2* (observer mission co-deployed with a UN mission); *Scenario 3* (stand alone AU observer mission); *Scenario 4* (regional peacekeeping force under Chapter VI); *Scenario 5* (AU peacekeeping force for complex multidimensional peacekeeping mission—low level spoilers); and *Scenario 6* (AU intervention, e.g., genocide situations where international community does not act promptly.)[127] *Scenario 6* is the only one in which the AU suggests an individual nation take the lead:

> Based on the level of coherence required at the field HQ [headquarters] level for an intervention mission, particularly those involving an opposed early deployment, such operations are best conducted by a coalition under a lead nation.... As a long term goal, the ASF should be capable of conducting such interventions without reliance on lead nations. This would require a standing AU Multinational military HQ at above brigade level, plus the capability to assemble and deploy rapidly with prepared and capable military contingents.[128]

Thus, the AU recognizes both its potential role in intervening against genocide and its current requirement to greatly expand its own capacities before it can conduct such missions.

In addition, the AU seeks to work with African regional groups to identify which missions will be conducted by whom, as well as the terms of reference and areas of responsibility for each regionally based brigade or equivalent force. The ASF is an extremely ambitious concept, and it should drive the

---

[126] African Union, *Protocol Relating to the Establishment of the Peace and Security Council of the African Union* (Durban: African Union, July 2002), 3. Specifically, its functions include peace support operations and intervention "pursuant to article 4(h) and (j) of the Constitutive Act."
[127] African Union, *Policy Framework for the Establishment of the African Standby Force and the Military Staff Committee (Part I)*, Adopted by the African Chiefs of Defence Staff (Addis Ababa: African Union, 15-16 May 2003), 3.
[128] Ibid., 5.

development of standardized doctrine and procedures for forces, equipment lists, the recognition of capacity gaps, and policy standardization.

To meet the AU vision of African regional forces taking the lead in interventions to stop crimes against humanity and genocide on the continent, regional organizations will need to adopt frameworks and develop the means to make them a reality. African organizations will have to align with the AU Policy Framework or define the specific types of missions in which they will engage. Progress has been slow; ECOWAS has moved forward with its own arrangements, for example, as has the Intergovernmental Authority on Development (IGAD) in Eastern Africa.[129] At the same, the AU framework contradicts the policies of the Southern African Development Community (SADC), which is theoretically non-interventionist.[130]

The Economic Community of West African States

The Economic Community of West African States is composed of 15 Member States. Its security-related responsibilities were outlined in the 1999 *Protocol Relating to the Mechanism for Conflict Prevention, Management, Resolution, Peacekeeping and Security*. The Mechanism seeks, among numerous objectives, to resolve internal and interstate conflicts, to strengthen conflict prevention, and to support the deployment of peacekeeping operations and humanitarian relief missions.

Authority to invoke the powers of the Mechanism lies primarily with the ECOWAS Mediation and Security Council (MSC). The MSC, along with the Executive Secretary and the supporting elements of the Defence and Security Commission, the Council of Elders, and the ECOWAS Monitoring Group (ECOMOG, the West African multilateral intervention force), applies the principles of the Mechanism at its discretion in the following situations:

- aggression or conflict in a Member State;
- conflict between Member States;
- internal conflict that threatens to trigger a humanitarian disaster or poses a serious threat to peace and security in the sub-region;
- serious and massive violation of human rights and the rule of law; and
- overthrow or attempted overthrow of a democratically elected government.[131]

---

[129] Mark Malan, *Developing the ECOWAS Civilian Peace Support Operations Structure*, Report of an Experts' Workshop convened at the Kofi Annan International Peacekeeping Training Centre, Accra, Ghana, 9-10 February 2006 (Accra, Ghana: KAIPTC, 23 February 2006), 7.

[130] Point made by Col. Festus Aboagye (ret.), interview with author, Institute for Security Studies, Pretoria, South Africa, June 2004.

[131] Economic Community of West African States, *Protocol Relating to the Mechanism for Conflict Prevention, Management, Resolution, Peacekeeping and Security* (Lomé: ECOWAS, 10 December 1999), Chapter V.

A response to one of the above situations can be initiated by the MSC, a Member State, the Executive Secretary, the UN, or the African Union, and can take the form of a peacekeeping or observer mission. ECOWAS thus has authority to intervene with military forces in a range of scenarios, including those that require enforcement action. In addition, ECOWAS humanitarian assistance is an integral part of its Protocol. Accordingly, ECOWAS will "intervene to alleviate the suffering of the populations and restore life to normalcy in the event of crises, conflict and disaster."[132]

'Coalitions of the Willing'

If a full-fledged intervention is launched to stop genocide, it might be led by a coalition of willing states, as opposed to any of the organizations listed above. By its very nature, such an *ad hoc* coalition would be "willing" to intervene and protect civilians. The legitimacy of a coalition's actions, however, stands on much shakier ground without authorization from the UN or another relevant international body.[133] The capacity of such a coalition, obviously, will depend on which countries join the multinational force, just as it would for a force of a recognized multinational organization.

BASELINE CAPACITY TO ACT

These multinational organizations have the foundational basis and willingness to deploy forces, but what is known about their abilities to take action? What are their capabilities to plan, organize, and sustain an operation? Do they have the means to rapidly and effectively deploy forces in a Chapter VII mission? The following is a brief analysis of the basic capacities of the UN, NATO, the EU, the AU, and ECOWAS. The utility of *ad hoc* coalitions is also discussed.

The United Nations

To implement the recommendations of the Brahimi Report, the United Nations has made significant efforts to strengthen its in-house capacity to organize and manage peace operations, and to recruit and deploy skilled forces more rapidly and effectively.[134] Useful improvements include an increase in headquarters staff, including the establishment of a small UN standing police and rule of law capacity; the integration of civilian and military training into one office; the development of Strategic Deployment Stocks to increase effective deployments

---

[132] Ibid.

[133] *The Responsibility to Protect* opens up the idea that a force can act without Security Council authority, but such issues of legitimacy and legality are not addressed here in depth.

[134] The Brahimi Report, officially the *Report of the Panel on United Nations Peace Operations*, offered specific recommendations to increase UN capacity for peace operations. For a review of the Panel's recommendations and their status, see Durch, Holt et al., *The Brahimi Report and the Future of UN Peace Operations*.

and a refurbished UN Logistics Base in Brindisi, Italy; and the creation of the DPKO Best Practices Section. The reforms were initially designed to help the UN organize and manage one new operation a year. Since 2003, however, the UN has set up five new peacekeeping missions, and substantially expanded a sixth operation. Jean-Marie Guéhenno, UN Under-Secretary-General for Peacekeeping Operations, outlined the modern challenges facing UN peace operations in 2004:

> Of the 17 current operations, five had yet to reach their mandated troop strength, and there were key gaps where the United Nations lacked critical enabling and niche capabilities, including in the maritime, helicopter, communications, and special forces fields. Rapid deployment of capable military forces was needed to help in the startup of new missions and to assist when existing missions were significantly challenged. The current United Nations standby arrangements did not provide for any such strategic reserve. The mere existence of such a capacity could deter spoilers in the first place, besides allowing for more certain risk management regarding the size of missions.[135]

By 2005, the UN was managing an amazing level of personnel, equipment, and resources: 120,000 military and civilian police personnel, representing over 100 countries, rotated through UN missions in one year. Guéhenno reported that reforms were underway, but that the pace was intense as the UN chartered 319 aircraft and 52 ships, operated an aircraft fleet with 57 fixed-wing and 114 rotary-wing aircraft, and transported 580,000 passengers, while running 14 military hospitals and 120 clinics.[136]

The UN continues to seek capable forces that can deploy rapidly and effectively and match the requirements of the mission upon arrival. In general, the UN cannot assume that the forces offered by Member States will have trained or operated together before arriving in an operation. There has been limited progress in regionally based training of brigades from troop contributing countries to provide the UN with more coherent forces for deployments. Despite its ability to draw on a variety of resources, the UN has yet to truly meet the Brahimi Report's recommended thirty to ninety day deployment goals for traditional and complex operations—goals that are intended to help establish operations faster and more effectively.[137] To improve the speed of deployment, the Stand-by Arrangements System (UNSAS) aims to provide the UN

---

[135] Jean-Marie Guéhenno, presentation to the UN Fourth Committee, "Present-day Peacekeeping Demands Exceed Capacity of Any Single Organization," United Nations, 25 October 2004.

[136] Jean-Marie Guéhenno, "Opening Remarks of Mr. Jean-Marie Guéhenno, Under-Secretary-General for Peacekeeping Operations to the Special Committee on Peacekeeping Operations," UN News Center, 31 January 2005.

[137] A recent exception is in Côte d'Ivoire, which went from having a UN political mission to a UN peace operation in 2004 with Nigerian forces already on the ground re-hatted for the UN force.

Secretariat with information about military resources that Member States are likely to offer for peace operations. While dozens of nations participate, only Jordan and Uruguay are listed at the most ready Rapid Deployment Level, having signed Memoranda of Understanding (MOUs) and agreed to deploy within an established timeframe. DPKO regularly calls on Member States to provide more enabling units, a linchpin for peace operations.

Further, DPKO requirements for effective deployment are shifting with the needs of more challenging, robust UN operations. One US military instructor of peace operations summed up the problem:

> What do you do when you tell a soldier on patrol to protect a victim of crime, and he doesn't know what to do? At the UN things are changing—they are saying, 'forget infantry battalions, we want to know who's got helicopter gunships, APCs, artillery.' In order to do it right they'd need intelligence, satellites, unmanned vehicles; the UN isn't going to put blue helmets in the field if they can't protect them.[138]

When UN mandates explicitly direct peacekeepers to protect civilians, this requirement adds a potential deterrent for troop contributors: some countries are not eager to provide contingents for missions beyond traditional peacekeeping in permissive environments.[139] While changing, the culture of UN operations usually presumes a relatively benign environment. Mandates to protect civilians may mean that national contingents are called on to use force and engage in potentially dangerous activities. Countries are reluctant to put their personnel in harm's way. Many countries have national guidelines that determine the conditions under which they provide forces to lead or participate in operations. Nations such as Japan are constrained from providing troops to *any* Chapter VII operation; other national contingents are prohibited from using force beyond self-defense, which affects their role in operations. While some countries take national pride in their military role in peace operations and have been consistent contributors to UN operations, mandating peacekeepers to protect civilian lives risks dissuading potential troop contributing countries from offering personnel.[140]

In the last decade, developed countries have reduced their military contributions to UN peacekeeping. The top troop contributors to UN-led operations are

---

[138] US Naval Captain (retired), lawyer, and instructor on military and peace operations, interview with author, May 2004.

[139] When a developed state such as the UK takes the lead, other countries may be more willing to offer troops.

[140] Lorraine Elliott and Graeme Cheeseman, eds., *Forces for Good: Cosmopolitan Militaries in the Twenty-First Century* (Manchester and New York: Manchester University Press, 2004). Some countries have cultural norms that embrace their national military involvement in peace operations.

developing nations, with Bangladesh, Pakistan, India, Jordan, and Nepal supplying the most peacekeepers as of March 2006.[141] Many of these countries, however, are willing and have deployed to tough missions, such as in the DRC, reflecting the fact that the UN will go where the Council sends it with the forces Member States provide it.

The North Atlantic Treaty Organization

NATO has conducted a number of peace support operations since the end of the Cold War. These have included the Implementation Force (IFOR) and Stabilization Force (SFOR) in Bosnia, the Kosovo Force (KFOR) in Kosovo, and ISAF in Afghanistan. NATO has also offered training to the Iraqi military since August 2004.

In recent years, NATO has significantly expanded its membership and embarked on ambitious attempts at military transformation. Following its 2002 summit in Prague, NATO eliminated the post of Supreme Allied Commander, Atlantic, and replaced it with a new head of Allied Command, Transformation, in charge of directing the transformation of alliance forces to meet evolving operational demands. The Alliance accepted seven new members in March 2004, bringing its total to twenty-six and asserted, in its 2004 Istanbul summit, that "the door to membership remains open."[142]

The newly operational NATO Response Force (NRF) represents the most high-profile result of NATO's efforts at transformation. It consists of 25,000 rapidly available, self-sustaining troops, deployable anywhere in the world within five days. The NRF includes air, land, and maritime components; it will reach full operational strength in October 2006. During its short history it has already deployed to two crisis response missions: providing relief for the victims of Hurricane Katrina in New Orleans in September 2005, and for those of the October 2005 earthquake in Pakistan.

As a highly mobile, self-sustaining rapid reaction force, the NRF appears uniquely prepared to respond to a fast moving genocide, such as occurred in Rwanda in 1994. According to NATO, possible NRF missions include everything from non-combatant evacuation to operations, including humanitarian and crisis response, peacekeeping, counterterrorism, and embargo

---

[141] UN Department of Peacekeeping Operations, "Ranking of Military and Police Contributions to UN Operations," 31 March 2006, www.un.org/depts/dpko/dpko/contributors/2006/march_2.pdf. There are varied reasons for this shift, including reticence to serve under UN command and military and peacekeeping commitments tying up forces elsewhere. National decisions also depend on funding, political leadership, and the perception of the last mission. Since Somalia, for example, the US has had a general aversion to US troops serving in UN-led operations.

[142] NATO, *Istanbul Reader's Guide* (Brussels: North Atlantic Treaty Organization, October 2004), 9.

operations.[143] There is room within this spectrum for forceful intervention to stop a genocide or mass killing, specifically as peace enforcement in a hostile environment.

The European Union

The EU has progressively taken larger steps towards developing its multilateral military capacity. One important driver of change has been the deployment of real world missions under the EU flag. The EU began in 2003 with Operation Concordia, a preventive military deployment of 350 troops in Macedonia, and can now also boast of having fielded missions in the DRC, Bosnia, and elsewhere. The EU Institute for Security Studies counts twelve EU missions altogether, although only a handful of these represent deployments of any significant size (Operation Artemis in the DRC and Operation Althea in Bosnia, for example); many more were exclusively civilian deployments (e.g., Operation Proxima in Macedonia and the EU Police Mission in Bosnia).[144] Moreover, the most impressive EU mission thus far, Operation Artemis in the DRC, was a French-led coalition in almost every meaningful respect—except its name. France provided the operational headquarters and most of the military personnel, including the operation commander and the force commander.[145] Nevertheless, the EU has offered substantial military assistance in a number of the world's key hotspots and may, in fact, be generating new multilateral capacity simply by so acting.

The EU is also engaging in a broad effort to expand and coordinate its constituent nations' military capabilities. The EU Headline Goals laid out capability targets, but these have not resulted in any significant increase in national military funding. One large-scale initiative is the EU's proposed 60,000-strong Rapid Reaction Force (RRF), which was targeted to be fully operational by 2003. In practical terms, however, the development of the RRF may have been postponed as states pursued the newer Battlegroups concept, first proposed by the UK and France in 2003 and adopted by the EU in June 2004 as part of Headline Goal 2010. The concept envisions the development of eleven multinational EU Battlegroups, or roughly 1,500-troop strong, self-sustaining, rapidly deployable crisis response battalions that could arrive on the ground outside Europe within ten days. These Battlegroups are provided for six month periods by EU Member States. As of February 2006, one EU Battlegroup was

---

[143] NATO, "Improving Capabilities to Meet New Threats," NATO Briefing, December 2004, 9, www.nato.int/docu/briefing/capabilities/html_en/capabilities09.html.

[144] Giovanni Grevi, Dov Lynch, and Antonio Missiroli, "ESDP Operations," European Union Institute for Security Studies, www.iss-eu.org/esdp/09-dvl-am.pdf.

[145] Catriona Mace, "Operation Artemis: Mission Improbable?" *European Security Review*, no. 18, International Security Information Service, Europe, July 2003.

reported to be operational, with the expectation that there will be two fully operational Battlegroups in place by January 2007.

The Battlegroups concept appears to mirror the force structure and size of Operation Artemis, a mission that had clear protection goals. Although never explicitly linked to civilian protection by the EU, the ability to respond quickly to an emerging crisis has been critical to efforts to protect civilian populations in the past. In addition, the UN has welcomed the development of the Battlegroups as either "Bridging Forces" (to help DPKO as it prepares a new mission or as it expands an existing one) or as "Over the Horizon Reserve Forces" (to respond under a UN mandate to contingencies beyond the capacity of the UN itself).[146] Both types of missions could potentially help stem a rapid spread of violence against civilians, a situation to which the slower moving UN would be less prepared to respond appropriately.

The European Defense Agency (EDA) helps Member States improve their military capacity in a coherent manner, with a continent-wide vision in mind. As EU defense budgets remain mostly static, the EDA effort is focused on improving efficiency rather than pursuing any significant expansion of capacity. It seeks to help improve the interoperability of forces, to change procurement patterns (so that fewer "logistics tails" are needed when equipment from multiple militaries is used in the same mission), to avoid an overlap in force capacities, to specialize according to comparative advantage, to develop niche capabilities, to augment much needed strategic lift capabilities, and to lower the percentage of conscripts in military ranks. The EU remains, however, a relatively small-time military player on the world stage in proportion to its economic might. Recent developments may reflect the emergence of new EU capacity or simply the reorganization of what is already there.

The African Union

The AU moved beyond declarations when its Peace and Security Council entered into force in December 2003. The PSC incorporates operational components, including a Continental Early Warning System and an African Standby Force.[147] The ASF is to be the means of intervention, with multidisciplinary civilian and military components on-call from their own countries and ready for rapid deployment. With troop contingents provided by Member States, the ASF will have the capacity to engage in a range of mission types, from observation, to peace support, to interventions in response to genocide. Cooperation with the UN and its agencies is encouraged, but the

---

[146] United Nations, "Non-paper: Employment of EU Battle Groups Concept in Support of UN Peacekeeping Operations," internal UN document, 4 June 2004.

[147] African Union, *Protocol*, Article 2.

Security Council's authorization is not required. The chain of command for the ASF will be through the Chairperson, the African Union Commission's appointment of a Special Representative, and a Force Commander.[148] Member States are expected to rapidly provide well-equipped contingents as well as "all forms of assistance and support" to their troops once deployed. The AU also plans to support the ASF to undertake "humanitarian activities" and to establish regional mechanisms in the form of five regional peacekeeping brigades.[149]

The African Union, however, recognizes its dependence on support from the United Nations:

> Where necessary, recourse will be made to the UN to provide the necessary financial, logistical and military support for the African Union's activities in the promotion and maintenance of peace, security and stability in Africa, in keeping with the provisions of Chapter VIII of the UN Charter on the role of Regional Organizations in the maintenance of international peace and security.[150]

This relationship is fundamental, since the AU has neither its own forces nor troops on-call prepared to deploy rapidly and effectively. The AU also lacks sufficient headquarters management and planning capacity (there are few military personnel on the Commission staff), logistics and enabling units, airlift, ground transportation, a mobile communications system, and teams of AU civilian experts and advisors that can deploy to the mission on short notice. "No country can self-deploy easily in Africa, except South Africa," reported a former Ghanaian military officer with AU experience, "It is not an unwillingness to go; its just that there is no capacity to send in troops and sustain them."[151]

The AU Commission, in its development of the ASF, is expected to collaborate with the UN Secretariat to assist in coordinating external support for its capacity-building in support of ASF training, logistics, equipment, communications, and funding.[152] The AU has declared that the ASF will be operational by 2010, with some regional capacity in place earlier. With the exception of ECOWAS, few regional groups currently have the capacity to organize such stand-by forces. Most regional organizations in Africa were started for economic purposes; those with peace and security mandates are just beginning to develop capacity, beyond diplomatic and early warning

---

[148] A military staff committee will also be established to advise the Peace and Security Council.

[149] African Union, *Protocol*, Article 15.

[150] Ibid., Article 17.

[151] Senior staff (and retired Ghanaian military) officer, interview with author, Institute for Security Studies, Pretoria, South Africa, June 2004.

[152] This is both a practical approach and one suggested in the AU *Protocol*, Article 13, African Standby Force.

functions.[153] Progress is underway in eastern Africa, where the development of the Eastern Africa Standby Brigade (EASBRIG) offers a regionally-based force. The Southern Africa Development Community may also move toward a more robust military capacity, part of a contribution to the ASF.

Increasing international attention is focused on providing support to the ASF and enhancing African peacekeeping capabilities. Capacity building for African-led peace operations has developed quickly through partnerships with the African Union in support of AMIS in Darfur, with major initiatives by the European Union, via the G-8 Africa Action Plan, and by bilateral initiatives.

The Economic Community of West African States

In the 1999 ECOWAS Protocol, the organization expressed its aim to deploy peacekeeping operations and humanitarian relief missions, including missions to intervene in humanitarian crises and threats equivalent to genocide. In part, however, the Protocol established a formal policy that reflected much of its operational reality for over a decade. ECOWAS deployed to Liberia in 1990 and remained embroiled in the civil war until its withdrawal in 1997. The organization also sent forces to Sierra Leone (1997-2000), Guinea Bissau (1998), Côte d'Ivoire (2002), and, once again, to Liberia (2003).

In addition to its frequent deployments since the 1990s, ECOWAS is developing the ECOWAS Standby Force (ESF). In 2004, the Defense and Security Commission approved the ESF concept, calling for a regionally based 6,500-strong force, made up of a 1,500-strong military "task force" and a 5,000-troop brigade. Plans call for the ESF to be able to deploy 1,500 troops within 30 days, to be followed by the remaining 5,000 troops within 90 days.[154] The ESF represents part of the continent-wide plans for the African Standby Force, although ECOWAS is moving forward without doctrine and training guidance from the African Union. Development of the ESF remains in the early stages, with funding and logistics posing challenges for the organization. A Peace Fund, established to finance the strengthening of ECOWAS capacity through contributions by Member States, remains largely unfunded. With focus and partner support, however, ECOWAS may yet meet its goal of having the ability to deploy and manage an effective complex peace support operation by 2010, coinciding with the ASF goals.[155]

---

[153] Including IGAD, SADC, the Economic Community of Central African States, the East African Community, the Arab-Maghreb Union, and the Common Market for Eastern and Southern Africa.
[154] Victoria K. Holt with Moira K. Shanahan, *African Capacity-Building for Peace Operations: UN Collaboration with the African Union and ECOWAS* (Washington, DC: The Henry L. Stimson Center, February 2005), 25.
[155] A 2005 workshop with ECOWAS leadership suggests this focus. Malan, *Developing the ECOWAS Civilian Peace Support Operations Structure,* 24.

'Coalitions of the Willing'

Coalitions also offer an option for countries to come together to use force. In comparison to multinational organizations such groupings have operational advantages and disadvantages.[156] In coalitions, nations commit to a particular mission, which can enhance the achievement of common goals and help to organize specific forces and support to accomplish the mission. This approach may increase unity of effort and reduce varied interpretations of mandate goals. Coalitions are usually led by a single, powerful country, which may provide more straightforward command and control arrangements than multinational organizations, in addition to increasing the commitment of military and civilian leadership and resources from the lead nation. In the long run, coalitions may have fewer costs, as they disband once the mission is completed.

Without a formal organizational structure, however, coalition forces are likely to face basic challenges in interoperability. Many factors need melding: equipment, training, doctrine, and communications systems, as well as leadership style and interpretations of rules of engagement. Militaries in a coalition typically will not have trained together prior to deployment. States may pull out of a coalition if their political circumstances change at home or the situation on the ground is more difficult than expected. They also may lack the legitimacy provided by participating in a mission led and authorized by a recognized multinational organization. Coalitions might suffer from higher costs without an institutional structure and face less coherent political decision-making if the situation changes abruptly.

Coalitions may be useful for short-term, urgent operations with specific goals.

Coalitions may be useful for short-term, urgent operations with specific goals. Because intervening to stop genocide and mass killing might require a rapid, short-term, large-scale response, and the robust use of force, coalitions are a likely and suitable approach. To achieve success, however, the coalition would need to be able to work in concert with other international efforts and hand leadership of follow-on peacekeeping responsibilities to a capable organization once the immediate crisis is resolved.

WHAT IS SUFFICIENT CAPACITY TO ACT AND PROTECT?

Any peacekeeping mission or intervention force can face major operational issues. Before deployment, for example, missions require authorization and

---

[156] William J. Durch and Tobias C. Berkman, *Who Should Keep the Peace? Providing Security for Twenty-first Century Peace Operations* (Washington, DC: The Henry L. Stimson Center, forthcoming), 62.

commitments for the provision of effective troops and personnel. Multinational operations may operate with limited logistical, planning, leadership, and rapid reaction capabilities. Analytic and intelligence data, communications systems, and public information are also important to mission success.

A large and thoughtful body of scholarly literature is written on *when* to intervene—and the legal, political, and normative implications of humanitarian intervention. Other studies have considered the broad capacities needed for any deployment of forces in peace and stability operations, presuming that capable forces are likely to be better at protecting civilians. There are relatively few practical, detailed analyses of *how* third-party intervention forces can best protect civilians caught in conflict; specific operational requirements are thus largely missing from the literature. Likewise, as discussed in subsequent chapters, there is a limited body of analysis considering such protection missions by military actors. What might a force designed to stop mass killing *look* like?

The ICISS report looked briefly at this question. It pointed out broad requirements for a successful intervention: a strong coalition with substantial political resolve; a unified military approach; and unified operational objectives. Effective interventions also need

> *There are relatively few practical, detailed analyses of how third-party intervention forces can protect civilians caught in conflict.*

clear and appropriate mandates, sufficient resources, a strong command structure, effective civil-military relations (including a recognition that military actions might undercut the distribution of humanitarian aid in the short term), the appropriate use of force (so as to save as many lives as possible and avoid alienating the local population), a willingness to incur casualties, and an effective public information campaign.[157] Forces need to be mindful that, in almost all cases, they will transition to peacekeeping and peacebuilding activities. To avoid creating a hostile local populace they should, for example, avoid using overwhelming force or excessive targeting of national infrastructure.

The ICISS recognizes that the protection of civilians remains important after a mass killing is abated. It points to key "protection tasks" in the post-conflict peacekeeping and peacebuilding phase, after an initial intervention force has established security. These include the protection of minorities; security sector reform (including the effective deployment of civilian police); disarmament, demobilization, and reintegration (including, potentially, coercive disarmament); de-mining; and the pursuit and arrest of war criminals. The Commission

---

[157] ICISS, *The Responsibility to Protect*, 58-64.

concludes that these operational issues need increased attention and that the Secretary-General should develop new doctrine to address them.[158]

Scholars who think about operations to prevent or stop genocide often start with the presumption of an effective military capacity capable of controlling the environment.[159] Micah Zenko, for example, notes the advantages of using robust, rapidly deployable forces to end genocide or mass violence in its earliest stages; and the need to move beyond the traditional components of peacekeeping (consent, impartiality, and minimum use of force)—and in some cases defeat a declared enemy.[160] Some analysts have offered views on how to structure missions to halt mass killing and to determine capacity requirements. Alan Kuperman focuses on the *limits* of humanitarian intervention primarily because "the killers" move so much faster than "the interveners," and most civilians could be dead before help arrives.[161] He thus emphasizes early warning and recommends the use of light, rapidly deployable forces. Michael O'Hanlon offers three main steps to gain control over a country experiencing extreme violence. First, intervening forces must "establish lodgments," and ensure their ability to defend themselves. Second, forces must establish strongholds in key population centers and seize key facilities to gain general control over the territory. Finally, they must pursue any residual elements of resistance and establish security in smaller cities and towns.[162] O'Hanlon is cognizant of the dangers of insurgency and argues that significant military resources and long-term deployment may be necessary.

---

[158] Ibid., 65-67.

[159] Michael O'Hanlon, *Expanding Global Military Capacity for Humanitarian Intervention* (Washington, DC: Brookings Institution, 2003); Michéle Flournoy, Julianne Smith, Guy Ben-Ari, Kathleen McInnis, and David Scruggs, *European Defense Integration: Bridging the Gap Between Strategies and Capabilities* (Washington, DC: Center for Strategic and International Studies, 12 October 2005); Patricia Taft with Jason Ladnier, *Realizing 'Never Again': Regional Capacities to Protect Civilians in Violent Conflicts* (Washington, DC: The Fund for Peace, January 2006); Colonel Scott R. Feil, *Could 5,000 Peacekeepers Have Saved 500,000 Rwandans? Early Intervention Reconsidered*, ISD Report, Vol. 3, no. 2 (Washington, DC: Institute for the Study of Diplomacy, Georgetown University, April 1997); Kristiana Powell, *Opportunities and Challenges for Delivering on the Responsibility to Protect: The African Union's Emerging Peace and Security Regime*, Monograph Number 119 (Ottawa: The North-South Institute, May 2005); Mike Denning, "A Prayer for Marie? Creating an Effective African Standby Force," *Parameters* 34, no. 4, (2004/2005); Paul D. Williams, "Military Response to Mass Killing: The African Union Mission in Sudan," *International Peacekeeping*, Volume 13, No. 2, June 2006, 168-183; Major Brent Beardsley, "Lessons Learned or Not Learned From the Rwandan Genocide," 7th Annual Graduate Student Symposium, Royal Military College of Canada, 29-30 October 2004; Michael O'Hanlon and Peter Singer, "The Humanitarian Transformation: Expanding Global Intervention Capacity," *Survival* 46, no. 1 (Spring 2004).

[160] Zenko, "Saving Lives with Speed: Using Rapidly Deployable Forces for Genocide Prevention," 3-19.

[161] Kuperman, "Humanitarian Hazard," 64.

[162] O'Hanlon, *Saving Lives with Force*, 18.

Two writers with defense experience, Cliff Bernath and David Gompert, suggest that new technology might reduce the force requirements for forcible humanitarian intervention.[163] They argue that "net-centric warfare," developed by the US primarily to fight terrorism, might be useful during humanitarian interventions. They suggest that small, mobile groups of highly trained soldiers can use aerial surveillance, satellite and human intelligence, and satellite-linked communications networks effectively to support an intervention at minimal expense—and thereby reduce political concern about large-scale troop deployments. Troops could track and predict the movement of "killing forces" and arrive in civilian population centers *before* those forces attack. In the event of a fast-moving genocide like in Rwanda, light net-centric forces could fly into theater faster than traditional forces. As a result, Bernath and Gompert believe new military technology may decrease the military requirements, and hence the necessary political will, for such successful military interventions.

William O'Neill, an international lawyer and human rights expert, examines current practice in peace operations and how troops have embraced their new protection-oriented tasks.[164] He details encouraging trends, finding that peacekeepers have begun to embrace more readily cooperation with humanitarian organizations, to promote the rights of IDPs, to conduct preventive patrols and to offer physical protection to civilians threatened by violence. For the most part, O'Neill does not try to design an intervention force *per se*, focusing instead on activities that peacekeeping missions can take to protect civilians across a range of threats.

The ICISS and these various studies are part of a valuable literature on aspects of the operational issues involved in the use of coercive protection missions for stopping violence against civilians. This literature, however, is only a start. Most studies do not offer details on what a potential mission looks like or its force requirements, or the preparation required for such operations. That job thus remains in the hands of today's practitioners, namely national militaries, civilian leaders, and multinational organizations.

Key Themes

Many experts judge readiness to stop mass violence by the ability to deploy forces in sufficient numbers quickly and effectively. (In Rwanda, 800,000 civilians were killed in 100 days.) To augment their responsive capabilities,

---

[163] Clifford H. Bernath and David C. Gompert, *"The Power to Protect": Using New Military Capabilities to Stop Mass Killings* (Washington, DC: Refugees International, July 2003). Gompert et. al., *Learning from Darfur: Building a Net-Capable African Force to Stop Mass Killing.*

[164] O'Neill, *A New Challenge for Peacekeepers*; O'Neill and Cassis, *Protecting Two Million Internally Displaced.*

multinational organizations and national militaries are increasing the speed at which they can get troops into regions of instability. As noted above, the EU is developing 1,500-troop strong Battlegroups of highly mobile forces that can deploy to crisis regions outside Europe within ten days, as needed.[165] The goals of other organizations are more modest. The UN target of deployment within thirty to ninety days would still be too late to prevent a large-scale campaign of violence or genocide. The AU and ECOWAS also strive to move quickly, but often rely on outside partners for lift and logistics support. Of the world's militaries, the US, UK, France, and NATO are the most capable of deploying rapidly, with sufficient logistics support and planning capacity to intervene, and presumably, to halt a quickly spreading, large-scale genocide in a country of any great size. Other nations have been willing to move quickly, however, especially if given support.

Some argue that the international community would need to deploy upwards of 100,000 well-trained and well-equipped troops to the DRC and 50,000 to Darfur to halt ongoing mass killings in those two countries alone.[166] Others contest that the number of troops necessary to protect civilians effectively is exaggerated, perhaps to mask a lack of political will. For example, General Roméo Dallaire has argued that expanding UNAMIR's force level to 5,000 could have halted the Rwandan genocide. Others are skeptical that such few troops could have made a significant difference.[167]

Military force levels alone can be misleading, since militaries are organized with assumptions about troop readiness and training. (Force-sizing is an area of study itself.) For every US soldier in the field, for example, one soldier is expected to be returning from a mission to retrain and another is preparing to deploy. But few active militaries have sustained this three-to-one ratio; Ghana and the US are both reportedly overworked at two-to-one ratios.[168] Thus, even when there is political and institutional will, certain kinds of forces might not be available. Limits on troop availability may result in tradeoffs between sending personnel to one mission and training them for another.

Another question is whether militaries can accurately inform political leaders of the capacity requirements for effectively protecting civilians in various circumstances. Political skepticism regarding humanitarian interventions might be fed by a military skepticism regarding the potential for success in such

---

[165] The US 82nd Airborne Division, in comparison, can be anywhere in the world in three days.

[166] O'Hanlon and Singer, "The Humanitarian Transformation," 81; Bradford Plumer, "Do Something...But What?" *Mother Jones*, 4 May 2005.

[167] O'Hanlon and Singer, "The Humanitarian Transformation."

[168] France also attempts to maintain this three-to-one ratio, which is one reason why it limits its deployments.

missions, given limited resources—a problem compounded by the lack of proper studies or evaluations of the operational implications of such missions.

Generally, even with ambitions to conduct more effective operations, multinational organizations face a global shortage of skilled troops available for peace and stability operations.[169] These organizations depend on the strength of the national contingents supplied by their members to succeed. UN operations routinely face delays in recruiting troops to meet authorized force levels. European military spending and force structure have not kept pace with the expansion of peacekeeping demands, and the US military has focused on warfighting and counterinsurgency. Increases in headquarters and operational capacity within regional organizations do not match their ambitions—yet. Nor have sufficient forces always filled the slots for coalition missions such as ISAF and AMIS. Moreover, many troops may not be prepared for robust activities involving civilian protection. With the modern shift toward "complex" UN peace operations, there is an important emphasis on militaries honing skills to support development, reconstruction, and long-term peacebuilding tasks. While these skills are needed for many peace operations, more traditional combat skills are also needed for missions involving the use of force to protect civilians.

Additional capacity questions include the availability of moving parts, such as transportation and logistics, areas often lacking in multinational organizations. The AU Mission in Sudan, for example, relies heavily on outside funding and such support from the EU, European countries, Canada, and the United States, among others. Without major assistance, even AMIS' halting deployment would have been impossible. For other organizations, such as the EU, the interoperability and efficiency of multinational forces remain serious concerns. EU Member States have historically procured military equipment from different sources to meet their national needs. As a result, the equipment available to the EU as a whole is duplicative, and this often results in inefficiencies. This is one reason why, despite the high number of total troops in its Member State militaries, the EU is still a relative military lightweight.

For the protection of civilians, therefore, the questions of tasks and strategy may make a greater difference in determining force requirements and evaluating success. If missions aim to provide physical protection to civilians with military force, then those operations *may* require large or highly mobile forces to protect

---

[169] For enumerations of such ambitions see *The National Security Strategy of the United States of America* (Washington, DC: The White House, September 2002) and European Union, "Security Strategy." For troop shortfalls, see O'Hanlon, *Expanding Global Military Capacity for Humanitarian Intervention.*

individuals dispersed over large, ill-defined areas.[170] An operation with too few forces could limit assistance to civilians outside specifically identifiable areas—a camp, for example—or exclude those in a neighboring town. Such limits were apparent in MONUC in the eastern DRC in 2003, which is one reason that the EU approved deployment of a French-led force to provide protection in a specific, highly volatile region where MONUC capacity was insufficient. Alternately, if the threat to civilians does not come from general lawlessness and numerous roving militias operating over vast areas, fewer forces might be sufficient. In some cases, defeating a single group of poorly trained and equipped militia might serve to end genocide—indeed, this may have been the case in Rwanda. The nature of the specific situation at hand and, therefore, the resulting strategy, likely determine the number and type of troops necessary for effective civilian protection.

> *A baseline capacity is central to a successful intervention, but the force structure alone does not provide for coercive protection.*

Is There Sufficient Capacity to Protect?

This broad overview of international operational capacity has highlighted the five organizations that have authority, and some capacity, to deploy military missions and to act to protect civilians from violence. Are they prepared to intervene against violence as suggested by *The Responsibility to Protect*, however? The UN, NATO, the EU, the AU, and ECOWAS generally are organized to take on peace support operations and/or military interventions. They have the components of presumed capacity: the authority to act; a capacity to organize and deploy military personnel; and some foundational basis to support missions in which the protection of civilians is a component of a peace operation or the goal of an intervening force. Without agreement on the force structure needed for such missions, it is best to judge these groups as somewhat capable, depending on the requirements of the operation.

Many recommendations to increase capacity are not unlike those for any successful military operation enabled to use force. This suggests that while a baseline capacity is central to a successful intervention, the force structure alone does not provide the full operational picture for coercive protection. When militaries prepare for their roles, they use key tools—rules of engagement, mandates, doctrine, and training—to get ready for their anticipated missions. What is the state of these tools, and what does that tell us about the preparedness

---

[170] The protection of IDP camps in Darfur, for example, requires covering an extensive area with poor roads, few airports, villages that are not all identified on maps, and little local capacity to sustain deployed forces.

of forces today and about how to prepare them for missions in the future? As O'Neill suggests, recent years have witnessed a marked effort within multinational organizations to improve their capacity to deploy forces effectively.[171] How do these groups—the UN, NATO, the EU, the AU, and ECOWAS—and their members measure up in the use of these tools to prepare forces for operations aimed at interrupting genocide or leading peace operations with coercive protection elements? This study now turns to those specific areas of military preparation and their treatment of the protection of civilians, a way of understanding what current troops serving in multinational operations or with intervention forces may have as guidance.

---

[171] O'Neill, *A New Challenge for Peacekeepers: The Internally Displaced.*

— 5 —
FROM THE COUNCIL TO THE FIELD: NAVIGATING MANDATES AND RULES OF ENGAGEMENT

A suicide attacker posing as a beggar wounded three soldiers from the NATO-led peacekeeping force and killed an Afghan girl Saturday on a street popular with Western souvenir shoppers.[172]

Soldiers must make split second decisions about whether and how to use force in the face of immediate threats to themselves or others. Military personnel make these difficult choices in environments in which it may be nearly impossible to differentiate aggressors and non-combatants.

Political and military leaders use two main tools to guide such determinations: the mandates provided for the mission and the rules of engagement (ROE)—legally binding instructions on when, where, and how soldiers may use force. Both mandates and ROE help the operation's leadership and field personnel define the mission and its goals. ROE ensure that national policy and objectives are reflected in the action of commanders in the field, particularly under circumstances in which communication with higher authority is not possible. Likewise, mission mandates provide a clear framework of the mission's goals and tasks to help guide decision making by actors in the field. Other components of mission planning provide guidance to forces—such as the formal strategic estimates, the commander's intent, contingency plans, and standard operating procedures. But at the core of shaping the operation are the mandate, from which all planning begins, and the ROE, where that mandate is put into action. The *UN Handbook* tells field personnel that:

> [U]se of force by the military component will depend on the mandate of the peacekeeping operation and the rules of engagement; sometimes the Security Council will authorize a peacekeeping operation to use armed force in situations other than in self-defense. The circumstances under which the operation may use armed force will then be spelt out in the relevant resolution in the Council. The rules of engagement for the peacekeeping operation will clarify the different levels of force that can be used in various circumstances,

---

[172] Wesal Zaman and Paul Watson, "Blast Kills Afghan Girl, Hurts 3 NATO Soldiers," *Los Angeles Times*, 24 October 2004.

how each level of force should be used and any authorizations that may need to be obtained from commanders.[173]

Appropriate use of force depends on a soldier's understanding of the ROE and the use of force allowed beyond self-defense. NATO defines ROE as "[d]irectives issued by competent military authority which specify the circumstances and limitations under which forces will initiate and/or continue combat engagement with other forces encountered."[174] UN guidance has defined ROE as "[d]irectives issued by DPKO that specify the way how units in PKO's [peacekeeping operations] have to act with hostile parties and the population."[175] Good decisions also require an understanding of the environment, knowledge of the mission goals, and prior training in dealing with potential threats. Even after deployment, military personnel may adjust their understanding of the parameters and compare notes on how to react to challenging situations. An entry on a website used by forces in Iraq, for example, identified ROE as the key to determining the appropriate course of action. [See Box 5.1.]

GETTING ROE RIGHT FOR PEACE OPERATIONS AND CIVILIAN PROTECTION

Modern peace and stability operations exist somewhere between traditional combat and traditional peacekeeping, presenting their personnel with particularly uneasy choices about how to act. ROE limit the use of force—and those for peace operations are more restrictive than those for regular combat. Consider, for example, a US Army view of the legal aspects of ROE:

> ROE provide restraints on a commander's action consistent with both domestic and international law and may, under certain circumstances, impose greater restrictions on action than those required by the law.[176]

---

[173] Peacekeeping Best Practices Unit, *Handbook on United Nations Multidimensional Peacekeeping Operations*, 57.

[174] NATO, "NATO Glossary of Terms and Definitions," AAP-6(V), North Atlantic Treaty Organization, 7 August 2000, www.dtic.mil/doctrine/jel/other_pubs/aap_6v.pdf.

[175] UN Department of Peacekeeping Operations, "Glossary of UN Peacekeeping Terms," DPKO Training Unit, September 1998, www.un.org/Depts/dpko/glossary/r.htm.

[176] Major Joseph B. Berger III, Major Derek Grimes, and Major Eric T. Jensen, eds., *Operational Law Handbook*, JA 422, International and Operational Law Department, The Judge Advocate General's Legal Center and School (Charlottesville, Virginia: US Army, 2004), 90. They point out that "[f]or many contemporary missions, particularly peace operations, the mission is stated in a document such as a UN Security Council Resolution, e.g., UNSCR 940 in Haiti or UNSCR 1031 in Bosnia. These Security Council Resolutions also detail the scope of force authorized to accomplish the purpose stated therein."

Box 5.1

SCENARIO: CHECKPOINT ROE TROUBLE

The following text appeared on a website used by US military personnel in Iraq in 2004:

You are a company commander deployed to Iraq after ground combat has ended.

Several weeks into your deployment, one of your soldiers at the vehicle checkpoint is searching a truck when he finds what he believes to be a gun in the floor of the cab. He locks and loads his weapon and points it at the driver standing near the vehicle, screaming for him to hit the ground. The squad leader searches the vehicle only to find that the gun is really a toy and not dangerous. The civilian is obviously shaken by the scare. Your battalion commander hears of the incident and wants to do an investigation to determine if the soldier has broken the rules of engagement by his actions. What should you do? Rate the following courses of action:

- *Let the platoon leader take care of the matter.*
- *Give the soldier an Article 15 for excessive display of force against a friendly civilian.*
- *Review the rules of engagement with your key leaders to ensure they are correct and that everyone knows them.*
- *Award the soldier for taking the appropriate action in this case.*
- *Convince your battalion commander that there is no need for an investigation.*
- *Wait for the investigation to determine if there was an actual violation.*
- *Ask your battalion commander to allow you to conduct an informal inquiry into the situation and give your recommendation to her.*

Of more than 200 respondents, the majority selected "review the rules of engagement" as the favored answer. Interestingly, one commentator wrote about the need for more ROE training for the scenarios troops face in Iraq:

I'd suggest using an incident where civilians were killed as a basis for your ROE training. The ROE situations the platoon commanders went over were good, but only as a start. Many of the ones from higher were simplistic and did not address real world issues and concerns of the troops. I'd say we were very successful—we did not have one Marine killed or wounded because he failed to act, or any ROE violations.

Source: US Department of the Army, Company Commander website, October 2004, www.companycommand.army.mil/cc.php.

Peacekeepers must strike a delicate balance between excessive and inadequate force, for example. One DPKO official described how he raised this issue with future peacekeepers by posing a scenario to military personnel: *Imagine a young teenage boy is pointing a Kalashnikov gun at you: do you shoot or not?* Future peacekeepers wonder if they should risk their own lives in such a situation, or face a potential court-martial for a hostile act against a child.

> *Peacekeepers' ROE have at times been too restrictive, limiting their ability to intervene to protect groups or individuals under threat.*

ROE will also be critical in situations where peacekeepers witness or are made aware of preventable abuses against the local civilian population; many ROE are the "bottom line" for using force to protect civilians in operations.[177] Additional factors—the wording of the mandate, the doctrine of the intervening force, the level of troop training—may matter less than having sufficiently robust and well-understood rules of engagement. NATO doctrine for peace support operations, for example, sees appropriate ROE as pivotal to forces' ability to protect civilians under threat:

> The sensitive issue for PSF [Peace Support Forces] is whether to intervene in response to human rights abuses directed at civilians "on the ground." Any authorization so to do [sic] would be found in applicable ROE. Such an intervention would only be legally permissible if authorized by applicable ROE and/or mandate. In formulating ROE, however, it should be borne in mind that a narrow and neutral concept of operations which limits itself to observation and reporting may not be appropriate in circumstances of widespread violations of human rights and ethnic cleansing even if it does reduce the risk of casualties to the PSF.[178]

This can be tough terrain for military forces directed to protect civilians in modern operations.

In situations where civilians face extreme violence, peacekeepers' ROE have at times been too restrictive, limiting their ability to intervene to protect groups or individuals under threat.[179] In 1994, during the US-led intervention in Haiti, US

---

[177] Colonel Michael Dooley, acting director, Peacekeeping and Stability Operations Institute, US Army War College, Carlisle, Pennsylvania, interview with author, June 2004.

[178] NATO, *Peace Support Operations*, AJP-3.4.1, Chapter 3 Fundamentals of Peace Support, North Atlantic Treaty Organization,
web.archive.org/web/20050325095751/http://www.pronato.com/peacekeeping/AJP-3.4.1/Chapter3.htm.

[179] Trevor Findlay, *The Use of Force in UN Peace Operations* (Oxford: Oxford University Press for the Stockholm International Peace Research Institute, 2002).

Army personnel stood by while personnel from the former Haitian army beat local people celebrating the arrival of the Americans. At the time, the US rules of engagement were understood to mean that the troops should not intervene in Haitian-on-Haitian violence—although the ROE were already under review at the time of the incident. This stance was attributed to the fact that the US Army was instructed not to get involved in law and order issues and to focus on its own force protection, both lessons from prior US experience in Somalia.[180] Televised internationally, the incident in Haiti changed the US posture, if not the actual ROE.[181] A Department of Defense workshop on the Haiti operation recognized the "hidden dangers" when troops and the chain of command have different understandings of the ROE, and urged that training be used to align those views more closely, especially during coalition operations.[182]

On the other hand, creative thinking and courage can sometimes work effectively despite restrictive ROE. Peacekeepers in traditional, Chapter VI missions have protected civilians while operating under mandates understood to allow force only in self-defense.[183] Various contingents in UNPROFOR in the former Yugoslavia sometimes intentionally positioned themselves in the line of fire when Serb forces bombarded Bosnian towns. They could then legally return fire as a form of self-defense to protect civilians. Similarly, in his memoir *Shake Hands with the Devil*, Canadian General Roméo Dallaire explains how he defended civilians without the ability to use force at all: he instructed his unarmed military observers within the undermanned and overwhelmed UNAMIR to stand guard in front of a hotel and protect the civilians inside it during the Rwandan genocide.[184] The Rwandan militias turned back rather than attack UN personnel. Even without bullets or Chapter VII authority, the UN observers managed to defend the hotel through sheer grit and presence.

DRAFTING MANDATES AND ROE

In missions led by multinational organizations like the United Nations or NATO, the drafting of ROE requires delicate political negotiation. For UN-authorized interventions, the mission's mandate and ROE are derived from Security Council resolutions.

---

[180] Margaret Daly Hayes and Rear Admiral Gary Wealty, eds., *Interagency and Political-Military Dimensions of Peace Operations: Haiti–A Case Study* (Institute for National Strategic Studies, National Defense University, February 1996), 21.

[181] Ibid., and US Army Colonel, JAG (retired), involved in the ROE negotiations for Haiti, interview with author, February 2006.

[182] Hayes and Wealty, eds., *Interagency and Political-Military Dimensions of Peace Operations*.

[183] British and Norwegian troops in UNPROFOR interpreted their mandate as one supporting the protection of civilians, and took action to do so, in contrast to other contingents who interpreted their mandates very narrowly as excluding response to human rights violations or threats to civilians. Findlay, *The Use of Force in UN Peace Operations*, 226-231.

[184] Dallaire, *Shake Hands With the Devil*, 268-269.

UN rules of engagement are not standardized. The United Nations has developed *draft* ROE that are then adapted for each operation, based on the authorizing resolutions. The mission ROE are formulated by the DPKO Military Advisor's office and the UN Office of Legal Affairs. The UN Under-Secretary-General for Peacekeeping Operations approves them and provides them to the mission's Force Commander, who can request changes to the rules of engagement.

Individual mission ROE include one or more general permissions for the use of force selected from the ten numbered options on the UN Master List. These include authorization to use force for self-defense and to protect other UN personnel; to defend UN or designated installations, areas, and goods; to prevent the escape of a detainee; and against those who limit freedom of movement. One rule (no. 1.8) allows force to protect civilians:

> Use of force, up to, and including deadly force, to defend any civilian person who is in need of protection against a hostile act or hostile intent, when competent local authorities are not in a position to render immediate assistance, is authorized. When and where possible, permission to use force should be sought from the immediate superior commander.[185]

Before approving a mandate for a UN-led peace operation, the Council is briefed by the Secretary-General and his staff, especially from DPKO, who offer recommendations for the mission and help shape an appropriate mandate. The Council then crafts mandates reflecting the views of its members and what the political environment will bear. The resulting resolution may provide greater or lesser responsibilities and authority than recommended by the Secretariat. The DPKO is next instructed to organize a peacekeeping force to achieve the goals established by the Council. The interpretation of the Council mandate by political leaders greatly influences the mission's organization and shapes how the use of force is understood by its leadership, including the Special Representative of the Secretary-General—who leads the peace operations—as well as by the DPKO and the Secretary-General. Peacekeeping contingents recruited for the operation, their commanders, and the UN Force Commander in turn also interpret the mandate.

When UN resolutions authorize the protection of civilians under imminent threat, there is little evidence that either the Secretary-General or the Council establishes the operational meaning of such language. The political leadership for a new mission or intervention is unlikely to have direct guidance about what

---

[185] UN Department of Peacekeeping Operations, "United Nations Master List of Numbered ROE," *Guidelines for the Development of ROE for UNPKO, Provisional Sample ROE*, Attachment 1 to FGS/0220.001, United Nations, April 2002.

is expected in terms of protecting civilians.[186] The transition of authority for the protection of civilians—and a clear understanding of what that authority means—from a Security Council mandate, to the negotiated official ROE for the mission, to the small, laminated ROE card provided each peacekeeper is not a clear and direct path.

"PROTECT CIVILIANS": AN EVOLUTION IN MANDATES AND ROE

Even before the end of the Cold War, the principle that peacekeepers could only use force in self-defense had broadened.[187] Personnel in UN peacekeeping operations were allowed to resist attempts to impede their duties and to defend the mission, for example. Mandates expanded further with the greater use of Chapter VII authorization in the 1990s.

Prior to 1999, however, no Security Council mandate instructed a UN peacekeeping or multinational force to "protect civilians." Mandates for operations typically authorized peacekeepers to promote a "secure and stable environment" or to protect the civilians associated with

> *Prior to 1999, no Security Council mandate instructed a UN peacekeeping or multinational force to "protect civilians."*

the mission, such as humanitarian aid workers or UN civilian personnel. UN resolutions sometimes called for the establishment of "humanitarian areas"[188] or "safe areas,"[189] but stipulated that peacekeepers defending these areas could use force only to reply to attacks and were expected to act in self-defense.[190] Sometimes it seemed that if the peacekeepers themselves were not directly threatened by attacks against a civilian population, such mandates seemed to require that they decline to act.

Beginning in late 1999, UN mandates began to change. The Security Council explicitly authorized the protection of civilians for the first time for the UN peace operation in Sierra Leone, UNAMSIL, stating that the mission:

---

[186] Translations of the Council's mandate into ROE can be hampered by the lack of a common peacekeeping doctrine, especially for missions with Chapter VII authority.

[187] Findlay, *The Use of Force in Peace Operations.*

[188] S/Res/918, 17 May 1994.

[189] S/Res/836, 4 June 1993.

[190] Findlay, *The Use of Force in Peace Operations*, 227. In his excellent study of the use of force in UN peace operations, Findlay points out that "UNPROFOR was never given the explicit mandate or the requisite forces or firepower to comprehensively and robustly protect the civilian population." Ibid., 226.

> [M]ay take necessary action to ensure the security and freedom of movement of its personnel and, within its capabilities and areas of deployment, to afford protection to civilians under imminent threat of physical violence, taking into account the responsibilities of the Government of Sierra Leone and ECOMOG.[191]

Since then, the Security Council has increasingly referenced the protection of civilians in operations; UN mandates and ROE have become more explicit in allowing—and directing—peacekeepers to protect civilians.

Table 5-1 lists UN-mandated peace operations that include "protect civilians" language, beginning with the first case, UNAMSIL in October 1999. The UN has cited the protection of civilians "under imminent threat of physical violence" for six other UN-led peacekeeping missions authorized under mandates for Chapter VII.[192]

The operations with civilian protection mandates have important caveats that limit what they are expected to do.

The table includes regionally-led operations, such as two African Union missions, in Burundi (AMIB) and Sudan (AMIS), which the Security Council endorsed but whose mandates are found in AU communiqués.

The operations with civilian protection mandates have important caveats that limit what they are expected to do. First, the Council usually recognizes that the protection of civilians is primarily the responsibility of the host government where the mission is operating—regardless of whether it is a highly functioning state or one bordering on collapse. The mandate for the UN Mission in Burundi (ONUB), for example, directs peacekeepers to protect civilians "without prejudice to the responsibilities of the Government of National Reconciliation." There are a few exceptions, such as mandates for MONUC in the DRC and the French-led *Operation Licorne* in Côte d'Ivoire.

Second, the Council also limits the realm of the mission's responsibility to protect civilians to "within its area of deployment" and "within its capacity" for nearly all operations. [See Table 5-2].

---

[191] S/Res/1270, 22 October 1999.

[192] Operations include Côte d'Ivoire (UNOCI), Burundi (ONUB), Haiti (MINUSTAH), Liberia (UNMIL), the Democratic Republic of Congo (MONUC), and the Sudan (UNMIS). Only three new peacekeeping missions since 1999 have not included this language: Ethiopia/Eritrea (UNMEE) and East Timor/Timor-Leste (UNTAET) and (UNMISET).

TABLE 5-1: UN MANDATES FOR PEACE OPERATIONS SINCE UNAMSIL
Since 22 October 1999

MISSION	COUNTRY	DATES	UN-LED	CHAPTER VII	"PROTECT CIVILIANS" MANDATE[193]
UNAMSIL	Sierra Leone	10/22/99 - 12/31/05	√	√	√
UNTAET	Timor-Leste	10/25/99 - 5/20/02	√	√	
MONUC[194]	DR Congo	11/30/99 - present	√	√	√
UNMEE	Ethiopia & Eritrea	6/31/00 - present	√		
ISAF	Afghanistan	12/20/01 - present		√	
UNMISET	Timor-Leste	5/20/02 - 5/20/05	√	√	
Operation Licorne[195]	Côte d'Ivoire	9/22/02 - present		√	√
ECOMICI	Côte d'Ivoire	2/4/03 - 4/4/04		√	√
AMIB	Burundi	4/2/03 - 6/1/04			
Operation Artemis	DR Congo	6/12/03 - 9/1/03		√	√
ECOMIL	Liberia	8/1/03 - 10/01/03		√	
UNMIL	Liberia	10/1/03 - present	√	√	√
MIFH	Haiti	2/29/04 - 6/1/04		√	
UNOCI	Côte d'Ivoire	4/4/04 - present	√	√	√
MINUSTAH	Haiti	4/30/04 - present	√	√	√
ONUB	Burundi	6/1/04 - present	√	√	√
AMIS[196]	Sudan (Darfur)	7/8/04 - present		√	√
EUFOR	Bosnia-Herzegovina	12/2/04 - present		√	
UNMIS	Sudan	3/24/05 - present	√	√	√
Percentage of operations with components in mandates			53%	89%	58%

[193] See Annex 1 for specific mandate language, which varies. Where mandates have changed since 1999, the most recent is cited here.

[194] Civilian protection language added to mandate on 24 February 2000.

[195] France began expanding its presence in Côte d'Ivoire in September 2002; the Council recognized its mission with S/Res/1464 in February 2003. Selections in table reflect language from S/Res/1528, 27 February 2004.

[196] The AMIS mandate is found in AU communiqués and mentions civilian protection; the Security Council also recognizes AMIS and its role.

The United Nations has authorized action by coalitions and regional organizations with similar "protect civilians" language. The Australian-led intervention in East Timor in 1999, for example, was authorized to "ensure the protection of civilians at risk."[197] Four coalition- and regionally-led missions in Africa have included protection language identical or similar to that of UN-led operations.[198] The French-led *Artemis* mission to the DRC in 2003 was authorized to use "all necessary measures...to ensure the protection of the airport, the internally displaced persons in the camps in Bunia, and if the situation requires it, to contribute to the safety of the civilian population."[199] The mandate for ECOWAS forces in Côte d'Ivoire (ECOMICI) directed it "to ensure, without prejudice to the responsibility of the Government of National Reconciliation, the protection of civilians immediately threatened with physical violence within their zones of operation, using the means available to them."[200]

There are exceptions too. Longstanding missions, such as those in Cyprus (UNFICYP) and in Western Sahara (MINURSO), are not organized under Chapter VII and have not been changed to include protection of civilians during mandate renewals. The mandate of ISAF operation in Afghanistan calls for the "maintenance of security." ISAF conducts patrols, often alongside Afghan security forces, to help provide security to protect civilians within Kabul and its surrounding areas, and aims to assist in the reconstruction of Afghanistan, slowly expanding to cover other parts of the country. The US-led multinational force *Operation Secure Tomorrow* intervened in Haiti in 2004 without such direction; its mission was to help provide security and stability, and to assist with humanitarian aid.[201] The UN mission that followed it there, however, has a clear mandate to protect civilians under imminent threat.[202]

Table 5-2 identifies language in UN mandates to "protect civilians," noting which mandates call for protecting civilians "without prejudice to the responsibility" of the host government, within the mission's "capabilities and areas of deployment," and using "all necessary means." Like Table 5-1, it includes AMIS and AMIB, whose mandates are in African Union communiqués.

---

[197] S/Res/1264, 15 September 1999.
[198] These four missions are: the French-led *Operation Licorne* in Côte d'Ivoire, the ECOWAS mission ECOMICI in Côte d'Ivoire, the EU and French-led *Operation Artemis* mission in the DRC, and the AU-led operation AMIS in Darfur, Sudan.
[199] S/Res/1484, 30 May 2003.
[200] S/Res/1464, 4 February 2003.
[201] S/Res/1529, 29 February 2004.
[202] S/Res/1542, 30 April 2004.

**TABLE 5-2: CHARACTERISTICS OF UN "PROTECT CIVILIANS" MANDATES
SINCE OCTOBER 22, 1999[203]**

MISSION	COUNTRY	DATES	UN-LED	"WITHOUT PREJUDICE TO RESPONSIBILITY" OF HOST	"WITHIN CAPABILITIES & AREA OF DEPLOYMENT"	"ALL NECESSARY MEANS"
UNAMSIL	Sierra Leone	10/22/99–12/31/05	√	√	√	√
MONUC[204]	DR Congo	11/30/99–present	√		√	√
Operation Licorne[205]	Côte d'Ivoire	9/22/02–present			√	√
ECOMICI	Côte d'Ivoire	2/4/03–4/4/04		√	√	√
Operation Artemis	DR Congo	6/12/03–9/1/03				
UNMIL[206]	Liberia	10/1/03–present	√	√	√	
UNOCI	Côte d'Ivoire	4/4/04–present	√	√	√	√
MINUSTAH	Haiti	4/30/04–present	√	√	√	
ONUB	Burundi	6/1/04–present	√	√	√	√
AMIS[207]	Sudan (Darfur)	7/8/04–present			√	√
UNMIS	Sudan	3/24/05–present	√	√	√	√
Percentage of mandates with component			64%	64%	91%	73%

Some mandates have also identified broad tasks and named categories of civilians under the rubric of civilian protection. The mandate for the UN Mission in Sudan stipulates that it may "coordinate international efforts towards the protection of civilians with particular attention to vulnerable groups including internally displaced persons, returning refugees, and women and children."[208]

While rules of engagement are not usually made public, interviews with DPKO personnel suggest that if the phrase "protect civilians under imminent threat" is in a UN mandate, such authorization also exists in the mission's ROE. In the case of the UN Stabilization Mission in Haiti (MINUSTAH), the ROE for that mission (as of May 2004) identified that force may be used beyond self-defense

---

[203] See Annex 1, *UN Security Council Resolutions for Missions Involving Aspects of Civilian Protection*, for specific mandate language, which may vary. Where mandates have changed since 1999, the most recent mandate is cited here.

[204] Civilian protection language added to mandate on 24 February 2000.

[205] Selections in table reflect language from S/Res/1528, which instructs forces to protect civilians within their deployment areas but does not include the caveat "within capabilities."

[206] Mandate language does not include "within its areas of deployment."

[207] The AU Communiqué in March 2006 makes no reference to the protection of civilians being the responsibility of the Government of Sudan, which the previous AU mandate included.

[208] S/Res/1590, 24 March 2005.

only in specific circumstances, including "to protect civilians under imminent threat of physical violence, within its capabilities and areas of deployment, without prejudice to the responsibilities of the Transitional Government and of police authorities."[209]

Annex 1 provides a chart, *UN Security Council Resolutions for Missions Involving Aspects of Civilian Protection*, which looks at selected mandates for UN-authorized or UN-led missions that involved resolutions providing for the use of force and the protection of civilians. These mandates are a good starting point for analyzing the actual application of the mandates and ROE in the field.

> *The specific civilian protection language of these mandates has grown clearer and more robust over time.*

The specific civilian protection language of these mandates has grown clearer and more robust over time in some cases, such as for MONUC (as described at length in Chapter 8 of this study.) For its first few months, MONUC operated without Chapter VII authority, making it a *de facto* Chapter VI operation. In February 2000, however, the Council added the direction and authority to protect civilians. Acting under Chapter VII, the Council authorized MONUC to protect UN personnel, facilities, installations and equipment; ensure the security and freedom of movement of its personnel; and protect civilians under imminent threat of physical violence.[210]

Even with a clear reference to civilian protection, however, the Council left the decision to protect civilians up to the mission leadership in the field, who were to "deem" if such protection was within MONUC's "capabilities." It was not clear whether the capabilities, from the beginning, were deemed sufficient to protect civilians—or were planned to be so. In essence, the mandate gave MONUC the *option* to protect civilians, but left it with a limited capacity since the Council authorized no more than 5,537 military personnel in a country the size of Western Europe.

As crises continued to occur and attacks on civilians persisted, the Council gave MONUC increasingly stronger civilian protection mandates throughout 2003 and 2004. In March 2005, the Council authorized specific, robust military tactics, and directly authorized the use of *preventive* force to protect civilians,

---

[209] UN Department of Peacekeeping Operations, "MINUSTAH-ROE: Rules of Engagement of the Military Component of the United Nations Stabilization Mission in Haiti (MINUSTAH)," UN Restricted, DPKO Military Division, 24 May 2004.

[210] S/Res/1291, 24 February 2000.

calling on MONUC to use "all necessary means, within its capabilities and in the areas where its armed units are deployed…to ensure the protection of civilians under imminent threat of physical violence, from any armed group."[211]

MONUC has the most assertive mandate yet regarding the protection of civilians, but other UN mandates have become increasingly robust and direct in their calls for civilian protection. The 2004 ONUB mandate stated without exception that the AU operation would use "all necessary means…without prejudice to the responsibility of the transitional Government of Burundi, to protect civilians under imminent threat of physical violence."[212] In Darfur, the AU mission was instructed to "[p]rotect civilians whom it encounters under imminent threat and in the immediate vicinity, within resources and capability, it being understood that the protection of the civilian population is the responsibility of the Government of Sudan."[213] In 2006 that role was revised to contribute to the "general security situation" for humanitarian assistance, provide support to IDPs and refugees, and "take all necessary steps…in order to ensure a more forceful protection of the civilian population."[214]

> *MONUC has the most assertive mandate yet regarding the protection of civilians.*

INTERPRETING MANDATES AND ROE

Political leaders also interpret Council mandates as they see fit, influencing mission organization and leadership, and thus, how the legitimate use of force is understood. There are many leaders within a UN operation in addition to the Special Representative of the Secretary-General (SRSG). The mandate interpretation is influenced by DPKO and the Secretary-General, and interpretations by the various peacekeeping contingents recruited for the operation, their commanders, and the UN Force Commander further impact their execution. Force commanders in multilateral operations also remain tied to their political leaders at home. All have understandings of what the mandate calls for and, without a single chain of command, those interpretations can tug personnel in different directions.

Thus, mandates and ROE that allow for the use of force to protect civilians do not guarantee that such force will in fact be exercised. The interpretation of ROE and the actual force capacity to protect civilians may be more important to their

---

[211] S/Res/1592, 30 March 2005.

[212] S/Res/1545, 21 May 2004.

[213] AU Peace and Security Council, Communiqué of the 17th Ordinary Session, 20 October 2004.

[214] AU Peace and Security Council, Communiqué of the 46th Ordinary Session, 10 March 2006.

implementation than their language. Even after UNAMSIL became the first UN operation mandated to "protect civilians under imminent threat," its peacekeepers themselves were taken hostage in 2000 by the brutal Revolutionary United Front (RUF) rebel group, which had terrorized the civilian population. The Secretary-General told the press that peacekeepers lacked cohesion and a common understanding of the force's purpose and rules of engagement, in addition to facing a difficult environment and logistical challenges.[215]

> *Thus, mandates and ROE that allow for the use of force to protect civilians do not guarantee that such force will in fact be exercised.*

Lacking a common understanding of the purpose and ROE of a mission is, unfortunately, familiar territory. Without common peacekeeping doctrine for UN missions, the translation of Council mandates into ROE can vary greatly, particularly for missions with Chapter VII authority where force is directly used to compel compliance or protect individuals.[216] For missions not led by the United Nations, NATO, or nations with advanced militaries, mission-wide rules of engagement for forces may not exist. When Nigerian troops deployed on the ECOWAS mission to Liberia, ECOMIL, in 2003, the force reportedly landed on the ground without any written ROE from ECOWAS because the regional organization had "none."[217]

Contingents in a peace support operation may operate under different national ROE as well and those ROE are interpreted differently—some nations consider them orders, others mere guidance. Interpretations of ROE can impact individual soldiers subject to multiple chains of authority (e.g., both a multinational institution and their home nation) whose understandings of ROE may not coincide. NATO doctrine states that "a commander at any level must always act within the ROE received but is not bound to use the full extent of the permission granted."[218] Even if robust, effective ROE are negotiated for a multilateral mission, a nation may order its forces to follow more restrictive national ROE or

---

[215] Edith Lederer, "UN Chief Calls Sierra Leone 'Dangerous and Volatile,'" Associated Press, 2 August 2000.

[216] Findlay makes this point in his comprehensive book, *The Use of Force in Peace Operations*, which reviews the specific mandates for UN operations and analyzes how UN-led or UN-authorized missions actually operated in the field in regards to force, and the variance of interpretation of ROE and mandates. Findlay, *The Use of Force in Peace Operations*, 360-361.

[217] Military advisor, DES-PADS, ECOWAS Secretariat, interview with author, Abuja, Nigeria, June 2004.

[218] NATO, *Peace Support Operations: Techniques and Procedures*, ATP-3.4.1.1, North Atlantic Treaty Organization, 28 May 2003, 1-9.

require permission from their national leadership for specific types of action. UN contingent commanders have been known to phone their capitals when situations require a robust response by peacekeepers.

Many countries are reluctant to send troops as peacekeepers to use force to protect civilians in violent trouble spots—or send personnel who are constrained by national limits on their use of force.[219] In some cases, troops may be prohibited from acting in more volatile regions, or in roles for which they are ill-prepared. Japan, for example, sent troops to Somalia and Iraq, but these troops were not permitted to use force except in self-defense.[220]

Interpretation is especially problematic when ROE themselves are silent or lack detail on key issues. The long version of the ROE for *Operation Restore Hope* in Somalia, for example, made explicit that troops can use force in self-defense—and to protect civilians. "Deadly force may be used to defend your life, the life of another US soldier, or the lives of persons in areas under US control," the ROE instructs troops. "You are authorized to use deadly force in self-defense if...armed elements, mobs and/or rioters threaten human life," it continues.[221] But this is not explicit in the "short" version of the ROE card, which is what most soldiers refer to in decision-making situations. [See Box 5.2.]

Troop actions may be affected by other agreements between the troop contributing country, the UN and the host country. For example, Status of Forces Agreements (SOFAs) between the receiving country and the UN may constrain how troops are deployed. Nations may negotiate separate Memoranda of Understanding (MOU) ordering that their forces not engage in certain types of behavior.

MONUC: INTERPRETATIONS MATTER IN THE DRC

Once again, MONUC demonstrates the challenges of protection. Effective civilian protection by MONUC suffered from cautious implementation of and internal confusion regarding the mission's ROE. Since 2000, MONUC had relatively permissive rules of engagement (under Resolution 1291) that allowed peacekeepers to use force beyond self defense to protect civilians under imminent threat of physical violence. Nevertheless, following the crisis in Ituri—in which a land dispute between armed factions associated with the Hema

---

[219] In nations such as the Netherlands and Italy, the parliament controls authorization of militaries to be offered to peace operations. Countries such as Ireland only provide troops if the UN authorizes the mission.

[220] Takahisa Kawakami, Japanese Mission to the United Nations, interview with author, June 2004.

[221] Excerpt from TF Mountain OPLAN 93-2 (*Operation Restore Hope*), TC-7-98-1, US Army Stability and Support Operations Training Circular, Slide 4.1.

and Lendu ethnic groups led to mass killings of civilians belonging to the 'wrong' group[222]—the Uruguayan battalion reported to the UN that it could not have done more to protect civilians because MONUC was a Chapter VI mission with ROE that proscribed the use of force beyond self defense.[223] Uruguayan soldiers in Bunia argued, for example, that ROE restricted them to simply controlling the UN compound, protecting UN personnel, and using force exclusively in self-defense. Uruguay and Morocco had issued MOU restricting their troops from participating in the more robust aspects of the MONUC mission. The Uruguayans were nationally barred from participating in Chapter VII UN operations and could not take part in certain types of mission tasks.[224] Even if a fighter pulled a pin from a grenade, argued one, the ROE proscribed any use of force until it was actually thrown. "And even then the threat is the

---

Box 5.2

ROE Card
ROE FOR OPERATION RESTORE HOPE
Joint Task Force for Somalia Relief Operations
Ground Forces Rules of Engagement

Nothing in these rules of engagement limits your right to take appropriate action to defend yourself and your unit.

1. You have the right to use force to defend yourself against attacks or threats of attack.
2. Hostile fire may be returned effectively and promptly to stop a hostile act.
3. When US forces are attacked by unarmed hostile elements, mobs, and/or rioters, US forces should use the minimum force necessary under the circumstances and proportional to the threat.
4. You may not seize the property of others to accomplish your mission.
5. Detention of civilians is authorized for security reasons or in self-defense.

Remember: The United States is not at war. Treat all persons with dignity and respect. Use minimum force to carry out the mission. Always be prepared to act in self-defense.

Source: Joint Chiefs of Staff, *Joint Tactics, Techniques, and Procedures for Peace Operations*, Joint Publication 3-07.3 (Washington, DC: US Joint Chiefs of Staff, 12 February 1999), A-D-6 from Annex D to Appendix A (Figure A-D-1).

---

[222] Amnesty International, "The Human Rights Crisis in Ituri," (no date), Amnesty International website, web.amnesty.org/pages/cod-040803-background_2-eng.

[223] Peacekeeping Best Practices Unit, *Operation Artemis: Lessons of the Interim Emergency Multinational Force*, Peacekeeping Best Practices Section, UN Department of Peacekeeping Operations, October 2004, 9.

grenade," he said. "We can't even shoot the person. We have to shoot the grenade."[225]

MONUC's revised mandate and rules of engagement in 2003 allowed the mission to pursue and challenge militia even when it was not directly attacked, to interpose peacekeepers between parties in conflict, and to arrest and detain civilian and militia elements caught committing obviously criminal acts.[226] ROE 1.7 reads, "Forces may use up to deadly force to protect civilians when competent local authorities are not in a position to do so."[227] According to Col. Lawrence Smith, Commander of MONUC Sector 5, however, the most important change was not in the ROE, but in the perceptions of

> *While MONUC had authority on paper to protect civilian lives, in practice mission personnel operated as a more traditional monitoring mission.*

soldiers and commanders on the ground. Prior to the 2003 Ituri crisis, not all MONUC personnel seemed aware of the permissive 2000 mandate. While MONUC had authority *on paper* to protect civilian lives, *in practice* mission personnel operated as a more traditional monitoring mission. "Although the previous Rules of Engagement did not need a major change with the new mandate," Col. Smith has argued, "their interpretation and application at ground level needed to be adjusted very quickly."[228] Even with the more robust ROE, the lack of a unified conception of MONUC's mandate and responsibilities continued to cause internal confusion and to a failure to protect civilians, as seen in Chapter 8.

MINUSTAH: USING FORCE IN HAITI

The importance of mandate and ROE interpretation is visible in other missions as well. In Haiti, UN forces from different contingents have varied considerably

---

[224] The Uruguayans' defense of civilians in Ituri in 2003 is noteworthy, where forces prepared for guard duty were deployed into a dangerous environment. They were not the right force for that mission, which was eventually taken on by the EU-authorized French-led forces.

[225] Sudarsan Raghavan, "UN forces watch bloodshed in Congo," Knight Ridder Newspapers, 2 July 2003.

[226] Henri Boshoff, "Overview of MONUC's military strategy and concept of operations," in Mark Malan and Joao Gomes Porto, eds., *Challenges of Peace Implementation: The UN Mission in the Democratic Republic of the Congo* (Pretoria: Institute for Security Studies, 2004), 136; Roberto Ricci, "Human rights challenges in the DRC: A view from MONUC's Human Rights Section," in Malan and Porto, eds., *Challenges of Peace Implementation*, 100; Alpha Sow, "Achievements of the Interim Emergency Multinational Force and Future Scenarios," in Malan and Porto, eds., *Challenges of Peace Implementation*, 216.

[227] MONUC military official, interview with author, 27 November 2005.

[228] Lawrence Smith, "MONUC's Military Involvement in the Eastern Congo (Maniema and the Kivus)," in Malan and Porto, eds., *Challenges of Peace Implementation,* 233.

in their use of force to protect civilians facing local violence. The Brazilian contingent has appeared to view its role in MINUSTAH as a traditional peacekeeping mission where force is used only in self-defense, while the Chilean and Sri Lankan contingents have engaged in robust combined military/military police operations targeting criminal gangs in Cap Haitien and elsewhere.

Events in Haiti demonstrate the difficult situation confronting peacekeeping missions where civilians face violence, and why clarity is needed for civilian protection mandates and the application of ROE. MINUSTAH has a mandate and ROE "to protect civilians under imminent threat of physical violence, within its capabilities and areas of deployment, without prejudice to the responsibilities of the Transitional Government and of police authorities."[229] It is also intended "to support the Transitional Government as well as Haitian human rights institutions and groups in their efforts to promote and protect human rights, particularly of women and children, in order to ensure individual accountability for human rights abuses and redress for victims."[230] The mission operates in an intense, insecure environment, where the state provides little security and the Haitian National Police (HNP) remain corrupt while gangs and former military adherents are still armed.

> **MINUSTAH has been criticized both for being too passive – and failing to fulfill its mandate to protect civilians – and for being too aggressive and harming civilians.**

MINUSTAH has been criticized both for being *too passive*—and failing to fulfill its mandate to protect civilians—and for being *too aggressive* in its actions and harming too many civilians. NGOs such as Refugees International and Amnesty International have called for the mission to take a more robust stance against spoilers, rather than be "neutral" during attacks on civilians.[231] The Brazilian UN commander expressed discomfort with such criticisms: "We are under extreme pressure from the international community to use violence. I

---

[229] S/Res/1542, 30 April 2004.

[230] Ibid., para. 7.

[231] Refugees International, "Haiti: Brazilian troops in MINUSTAH must intervene to stop violence," *Refugees International Bulletin*, 17 March 2005; Amnesty International, "Haiti: Disarmament Delayed, Justice Denied," *AI Index: AMR 36/005/2005*, 28 July 2005. One human rights group accused the mission of being in legal breach of its mandate by failing to use force to protect civilians under imminent threat. Pooja Bhatia and Benjamin S. Litman, *Keeping the Peace in Haiti? An Assessment of the UN Stabilization Mission in Haiti Using Compliance with its Prescribed Mandate as a Barometer for Success* (Harvard Law Student Advocates for Human Rights & Centro de Justica Global, March 2005), 19-20, 27-34.

command a peacekeeping force, not an occupation force... We are not there to carry out violence."[232] Indeed, the UN reported that in January 2005 UN police officers were coming under attack during patrols.

Beginning in March 2005, MINUSTAH demonstrated a more robust view of its mandate, by trying to disarm ex-soldiers and their supporters with raids on three towns. MINUSTAH and the Security Council declared the effort a success while critics complained that the results were meager.[233] One day later, Special Representative to the Secretary-General Juan Gabriel Valdes demanded that Haitian gangs disarm or MINUSTAH would deal with them "with the same line of firmness that we have followed in the last week vis-à-vis the former military."[234] The UN force commander again defended MINUSTAH's position: "'I have been accused of not being aggressive enough, and now I have been labelled as timid. I don't know if that's true, but I do know that I am prudent, thank God, because imprudence can lead to a court martial,'" the Brazilian general reportedly told a Uruguayan media delegation.[235]

MINUSTAH struggled to disarm armed gangs and militias without harming civilians in the crossfire, but it came under criticism for its aggressive operations in poor neighborhoods friendly to former Haitian President Jean-Bertrand Aristide.[236] Highly robust MINUSTAH operations began in July 2005, with a raid in Cité Soleil aimed at uprooting a key gang leader, and involving over 300 soldiers and 41 troop transports and armored vehicles. The UN acknowledged that many shots were exchanged and the gang leader and four colleagues were likely killed, but denied outside reports that non-combatants were injured and killed and that force was used indiscriminately.[237] MINUSTAH pledged to investigate any use of unnecessary force, maintained that it did not target civilians, and reported unconfirmed HNP accounts that gang killings of civilians

---

[232] Sarah Martin, Peter Gantz, and Braun Jones, "Haitian Voices: Response to the Brazilian Peacekeepers," Refugees International, 4 March 2005, www.refugeesinternational.org/content/article/detail/5297?PHPSESSID=5ce00f92779c166324e1d.

[233] Jane Regan, "Peacekeepers Stage Raids to Disarm Thugs," Miami Herald, 22 March 2005.

[234] Nick Wadhams, "UN Official Warns Haiti Gangs to Disarm," Associated Press, 23 March 2005.

[235] Darío Montero, "UN Mission Walks Thin Line Between Peacekeeping and Repression," Inter Press Service, 15 June 2005, www.ipsnews.net/news.asp?idnews=29085.

[236] Haiti Information Project, "UN Troops Massacre Civilians in Cité Soleil," Haiti Information Project, 13 July 2005.

[237] Andrew Buncombe, "UN Peacekeepers Kill 5 in Crackdown on Haiti's Gangs," The Independent (London), 8 July 2005. Others charged that more were killed by a "UN massacre." Haider Rizvi, "Group Charges 'Massacre' in UN Raid," Inter Press Service, 14 July 2005. Human Rights Watch noted allegations of indiscriminate force used by UN troops in its overview of human rights developments in 2005. Human Rights Watch, World Report 2006, (New York: Human Rights Watch, 2006), 198.

were attributed to MINUSTAH.[238] *The Washington Post* later reported that a confidential UN investigation concluded that "dozens" of civilians were injured.[239]

Médecins sans Frontières, which opened a trauma center in Port-au-Prince in December 2004, reported that almost half of those it treated by early July 2005 were women, children, or elderly who were most often injured during violent confrontations between the HNP or MINUSTAH and armed gangs.[240] The organization claimed that MINUSTAH was becoming an armed actor in the conflict, and that its use of force had caused an increase in threats to civilian lives.[241]

Such problems demonstrate the difficulty peacekeeping missions face in trying to integrate various contingents, uphold the mandate and establish greater security with some use of force. In a place like Haiti, where consent is partial, the mission needs a clear concept of civilian protection and of the use of coercive protection. Differing interpretations of ROE and mandates further complicate this job. Further, those on the ground may be left frustrated by the situation of insecurity while remaining equally ill at ease with peacekeepers using force.

GAINING CLARITY ON PROTECTING CIVILIANS

The specific authorization to protect civilians in UN mandates and ROE is an important step forward. Many missions no longer lack sufficient legal authority for troops to use force to protect civilians. As the Brahimi Report suggested, ROE must be more than just responsive in nature:

> Rules of engagement should not limit contingents to stroke-for-stroke responses but should allow ripostes sufficient to silence a source of deadly fire that is directed at United Nations troops or at the people they are charged to protect and, in particularly dangerous situations, should not force United Nations contingents to cede the initiative to their attackers.[242]

At the same time, troops on the ground may still not use force to protect civilians in areas of violence, and cite restrictive ROE and mandates to explain

---

[238] UN News Service, "In Robust Fight Against Haiti's Gangs, UN Peacekeepers Seek to Avoid Civilian Casualties," UN News Center, 25 July 2005, www0.un.org/apps/news/story.asp?NewsID=15135&Cr=Haiti&Cr1.

[239] Colum Lynch, "UN Peacekeeping More Assertive, Creating Risk for Civilians," *The Washington Post*, 15 August 2005.

[240] Pierre Salignon, "Violence Intensifies in Port-au-Prince, Haiti," Médecins sans Frontières Press Release, 30 July 2005.

[241] Ibid.

[242] A/55/305-S/2000/809, paras. 62-64.

their behavior. Addressing the known areas of confusion—differing national ROE, for example, or a lack of capacity to act—could help improve the performance of missions with civilian protection mandates. Where troop contingents are operating under ROE that allow them to protect civilians with force, they should be well trained on these ROE; their political leadership should also be clear in understanding what application and use of coercion the ROE may engender. Current training programs to prepare peacekeepers, such as training by the UN Integrated Training Service and bilateral and regional training efforts, could better address how ROE work in the field. Recognition of military polices' use of "rules of contact" for interacting with civilians, as opposed to ROE, could expand this area of research.

In many missions, the letter of ROE is less important than a clear, overall understanding of mission strategy and mindset. While improvements in the official, legal documents that dictate troop behavior are necessary for effective civilian protection, they are by no means sufficient. Effective communication with troops and contributing countries should ensure that all forces understand their responsibilities, the nature of the mission, and the types of situations they may encounter on the ground. Civilian leaders may also misunderstand mandates and rules of engagement. One UN official noted that political leaders would benefit from training in both ROE and mandates, since they direct missions and may easily misread the parameters of a peacekeeper's legitimate use of force.

> *The exact rules of engagement may be less important than a clear understanding of the mission's strategy.*

Development of common ROE associated with specific mandates could also help improve understanding of how forces can and should operate in hostile environments with civilians under threat. In turn, this could assist in the development of doctrine, training for deployment, scenario-building, simulations, and the better understanding by political and military leaders of the use of force in pursuit of civilian protection.

— 6 —
TRANSLATING CONCEPTS: DOCTRINE

The development of military doctrine helps establish an institutional basis to prepare forces for specific missions. Both NATO and the US Department of Defense define doctrine as "fundamental principles by which the military forces or elements thereof guide their actions in support of national objectives. It is authoritative but requires judgment in application."[243] In many countries, doctrine provides armed forces a broad set of principles and guidelines for their assignments. A former officer involved in developing doctrine in Africa suggested that it provides the written-down, big picture description of a potential operation, the manner in which it should be conducted, and the types of situations for which forces should anticipate and plan. From doctrine, training goals are developed; doctrine also leads to tactics, techniques and procedures, and standard operating procedures.[244]

In preparing forces for operations, military doctrine is designed at many levels, from the strategic to the tactical, from single service to joint operations, from the national to the multinational. However, policy shapes the use of such doctrine, as political leaders establish the goals of a mission and may direct what forces are to do—and not to do—to achieve those goals.[245] Some blurriness also exists between formal military doctrine and policies widely viewed as doctrine, such as

---

[243] US Department of Defense, *DoD Dictionary of Military and Associated Terms*, JP 1-02 (US Department of Defense, 12 April 2001, as amended through 31 August 2005), www.dtic.mil/doctrine/jel/doddict/.

[244] This list reflects US military thinking and terms; most Western countries have organizational doctrine and components that are derived from it, but terminology differs. Dr. Charles Grimm, US advisor, ECOWAS, June 2004; Col. Tim Parks (UK), Kofi Annan International Peacekeeping Training Center, Accra, Ghana, June 2004; and Col. Michael Larmas Smith (retired), interviews with author. Workshop, *Operational Capacities for Civilian Protection Missions*, The Henry L. Stimson Center, Washington, DC, 8 December 2004.

[245] For *Operation Enduring Freedom* in Afghanistan, for example, the initial US decision not to focus on nation-building or peace operations "affected the strategic direction of the operation" and was "an outgrowth of the lack of a political/military planning process.... [that] stunted the development of a coherent approach to address the reality on the ground in Afghanistan." Col. William Flavin, *Civil Military Operations: Afghanistan Observations on Civil Military Operations During the First Year of Operation Enduring Freedom* (Carlisle, PA: US Army Peacekeeping and Stability Operations Institute, Army War College, 23 March 2004), 11.

the guidance developed for most multinational organizations like the United Nations.[246]

The development of doctrine is recognition itself that forces may be directed to conduct a particular type of operation. The problem with writing doctrine, suggested by more than one officer, is that it makes it more likely that the military would be called on to perform that kind of mission again. While there is no doubt that the United States could intervene to stop a genocide, for example, some have suggested that this is a reason the US resisted new military doctrine explicitly for "humanitarian interventions" after the American experience in Somalia in the 1990s.[247] On the other hand, the 2006 US National Security Strategy declares that: "The world must act in cases of mass atrocities and mass killing that will eventually lead to genocide even if the local parties are not prepared for peace."[248] The decision to intervene militarily is fundamentally a policy decision, of course. The doctrinal question is how prepared personnel and their leaders are for operations and what their understanding of those operations entails.

Doctrine is not a silver bullet, however, to ensure military capacity for specific mission types. Experts point out that not all doctrine has equal weight. Its development alone ensures neither awareness nor use by the relevant forces. Much doctrine, frankly, is ignored. The content of doctrine matters, but its importance is determined by whether, and how, it is used.

Gaps in military doctrine for a particular situation do not necessarily indicate that troops are ill-prepared. In some circumstances, doctrine may not address a specific situation, but personnel can develop techniques in the field.[249] US personnel serving in Iraq have used the Internet to share ideas about how to handle scenarios they face, for example, creating new guidelines in real-time.[250]

---

[246] Some consider "doctrine" to be guidance at many levels, such as the supranational (e.g., the UN Charter), the national (e.g., policy guidelines), the operational (specific to missions) and the tactical (instruction, training, commander level). Observation by Mark Malan, quoted in The Challenges Project, *Challenges of Peace Operations: Into the 21st Century, Concluding Report, 1997-2002*, Swedish National Defence College and Challenges Project Partner Organizations (Stockholm: Elanders Gotab, 2002), 91.

[247] Military officers suggest that the US would turn to doctrine for actions similar to humanitarian intervention, but not labeled as such.

[248] *The National Security Strategy of the United States of America*, 2006, 17.

[249] There is a debate about what is doctrine, seen as a set of enduring principles to guide action, and whether that includes tactics, techniques, and procedures (TTPs), which are based on doctrinal principles. Observation by Col. William Flavin, Peacekeeping and Stability Operations Institute, Army War College, interview with author, 9 June 2006.

[250] Websites such as *http://platoonleader.army.mil* and *www.companycommander.com* offer an opportunity for company commanders and platoon leaders to share information about present day operations. Both sites were open to public viewing in 2004 but are now unavailable to the public or operate under restricted access.

Militaries also have a certain degree of flexibility and can "train up" for specific missions when necessary. In other cases, doctrine for one kind of operation may be applied to another. Doctrine for the emergency evacuation of a nation's citizens from a foreign country (non-combatant evacuation operations, or NEO), for instance, could apply to providing immediate protection to civilians from other nations as well.

One gap is clear, however. There is little well-developed or well-known doctrine addressing operations authorized to use force to protect civilians under imminent threat either in the context of a peace support operation or as a stand-alone mission. Further, there is no common terminology to identify such missions or the likely tasks

> *Little doctrine addresses operations authorized to use force to protect civilians under imminent threat either in the context of a peace support operation or as a stand-alone mission.*

"triggered" by a mandate to protect civilians. As a result, doctrine most applicable to missions requiring personnel to protect civilians in non-permissive environments is usually called something else. Likely scenarios are covered in part by doctrine for missions such as counterinsurgency, peace support, peace enforcement, peacekeeping, operations other than war, humanitarian assistance, non-combatant evacuations, small wars, military policing, and civil-military cooperation. Such doctrine encompasses traditional military and humanitarian concepts of protection: as an obligation of warfighting, as observance of international humanitarian and human rights law, and as support to the provision of humanitarian space. Some peace operations doctrine also provides limited lists of military tasks for protecting civilians.

Almost no doctrine, however, addresses the concept of civilian protection as the goal of a military mission. There are areas where doctrine identifies coercive tactics to protect civilians, but they are not categorized as such. Thomas G. Weiss rightly argues that "there seems to be a lack of institutional adjustment, at least as is indicated by military doctrines, that, to date, have failed to specify ways to meet the needs for coercive protection of civilians, the challenge of the responsibility to protect."[251] That gap is also true for peace operations with mandates to protect civilians under imminent threat.

Therefore, existing doctrine offers only a partial roadmap for armed services faced with preventing deadly violence against civilian populations. There is a

---

[251] Weiss, "The Humanitarian Impulse," in Malone, ed., *The UN Security Council: From the Cold War to the 21st Century*, 48.

clear baseline of preparation for peace operations involving the use of force, and for combat missions with tasks applicable to protecting civilians. At the same time, significant changes in doctrine are underway, as countries and multinational organizations are developing new and revised doctrine for forces across the range of peace and stability operations. Thus, this chapter reviews some examples of military doctrine, considers their core ideas for national and multinational forces in situations where civilians require protection, and looks at how that impacts preparedness for operations mandated to protect civilians in hostile environments or to intervene on behalf of populations facing mass violence.

RECURRING THEMES IN EXISTING DOCTRINE

National and multinational doctrines embrace a variety of approaches to peace operations, non-combatant evacuations, civil-military cooperation (CIMIC), and other related missions. It is nonetheless possible to identify patterns in how such doctrine treats the protection of civilians. The following is a broad outline of existing categories of doctrine and how each touches on, but rarely addresses directly, civilian protection.

Peace Support Operations Doctrine

Peace operations or peace support operations (PSO) doctrine usually focuses on building a political peace and promoting host-state governance capacity. Historically, PSO doctrine divided into two broad categories—relative to the level of consent among parties to the conflict and the anticipated need to use force. The first type, often called "traditional" or "Chapter VI" peacekeeping, assumes a high degree of consent locally, little requirement for peacekeepers to resort to force, and the steadfast impartiality of peacekeepers. Typically led by the UN, such operations involved troops in tasks such as observing a ceasefire or monitoring compliance with a peace agreement. Peacekeeping was thus different from "peace enforcement" which was conducted primarily by militarily-led coalitions authorized to use force to achieve its goal.

> *National and multinational doctrines embrace a variety of approaches to peace operations, NEO, civil-military cooperation, and other related missions. It is possible to identify patterns in how such doctrine treats the protection of civilians.*

In the 1990s, peacekeepers were increasingly sent to support stability within states and help governments find their footing after civil war. These missions, termed "complex" or "multidimensional," assumed that fighting had ceased and that troops would operate in permissive environments where they were tasked to rebuild governance. Following the serious challenges to peacekeeping in Rwanda, Bosnia, Kosovo, Angola, Sierra Leone, and elsewhere, however, many states and multinational organizations came to recognize that missions needed more tools—and force—to succeed. Peacekeepers confront the challenge of determining whether and how to employ force, for example, when:

- a ceasefire is signed but groups are not fully committed to it;
- warring parties have factions that disagree with the decisions of their leadership;
- local governance is weak and violent crime is not suppressed by national forces alone; or
- powerful economic interests spur a return to warfare absent an effective deterrent force.

In their most robust state, peace operations have also been called "peace enforcement" or "coercive missions," among other labels.[252] For the most part, such missions are considered interventions rather than peace support operations; the UN traditionally leaves peace enforcement to coalitions or multinational organizations like NATO. Some current UN missions, however, use significant force and may thus bridge the gap between peacekeeping and peace enforcement.

The doctrine for such peace support operations has evolved as well. While recognizing basic principles of consent, impartiality, and the minimal use of force, standard doctrine now allows for more ambitious peacekeeping activities. Full consent may not be presumed before peacekeepers deploy; rather, doctrine may require promotion or management after arrival. Impartiality becomes active impartiality, whereby peacekeepers are to take action when parties contravene peace agreements or the mission mandate. The use of force for self-defense is clarified to include the use of force in defense of the mandate or the mission.

By late 2004, the framers of some national doctrine abandoned distinct PSO categories, concluding that boundaries between "peacekeeping" and "peace enforcement" were arbitrary or potentially harmful. They saw the need for PSOs to be ready for diverse and shifting environments—to engage in patient negotiation one minute and aggressive enforcement action the next. Even in environments that appear to be non-threatening, troops should be prepared for combat activities and have sufficient firepower to dominate the local security

---

[252] The lack of universal terminology and definitions causes confusion among analysts and policymakers alike. See William J. Durch, with Tobias C. Berkman, "Restoring and Maintaining Peace: What We Know So Far," in William J. Durch, ed., *Twenty-first-Century Peace Operations* (Washington, DC: US Institute of Peace Press, forthcoming), Table 1.1.

environment. This "unified" depiction of PSOs is innovative, if not universally endorsed.

Most PSO doctrines approach the protection of civilians cautiously, remain vague about their specific requirements, and do not address tactics for stopping *génocidaires*. There are good reasons for this. The fundamental principles of PSOs seem to run counter to robust, coercive civilian protection. PSOs are expected to be impartial. Although they may use force to uphold their mandate, PSOs do not seek to defeat a party to a conflict, regardless of how abhorrent its behavior. Similarly, PSOs focus on managing consent and hence providing support to a political agreement, not taking sides.

Active intervention by a PSO to defend civilians under threat could build consent among the local populace—a group that likely thinks that the international force is there to protect them. But PSOs generally do not aim to defeat a particular group—even if it would serve to end ongoing violence. The direct use of force to stop mass killing requires either interpretation of a PSO mandate authorizing "defense of mission" to protect civilians or a more explicit mandate to stop an abusive armed attack. This kind of mandate is possible, but not uniformly anticipated in current doctrine and practice. Thus, if genocide occurs, many forces lack a recognizable strategy to act—since mass violence is not presumed to be a threat for most peacekeeping operations and its prevention lies outside their usual goals. Certainly, including civilian protection in a PSO mission or mandate makes it easier to justify aggressive action against a murderous militia as an impartial act in defense of the mandate. But arriving at more active types of civilian protection through PSO doctrine nonetheless requires a shift in traditional interpretations of mandates and an exercise in leadership not often found in peace operations.

> *If genocide occurs, many forces lack a recognizable strategy to act, since mass violence is not presumed to be a threat for most peacekeeping operations and its prevention lies outside their usual goals.*

Most PSO doctrine steers clear of traditional warfighting strategies and tactics to secure an area. To protect civilians under threat, PSO doctrine is more likely to touch directly on dissuasive, limited, and "defensive," rather than coercive, strategies for protecting civilians—that task is left to others. It usually includes direction on the support of local governance capacity, including the provision of public security to the local population, the establishment of an atmosphere of law and order, the promotion of a secure and stable environment, and the assistance of humanitarian groups. In more benign environments, therefore, PSOs help protect civilians from crime, lawlessness, and low-end physical threats. There is also room for more active (if not strategic) protection tasks, such as the defense of safe areas, humanitarian corridors, or IDP camps. Many of these tasks are precisely those that militaries are often unprepared and unwilling to fulfill, as they are often perceived as the domain of military police (and thus the job of the local government).

CIMIC Doctrine

Doctrine on CIMIC or civil-military operations (CMO) typically touches on activities relevant to civilian protection. CIMIC addresses military interaction with a broad range of civilian actors, including the host state government, NGOs, and local civilians. Most CIMIC is designed to ensure that military operations have a limited negative, if not positive, effect on local civilians—and vice-versa. CIMIC thus involves tasks important to the "indirect" protection of civilians, such as minimizing harm during operations, building up local infrastructure, distributing emergency aid and medical assistance, and other "hearts and minds" actions.

Cooperation with humanitarian groups and NGOs remains an important aspect of CIMIC doctrine. Especially in lower threat environments, the military liaises with these groups to support the physical safety and well-being of civilians. CIMIC doctrine can provide important guidance for civilian protection in places such as the DRC, where lives are threatened less by direct, violent massacres than by disease and malnutrition due to instability. Lessons address the protection of humanitarian space, respecting humanitarian neutrality, and cooperating with relief groups when appropriate. Although humanitarians are concerned about aligning themselves with the military and jeopardizing their neutrality, some may take advantage of the military's logistics and rapid response capacity to serve their missions. Likewise, militaries can benefit from NGO knowledge about local concerns. CIMIC doctrine explains these issues— outlining the need for measured cooperation and information exchange among military and humanitarian actors, combined with a respect for humanitarian space—and aims to create a more effective international response on the ground, particularly in regards to non-violent threats to civilian life such as displacement, disease, and hunger.

CIMIC doctrine, however, implies that the *primary* military mission is something *other* than improving or protecting civilian lives. CIMIC is most often used to enhance its success in pursuing its goals; it is not likely to be the goal of the mission itself. Like PSO doctrine, therefore, it is used in the protection of civilians, but does not address the topic directly or fully.

NEO Doctrine

Non-combatant evacuations doctrine is specifically about protecting civilians—in limited groups and in unique situations. It describes military operations to remove citizens from a threatening environment, such as the evacuation of either one's nationals or local VIPs from a country. Most NEO missions do not address threats to the general population, natural or otherwise. For example, the US, France, and Belgium sent a NEO mission to Rwanda in 1994, which arrived days after the genocide began, to evacuate US and European citizens, but did not take action to protect Rwandan Tutsi or moderate Hutus under attack.[253] Indeed, for a large-scale emergency, NEO doctrine is only partly applicable—a foreign force could not have evacuated over one million Tutsis from Rwanda. The principles in NEO doctrine, however, start with protecting civilians and in providing immediate security to them. These principles, including organizing the physical protection and evacuation of defined groups, could be applied to vulnerable civilians, such as refugees or IDPs, if the threats to life were localized and contained.

Civil Order Doctrine

Civil order doctrine, sometimes referred to as "crowd control" or "crowd confrontation," addresses a scenario of mass civil disorder, such as a violent riot. At its most extreme, civil disorder could devolve into mass ethnic-based killings or genocide. A robust form of civil order doctrine could therefore do much to inform efforts at protecting civilians, by preparing troops to quell mass hysteria, violence, and looting (as seen in Iraq following the US invasion in 2003, or in Kosovo in March 2004) through the appropriate, graduated use of force. Most civil order doctrine is designed for domestic rather than international use, however. In addition, civil order doctrine might not address large-scale violence organized and directed from the top down by a powerful political actor.

Small Wars and Counter-Insurgency Doctrine

In the face of political actors bent on killing large numbers of civilians, some countries might respond by declaring war, albeit on a limited scale. Most militaries see warfighting as their primary mission, but some have returned to

---

[253] That US Marines were on the ground so quickly and in such force belies the idea that no international response could have arrived in time to stem the genocide, although deploying a small NEO force is less challenging than sending one to counter large-scale genocide. For a comprehensive account of the US response to the Rwanda genocide, see Samantha Power, *A Problem From Hell: America and the Age of Genocide* (New York: Basic Books, 2002), 329-390.

look at doctrine for asymmetrical warfare, counterinsurgency, or small wars. These involve the defeat of an under-resourced enemy that survives using guerilla tactics and knowledge of the local landscape. They also potentially involve the occupation of foreign lands.

Within such doctrine, there is little explicit mention of a *civilian protection* imperative. As described, small wars and counter-insurgencies are fought for *political* aims; they involve winning local support for the aims of the invading party, irrespective of the humanitarian cost. Minimizing harm to civilians may be an important objective within such operations—and it may increase support—but it is not *the immediate aim* of the mission. If such missions were redefined to protect civilians as the central goal, they would involve new humanitarian requirements for military actions and tactics designed to eliminate "the enemy's" capacity to kill. The importance of *how* a protection mission is conducted (e.g., its adherence to the laws of war, its ability to minimize civilian collateral damage, and the number of troops available on the ground to impose general law and order or counter a nascent insurgency) would increase, as would its link to the success of any follow-on peace support operation.

There is a strong argument behind these doctrinal approaches that the protection of civilians is *the result* of functioning, effective government and, therefore, that military support to help improve the conditions for such institutions to succeed is the best way to protect a population. While there is little dispute over the wisdom of this longer-term approach, it does not address the means to support physical protection to civilians facing immediate violence.

EXISTING DOCTRINE:
THE UNITED NATIONS, KEY STATES, AND NATO

Militaries and multinational organizations are at different stages in the degree to which they use doctrine, which is developed primarily for military organizations, and how that doctrine addresses the protection of civilians. Many leading nations engaged in peace operations supported the work of the Challenges Project, which argued in 2002 that:

> [T]here are many different, and sometimes overlapping, opinions about doctrine for complex peace operations—but as yet no clear UN guidance on the subject... There should be a multinational and inclusive effort to define the meaning and scope of doctrine applicable to UN peace operations; troop contributing countries should then take steps to build common doctrinal statements into their national doctrines; led by the Department of Peacekeeping Operations, specific efforts should be made to apply lessons learned in the

formation of peace operations doctrine, paying particular attention to the need to enhance military, police and civilian coordination.[254]

Generally speaking, protection is addressed by most doctrine in traditional approaches, such as part of international humanitarian law, and has little recognition within strategic doctrine.

UN Doctrine

The United Nations does not—yet—have official doctrine for its peace operations, let alone doctrine for missions with mandates "to protect civilians under imminent threat." Doctrine traditionally is viewed as a national responsibility. In the past, UN Member States have been suspicious of efforts to develop UN doctrine, reflecting their national sensitivities and concern about a more autonomous, empowered UN military capacity. This attitude is shifting, however, and the UN is moving to develop greater guidance, and doctrine, for those serving in its missions.

> *The United Nations does not – yet – have official doctrine for its peace operations, let alone for missions with mandates "to protect civilians under imminent threat."*

Without doctrine, the UN has published a series of reports outlining a basic philosophy for peace operations. In 1992, UN Secretary-General Boutros Boutros-Ghali's *An Agenda For Peace* provided a definition of peacekeeping as "the deployment of a United Nations presence in the field, hitherto with the consent of all parties concerned, normally involving United Nations and/or police personnel and frequently civilians as well."[255] The report, written amidst the post-Cold War, post-Gulf War high of the early 1990s, set an ambitious agenda for UN forces to promote international peace and security, but gave little practical guidance. Boutros-Ghali's January 1995 *Supplement to An Agenda For Peace* updated the original, taking into account contemporary UN struggles with peacekeeping and efforts to mount complex, multidimensional missions in the mid-1990s. The report affirmed "consent of the parties, impartiality, and the non-use of force except in self-defense" as the key definitional characteristics of peacekeeping. It also kept the more active use of force at arms-length, emphasizing that "peace-keeping and the use of force

---

[254] The Challenges Project, *Challenges of Peace Operations*, 16-17.

[255] United Nations, *An Agenda For Peace: Preventive diplomacy, peacemaking and peace-keeping*, Report of the Secretary-General pursuant to the statement adopted by the Summit Meeting of the Security Council on 31 January 1992, A/47/277 – S/2411, 17 June 1992, para. 20.

(other than in self-defense) should be seen as alternative techniques and not as adjacent points on a continuum, permitting easy transition from one to the other."[256] The *Supplement* thus left little room within peacekeeping for the use of force to protect or provide security for local civilians.

In 2000, the pivotal *Report of the Panel on Peace Operations* (or, "Brahimi Report") outlined a strategy for improving UN peacekeeping, and recognized Secretary-General Annan's desire to extend more protection to civilians in armed conflict. It urged that peacekeepers who witness violence against civilians "be presumed to be authorized to stop it, within their means," in support of "basic United Nations principles." But it also cautioned against a "blanket mandate" as potentially unachievable, especially given the scale of threats to civilians in the areas of UN deployments, noting:

> The potentially large mismatch between desired objective and resources available to meet it raises the prospect of continuing disappointment with United Nations follow-through in this area. If an operation is given a mandate to protect civilians, therefore, it also must be given the specific resources needed to carry out that mandate.[257]

On one hand, the Brahimi Report urged that peace operations be capable of meeting the requirements of their UN mandates and employing robust rules of engagement when needed to support the mission. But the report also pointed out fundamental problems for the UN: force deficits, shortfalls in capacity, and increasingly ambitious mandates from the Security Council. In their more challenging environments, UN forces had trouble protecting even themselves, let alone UN civilian employees, humanitarian workers, and resident civilians. Nor could they assume that troop contributing countries would be keen to take on assignments.[258]

Since the Brahimi Report, formal UN guidance has improved. The DPKO, through its Peacekeeping Best Practices Section (formerly Unit), has spearheaded efforts to analyze and incorporate lessons from past missions and to codify guidance on conducting operations. In 2003, it released the *Handbook on United Nations Multidimensional Peacekeeping Operations*, developed to inform personnel of what to expect during deployments. The *Handbook*, for example, includes definitions of "impartiality," "consent and cooperation," and "appropriate use of force" that allow for robust UN peacekeeping. Impartiality,

---

[256] United Nations, *Supplement to an Agenda for Peace: Position Paper of the Secretary-General on the Occasion of the Fiftieth Anniversary of the United Nations*, A/50/60 – S/1995/1, 25 January 1995, 6-7, 9.

[257] *Report of the Panel on United Nations Peace Operations*, A/55/305 – S/2000/809, para. 63.

[258] The report included recommendations for UN operations in non-permissive environments. See Durch, Holt et al., *The Brahimi Report and the Future of UN Peace Operations*, 23-25.

for example, "does not mean inaction or overlooking violations." Rather, the *Handbook* urged UN peacekeepers to "actively pursue the implementation of their mandate even if doing so goes against the interests of one or more of the parties." While consent remains a key requisite for "[p]eacekeeping and progress towards a just and sustainable peace," if it is "withdrawn or uncertain from the outset, the Security Council may also exercise the option of authorizing a robust, deterrent military capability to promote consent by closing the option of war."[259] From the United Nations, these are strong words.

The *Handbook* provides some basic guidance on tasks related to the protection of civilians. On "providing a secure environment," for example, the *Handbook* explains:

> Military forces, as part of a UN peacekeeping operation, are often tasked with providing a secure environment to allow other aspects of the mission's mandate or peace process to be implemented. A secure environment is generally a precondition for moving ahead on several elements of peace agreements, such as safe return of refugees and internally displaced persons, cantonment, disarmament and demobilization, the free flow of persons and goods and delivery of humanitarian assistance. As part of the task of providing a secure environment, the military component may be asked to provide a visible deterrent presence, control movement and access through checkpoints, provide armed escort for safety and to facilitate access, conduct cordon and search operations, control crowds or confiscate weapons.[260]

This description of distinct, recurring tasks in peacekeeping mandates usefully identifies tasks for operations requiring the protection of civilians. While cast as the means for providing a secure environment, the list covers roles for peacekeepers that range from dissuasive to coercive means of providing protection to civilians, such as traditional strategies (i.e., the provision of support to humanitarian assistance and space) and more coercive measures (i.e., cordon and search). This section does not link the provision of "a secure environment" to civilian well-being explicitly, however. Rather, protection is likely to result from support to peace agreements, which require a secure environment. Implicitly, then, the protection of civilians is considered a task toward another goal. Certainly the phrase "secure environment" can be interpreted in a number of ways that leave civilians out of the equation.[261]

---

[259] *Handbook on United Nations Multidimensional Peacekeeping Operations*, 56-57.
[260] Ibid., 60.
[261] The *Handbook* does not suggest addressing the protection of civilians as part of the restoration of law and order either, something which "is not normally a military task and requires significant specialized training," and will be "only in exceptional circumstances, with the goal of returning to civilian policing as soon as possible." Ibid., 63.

Indeed, the *Handbook* directly addresses the task to "protect civilians" only to say:

> In specific circumstances, the mandate of a peacekeeping operation may include the need to protect vulnerable civilian populations from imminent attack. The military component may be asked to provide such protection in its area of deployment only if it has the capacity to do so.[262]

The premise is that UN missions with this mandate are *overtly* dependent on capacity. Forces are not *presumed* to have the ability to act in support of the mandate. So, even when the Security Council includes "protect civilians" in its mandates, additional factors—actual capacity, perceived capacity, and location—are expected to impact whether and how a peacekeeping force carries it out. Indeed, Council mandates often include such caveats.

Unfortunately, the *Handbook* offers no further details on tasks for protecting civilians. It cites the examples of UNAMSIL and the MONUC as missions mandated to afford protection to civilians under physical threat "within their capabilities and areas of deployment"—without suggesting exactly what these operations did, or could have done, to implement this mandate.[263] Moreover, it does not address more aggressive, proactive strategies that may be needed to protect civilians, such as directly eliminating the capacity of abusive armed groups. The implication is that such activities are outside the scope or capacity of UN peacekeeping.

More changes are underway at the UN, however. Within DPKO, efforts include developing guidance on the use of force and on military involvement in humanitarian and development activities, to clarify the responsibilities of actors in peacekeeping operations.[264] The Peacekeeping Best Practices Section completed assessments of the crises in the DRC in Ituri and Bukavu, which address important issues of civilian protection.[265] Prior to getting a green light for official, unified doctrine, Best Practices embarked on a "guidance project" to provide structured guidelines to personnel on common tasks within peacekeeping operations, such as DDR. The project may produce the most detailed and substantive DPKO guidance on the conduct of forces in peacekeeping operations ever developed.[266]

---

[262] Ibid., 64.

[263] Ibid.

[264] Department of Peacekeeping Operations Directive, "Military Involvement in Humanitarian and Development Activities," draft document on file with authors, February 2006.

[265] Peacekeeping Best Practices Unit, *Operation Artemis*; and MONUC, *MONUC and the Bukavu Crisis 2004*, Best Practices Unit, DPKO, on file with authors, March 2005.

[266] DPKO official, interview with author, 27 November 2005.

In December 2005, the Secretary-General highlighted doctrine for UN peacekeeping, suggesting the need to inventory and establish doctrine, and to address questions, such as "What are the conditions under which we adopt particular approaches to the protection of civilians?"[267] In March 2006, Member States signaled their general consent, and a change in attitude, toward development of UN doctrine and offered this as a definition:

> The evolving body of institutional guidance that provides support and direction to personnel preparing for, planning and implementing UN peacekeeping operations, and which includes guiding principles and concepts, as well as the policies, standard operating procedures, guidelines and manuals that support practitioners.[268]

The Secretariat was asked to prepare an interim glossary of terminology for "further development of a peacekeeping doctrine, guiding principles and concepts."[269] This request may match a desire by many to see the UN develop more formal guidance and to address the protection of civilians in that effort.

Key Nations

Without its own doctrine, the UN relies on what is developed by Member States. Some countries have sophisticated doctrine for peace support operations; others have none. Canada and Great Britain come closest to providing guidance to their armed forces on coercive protection and reflecting the language of *The Responsibility to Protect*. Few others have the protection of civilians identified strategically and as an overall goal of military operations, although they offer strategies akin to coercive protection. To see where current doctrine may already prepare forces for protecting civilians as a major task or as the goal of a mission, it is useful to consider selected national doctrines.

Canadian Doctrine

Canadian doctrine includes four types of military operations other than war (MOOTW): peace support operations, humanitarian operations and disaster response operations, non-combatant evacuation, and crowd confrontation. Except for PSOs, there is little in this doctrine that relates to coercive civilian protection in non-permissive environments. As discussed earlier, NEO and crowd confrontation have tangential relevance to such protection. Humanitarian

---

[267] UN General Assembly, *Implementation of the recommendations of the Special Committee on Peacekeeping*, Report of the Secretary-General, A/60/640, 29 December 2005, 11.

[268] UN General Assembly, *Report of the Special Committee on Peacekeeping Operations and its Working Group at the 2006 substantive session*, A/60/19, 22 March 2006, para. 7.

[269] UN General Assembly, "Special Committee on Peacekeeping Operations Concludes Current Session," GA/PK/189, UN Department of Public Information, 20 March 2006, www.un.org/news/Press/docs/2006/gapk189.doc.htm.

and disaster response operations primarily involve using "military resources to assist in the alleviation of human suffering," and are meant "to augment and complement the capabilities of humanitarian agencies" presumably in permissive environments.[270] The military may provide logistics, airlift, and rapid response capacity, but has no potential combat or coercive role.

Yet Canadian PSO doctrine includes some of the only direct references to humanitarian intervention—or to a mission with a comparable overriding civilian protection mission goal—found in the doctrine of major developed state militaries. The 2002 Canadian joint doctrine publication *Peace Support Operations* briefly describes humanitarian intervention as a non-PSO "enforcement action," and outlines how force may be used by the military to protect populations at risk of deadly violence:

> Humanitarian interventions are launched to gain access to an at risk population when the responsible actors refuse to take action to alleviate human suffering or are incapable of doing so and where actors internal to a state are engaging in gross abuses of human rights. Intervention is a combat operation intended to provide protection to the at risk population and aid workers by imposing stable security conditions that permit humanitarian access. These operations can be precursors to complex peacekeeping operations.[271]

The doctrine provides a few further details, linking humanitarian intervention to peacekeeping:

> Humanitarian intervention can establish the conditions for [a] successful peacekeeping operation. Many of the same tasks performed in a CPKO [Canadian Peacekeeping Operation] would be carried out during a humanitarian intervention. Though the presence of overwhelming force may be necessary it may be best applied in the same restrained manner as in a PSO.[272]

Importantly, "humanitarian intervention" here is explicitly aimed at providing protection to civilians rather than serving a larger political goal. This formation places it outside the realm of peace support operations. At the same time, the doctrine makes clear that humanitarian intervention requires restraint—a different approach to the use of force than in warfighting.[273] Canadian doctrine also makes a direct reference to *The Responsibility to Protect* framework for triggering international intervention:

---

[270] Chief of Defense Staff, Canadian Forces, *Peace Support Operations*, Joint Doctrine Manual, B-GJ-005-307/FP-030 (Canada: National Defense, November 2002), 2-5.

[271] Ibid.

[272] Ibid., 5-12.

[273] Canadian doctrine describes PSOs as "authorized in support of the political objectives of internationally recognized organizations such as the United Nations (UN) or the Organization for Security and Co-operation in Europe (OSCE)." Ibid., 2-1.

As well described in the Report of the International Commission on Intervention and State Sovereignty, *The Responsibility to Protect*, nation states have certain fundamental obligations to their citizens. If a state fails to carry out these obligations to the extent where there is serious and irreparable harm occurring to human beings, in particular, large-scale loss of life or ethnic cleansing, the UN may mandate intervention.[274]

There are no more detailed descriptions of humanitarian intervention found in Canadian doctrine, however. Its discussion of peace support operations describes tasks relevant to protecting civilians, framed within their broader political aims. They include:

- the provision of security to protect humanitarian activities and to provide a "security shield behind which international agencies and NGOs attempt to construct a stable state;[275]
- temporary "Military Civil assistance" to provide emergency food or health aid when capable NGOs are not immediately available;[276] and
- "Public Security assistance" to local law enforcement in the absence of capable police forces.[277]

Canadian doctrine clearly states that the role of the PSO includes re-establishing security in a mission area and, depending on the compliance of parties, suppressing well-armed and violent groups.

Interestingly, this doctrine discards the traditional use of Chapter VI and VII to frame the use of force, arguing that it is unimportant in considering the actions of military forces in the field. Rather it distinguishes between "traditional" peacekeeping operations, which have been in existence since the 1956 Suez Crisis, and more modern, "complex" peace operations that may be mandated to protect civilians. Moreover, the latter form of PSO must be ready for challenging contingencies and significant use of force: "The full employment of combat power may be required if the situation on the ground deteriorates during a PSO."[278] Likewise, complex peacekeeping forces "must be structured for the worst-case scenario. These operations are established to deal with complex emergencies, gross violations of human rights or genocide."[279] How, exactly, a peacekeeping force should "deal with genocide" is not further elaborated.

---

[274] Ibid., 1-5.
[275] Ibid., 4-11, 2-4.
[276] Ibid., 4-10.
[277] Ibid., 4-14.
[278] Ibid., 3-7.
[279] Ibid., 5-8.

A 2003 Canadian workshop between government and NGO participants suggested that this doctrine be a "base" for developing further doctrine, strategy, and tactics, including a new manual on humanitarian operations.[280] By late 2005, the Canadian government was reportedly revising its military doctrine to include greater application to missions involving the protection of civilians.[281]

UK Doctrine

The United Kingdom's *Peace Support Operations* includes tactical, operational, and strategic considerations for a range of activities with relevance to civilian protection. In a section on "humanitarian operations and human rights," it details a number of "protection tasks":

> The foremost task for the military force may be to restore the peace and create a stable and secure environment in which aid can run freely and human rights abuses are curtailed. Specific protection tasks may include Non-combatant Evacuation Operations (NEOs) but will more normally apply to the protection of convoys, depots, equipment and those workers responsible for their operation. Conditions of widespread banditry and genocide may exist, and when aid operations are being consistently interrupted there may be a requirement to use force in large measure to prevent the genocide and achieve the mission.[282]

Here, the turn of phrase, despite referencing measures to prevent genocide, reveals caution in the British approach to the protection of civilians as a mission for its own sake. Taken literally, the doctrine holds that "widespread banditry and genocide" are not sufficient grounds to require the use of force—only when "aid operations are being consistently interrupted" must the military act. This frame for action may reflect a presumption that the mission is to support aid delivery, not protection or genocide prevention. Additional tasks in the "humanitarian operations and human rights" section include conflict containment, the forcible separation of belligerent parties, the establishment of protected or safe areas, the guarantee and denial of movement, and sanctions enforcement.

---

[280] *The Responsibility to Protect as part of Canada's Defence Effort*, Report from NGO-Government Roundtable (Ottawa: Peace Operations Working Group, Canadian Peacebuilding Coordinating Committee, 22 September 2003), www.worldfederalistscanada.org/R2Ppapers.htm.
[281] Senior official, Canadian Mission to the United Nations, interview with author, 29 November 2005.
[282] Chief of Joint Operations, Permanent Joint Headquarters, Peace Support Operations, Joint Warfare Publication 3-50 (JWP 3-50) (United Kingdom, as directed by the Chiefs of Staff, 1998), 6-11 through 6-12.

The United Kingdom issued a revised 2004 version of its doctrine, *The Military Contribution to Peace Support Operations*, aimed at the operational level.[283] The publication promotes a unified, "one doctrine" concept of peace support operations. Rather than divide PSOs into separate mission-types, it argues that all PSOs should observe the same basic principles. PSOs are defined by the desired effect they hope to achieve, namely, "to uphold international peace and security by resolving conflicts."[284] They encompass activities across a spectrum between war and peace. In such operations, adaptability and multifunctionality are keys to success. Forces should be prepared to engage in a variety of tasks and switch quickly from "enforcement" to "stabilization" and "transition" stances.

The doctrine provides some minimal guidance on how the military should engage in the "provision of protection." "Protective tasks," it states, "include protection and safeguarding of individuals, communities and installations.... Commanders should be aware of the need to balance protective tasks against the need for more active operational measures."[285] Here, "protection" is a mostly passive activity, akin to guard duty. No elaboration on either "protective tasks" or "more operational measures" is offered.[286] Other, somewhat more active tasks related to civilian protection, include: the establishment of "restricted areas," which can include "centres of population;" "crowd control;" "interposition" as a "short-term emergency response to forestall or manage a local crisis;" and the establishment of "protected or safe areas."

In no section does the UK bundle relevant tasks under a single heading about the protection of civilians. Indeed, the doctrine explicitly points out the need for further guidance on the concept, with language that echoes the *The Responsibility to Protect* report:

> There are occasions when a national government or sub-national organs of government fail to uphold international norms. They may be unable or unwilling to prevent a faction or group being subject to, or threatened with, significant harm.... Consequently, a responsibility to provide protection may fall upon the international community.... To respond to these changes, and the associated responsibilities, those who are tasked with, or choose to assist with,

---

[283] United Kingdom Ministry of Defense, *The Military Contribution to Peace Support Operations*, Joint Warfare Publication 3-50 (JWP 3-50) (UK Ministry of Defense, Joint Doctrine and Concepts Center, Second Edition, June 2004).

[284] Ibid., 2-3.

[285] Ibid., 5-22.

[286] Workshop, *Operational Capacities for Civilian Protection Missions*, The Henry L. Stimson Center, Washington, DC, 8 December 2004.

upholding, renewing or restoring acceptable governance need an expansion of the concepts and doctrine that guide their actions.[287]

US Doctrine

The United States has extensive doctrine at many levels for peace support operations (tactical, operational, service-oriented, and joint, among others). The Army first developed much of this doctrine in the 1990s. Organized for long-term missions, the Army is, perhaps, the military branch most prepared for peace and stability operations. In contrast, given its expeditionary nature, the Marine Corps is often the first to arrive in a crisis. As a result, civilian protection tasks might be more relevant to Marine Corps responsibilities, as a large-scale genocide or ethnic cleansing campaign could require a rapid, responsive intervention.

In a section devoted to MOOTW, the Marine Corps doctrine, *Marine Corps Operations*, explains that Marine Air Ground Task Forces (MAGTFs) "are usually the first forces to reach the scene and are often the precursor to larger Marine and joint forces."[288] Where large-scale violence breaks out, therefore, forward-deployed, quick-reacting MAGTFs could play a significant role in organizing an immediate response. In addressing "MAGTF Reconnaissance and Security Operations," *Marine Corps Operations* acknowledges that the protection of civilians may be a necessary task for many MOOTW: "Security operations in MOOTW are complicated by the requirement to extend the protection of the force to include civilians and other nongovernmental organizations."[289] It is not clear if the referenced civilians are local people or those affiliated with the mission, but their protection is construed as a "requirement" imposed on the military and a complication rather than the explicit goal. *Marine Corps Operations* further recognizes that the MAGTF could be called to uphold the rule of law when a local government is incapable of providing "the necessary security and law and order for itself or its population." Although military police remain the preferred forces for such "law-and-order missions," the MAGTF can be used "to maintain general law and order, establish a civil defense effort, and protect the government infrastructure."[290]

The Marine Corps also has doctrine addressing specific types of operations. These include hypothetical examples of future missions. *Expeditionary*

---

[287] *Peace Support Operations,* JWP 3-50 (revised, 2004), 1-6.

[288] US Marine Corps, *Marine Corps Operations,* MCDP 1-0 (Washington, DC: Headquarters US Marine Corps, Department of the Navy, 27 September 2001), 10-2.

[289] Ibid., 11-17.

[290] Ibid., 10-19. A large-scale break down in law and order could be a contributing factor to genocide or ethnic cleansing, as seen in the Rwanda genocide of 1994.

Operations doctrine, for example, describes an intervention into a chaotic West Africa in 2017 to defeat forces that led a coup and launched genocide. The goal is to defeat those forces and "stop the tribal slaughter."[291] This scenario would require skills associated with warfighting but, with the aim of protecting civilians, it reflects the Marine Corps posture of preparing to respond to a wide range of crises. The doctrine does not, however, detail the tasks and training necessary for such an operation.

US Army doctrine, *Stability Operations and Support Operations* of February 2003, addresses civilian protection tasks for the military. It divides peace operations into peacekeeping and peace enforcement based on the level of consent among local parties. Likewise, it also distinguishes peacekeeping and peace enforcement missions from warfighting operations, based on their impartiality. The doctrine identifies various tasks within peace enforcement, many of which support the goal to "establish a safe and secure environment" and relate to civilian protection scenarios.[292] They include: "forcible separation of belligerents," "establishment and supervision of protected areas," "sanction and exclusion zone enforcement," "movement denial and guarantee," "restoration and maintenance of order," and "protection of humanitarian assistance."[293] The principle of restraint does not preclude use of "overwhelming force" when there is a need to "establish dominance," demonstrate resolve or "protect US or indigenous lives and property, or to accomplish other critical objectives."[294]

Army doctrine describes other operations that touch on civilian protection, but none fully suggests a military intervention to halt ongoing abuses in a hostile environment. For example, the doctrine categorizes "relief operations" as a type of "support operation" in which troops "respond to and mitigate the effects of natural or man-made disasters." Here the focus is to "mitigate damage, loss, hardship, or suffering," but these operations are undertaken "[t]o support the efforts of local authorities or the lead agency."[295] This framework presumes that "local authorities" are not themselves responsible for abusing civilians, and that the environment is calm enough to allow a "lead agency" other than the military to effectively intervene.

---

[291] US Marine Corps, *Expeditionary Operations*, MCDP 3 (Washington, DC: Headquarters US Marine Corps, Department of the Navy, 16 April 1998), 134.
[292] US Army, *Stability Operations and Support Operations*, FM 3-07 (Washington, DC: Headquarters, Department of the Army, February 2003), 4-6.
[293] Ibid., 71.
[294] Ibid., 4-16.
[295] Ibid., 6-9.

Likewise, the requirement to offer "support to civil law enforcement" in response to "civil disturbances" touches on, but does not encompass, the protection of civilians. While bringing a halt to the genocide in Rwanda in 1994 could be conceived of as quelling an extreme "civil disturbance," the Army focuses on domestic disturbances where local agencies are cooperative:

> In extreme cases, civil disturbances may include criminal acts of terrorism and violence.... The Army has a role in assisting civil authorities to restore law and order when local and state law enforcement agencies are unable to quell civil disturbances. Under provisions of the Constitution and selected federal statutes, the president may order federal armed forces to aid local and state civil authorities to protect the Constitutional rights of citizens.[296]

The more relevant case for such operations is the Los Angeles riot of 1992, rather than Bosnia or Rwanda in the 1990s, or Darfur today. Yet this approach to mass violence in foreign states might approximate a civilian protection mission. The Army has addressed this gap in offering protection in part by assigning its military police the roles of providing protection to refugees; supporting a secure environment for humanitarian relief efforts; dealing with crimes, persons, and property; performing patrols; and other "law and order" functions while deployed overseas.[297]

An appendix in *Stability Operations and Support Operations* on "Refugees and Displaced Persons" addresses some protection issues of concern to humanitarian actors:

> Military forces have been called on to secure displaced persons within their country of origin. Support for IDPs can take several forms. Often, relief convoys need military security. At times, military forces must insulate internally displaced groups from the population at large. Safe areas may be established to ensure the safety of the targeted group. As with military support to refugee operations, the military forces operate with their civilian partners.[298]

Such tasks, often labeled "civilian protection" by both military actors and civilian humanitarians,[299] could be important for saving lives in hostile environments with violence against civilians. By themselves, however, the protection of IDP camps, relief convoys, and safe areas would be unlikely to halt genocide or ethnic cleansing. Indeed, US doctrine views the use of military intervention alone to protect civilians abroad as an inadequate response to the

---

[296] Ibid., 6-21.

[297] US Army, *Military Police Internment/Resettlement Operations, Field Manual No. FM 3-19.40* (Washington, DC: Headquarters, Department of the Army, 1 August 2001). Reportedly this doctrine was updated in 2005 to include international deployments by military police.

[298] US Army, *Stability Operations and Support Operations*, F-3.

[299] UN Office for the Coordination of Humanitarian Affairs, "Protection of Civilians in Armed Conflict," OCHA, www.reliefweb.int/ocha_ol/civilians/.

threat to civilians. US doctrine aims to support civilians by addressing the structural problems and viable institutions (political, economic, social, and military) first, and then to establish law and order, governance, and security to a population.[300]

Thus, overall, the United States does not have a clear doctrine for missions suggested by *The Responsibility to Protect*, or for peace enforcement and peace support operations in which the protection of civilians is the central goal. But as described here, US doctrine addresses many tasks associated with such missions, including support to humanitarian space, support to law and order, and the explicit and active protection of vulnerable populations. Even without explicit US doctrine for civilian protection missions, the US could conduct a well-organized military intervention. One US military expert was optimistic. "It's not that bad," he suggested. "You can draft all the doctrine you would need."

With a 2005 Defense Department directive to integrate preparation for stability operations more squarely within US military preparedness for traditional combat operations, doctrine is slated for review and revisions across the armed services.[301] As the US moves to revise its doctrine, there is an opportunity for a more explicit recognition of how US forces should deal with vulnerable populations in conflict—and more explicitly address the protection of civilians in imminent threat and with the means of coercive measures, as needed. A US Army officer with expertise in military doctrine suggested that, for the US, the decision to act was in policy hands, since "the door is open" in American doctrine.[302]

French Doctrine

By the mid-1990s, French military doctrine began to embrace the robust use of force to prevent and control international crises as part of peace support operations, well before the US, the UK, and Canadian militaries. A March 1995 directive issued by General Jacques Lanxade, chief of staff of the French armed forces, outlined three main types of PSOs and "international law enforcement operations," from consent-based peacekeeping all the way up to limited war.[303]

---

[300] US doctrine, *Foreign Internal Defense*, for example, describes US support to foreign governments for their internal defense and development with a mixture of civilian and military support to protect against subversion, lawlessness, and insurgency. US Joint Chiefs of Staff, *Joint Publication 3-07.1, Joint Tactics, Techniques and Procedures for Foreign Internal Defense* (Washington, DC: US Department of Defense, revised, 30 April 2004), www.dtic.mil/doctrine/jel/new_pubs/jp3_07_1.pdf.

[301] DoD Directive 3000.05, *Military Support for Stability, Security, Transition, and Reconstruction (SSTR) Operations* (Washington, DC: US Department of Defense, 28 November 2005).

[302] US Army Colonel, interview with author, July 2006.

[303] Thierry Tardy, "French Policy Towards Peace Support Operations," *International Peacekeeping*, 6, no. 1 (Spring 1999), 73; Joseph P. Gregoire, "The Bases of French Peace Operations Doctrine,"

Opérations de maintien de la paix, or "peacekeeping," were authorized under Chapter VI of the UN Charter and based on the consent of local parties "following the cessation of hostilities." *Opérations de restauration de la paix*, or "peace implementation," were authorized under Chapter VII of the UN Charter and involved impartial efforts to bring peace to a country "experiencing civil war where the safety of the civilian population is gravely threatened but where no aggressor can be identified" (roughly equivalent to "peace enforcement" in NATO doctrine). *Opérations d'imposition de la paix*, or "peace enforcement" (but not in the NATO or US sense of the term), involved limited warfare under Chapter VII, and could involve "opposing with force a well-identified aggressor" in order to "impose or re-establish peace."[304]

Notably, the French definition of "peace implementation" explicitly denotes civilian safety, rather than political concerns, as the motivation behind deployment. Likewise, French "peace enforcement" appears to span the doctrinal boundary between peacekeeping and warfighting, in which coercive protection might be situated.

Elsewhere, French doctrine endorses a concept of "active impartiality," through which forces can aggressively target any actor preventing the implementation of their mission. This implies that French forces would have few qualms about defeating a group of *genocidaires* outright if their mission included the protection of civilians.[305] Moreover, France does not see PSOs as wholly distinct from warfighting. All missions exist on "a continuum of possibilities" where "the principles of war fighting" are "the foundation of action."[306] French missions should also include "undisputed military superiority" over any potential adversary.[307] French doctrine, in this sense, anticipated changes in UK and Canadian doctrine, which came to embrace such robust PSO concepts only after the turn of the century.

Dutch Doctrine

Netherlands doctrine is heavily influenced by the 1995 massacre in Srebrenica, where Dutch peacekeepers failed to take action against Serb forces committing atrocities against Muslim men and boys.[308] The Royal Netherlands Army's

---

Carlisle Papers in Security Strategy Series (Carlisle, PA: Strategic Studies Institute, US Army War College, September 2002), 4.

[304] Etat-Major des Armées, *The French Force Commitment Concept*, No. 827/DEF/EMA/EMP.1/NP, 23 July 1997, 27.

[305] Gregoire, "The Bases of French Peace Operations Doctrine," 5.

[306] Steve Rynning, *Changing Military Doctrine: Presidents and Military Power in Fifth Republic France, 1958-2000* (Westport, CT: Praeger, 2001), Ch. 5.

[307] Gregoire, "The Bases of French Peace Operations Doctrine," 6.

[308] A/54/549, *The fall of Srebrenica*, paras. 470-474.

(RNLA) *Peace Operations* doctrine was updated in June 1999, and has a more traditional approach towards peacekeeping than its Canadian, British, and French counterparts. Within this framework, however, it recognizes the potential need for coercive action to protect civilians.

The doctrine allows that part of a peace operation's "political success" consists in "creating a safe environment for the population in the conflict area," and that a peace force "may...be charged with the protection of...the civilian population."[309] It also states that peace operations must adhere to the laws of war, including taking care to minimize civilian casualties. The doctrine also requires contingency plans for the protection of civilians in areas of operation.[310] However, several elements of the doctrine limit the extent to which the RNLA is likely to engage in active civilian protection.

As with other PSO doctrine, the RNLA focuses on consent and impartiality as essential elements of peace operations. The doctrine distinguishes peacekeeping from peace enforcement on the basis of consent, or its absence. But the doctrine stresses that where consent is missing or in doubt, "direct efforts must be made at all levels to *stabilise and promote this consent*."[311] All peace-enforcing activities are considered to jeopardize the operation by making consent more difficult to obtain or re-establish. Furthermore, mandates for peace operations will not designate enemies or set military victory as a condition of success.[312] Thus, the RNLA appears highly unlikely to undertake an operation to destroy or defeat a force threatening civilians as part of a peace operation, though it will in some cases guard civilians against such threats.

The most robust forms of civilian protection considered in the doctrine are the establishment and maintenance of protected areas and non-combatant evacuations.[313] In a protected-area operation, the peace force guards a specified geographic area against attack. The operation is authorized to use force to disarm military elements within the protected area and to defend the area in the event that one or more parties do not consent to the safe area or temporarily suspend their consent.[314] Active operations are confined to controlling approaches and conducting patrols.[315]

---

[309] Royal Netherlands Army, *Peace Operations: Army Doctrine Publication III* (The Netherlands: Royal Netherlands Army, approved 29 June 1999), 61, 89.
[310] Ibid., 102, 111.
[311] Ibid., 16-17, 83, emphasis in original.
[312] Ibid., 77.
[313] Ibid., 201-216, 287-306.
[314] Ibid., 202-204.
[315] Ibid., 207.

NEO missions remove civilians or unarmed military personnel from conflict areas. The doctrine focuses heavily on issues related to the evacuation of Dutch nationals, but it does contemplate facilitating movement of refugees out of a conflict zone.[316] Depending on the situation, the evacuees may use civilian transport protected by a military escort or they may be evacuated using military assets. Evacuations may take place where the host government does not consent and/or does not control the security situation; such situations may call for a full-scale combat operation.[317]

Several other operational tasks in RNLA doctrine may involve civilian protection directly or indirectly: monitoring human rights violations; securing the freedom of movement of humanitarian agencies; and assisting civilian police in the protection of individuals, groups, or installations. The military may be called on to

> *Few developing states have written doctrine for peace operations. India, a country with significant peacekeeping experience, is one of the exceptions.*

protect civilian humanitarian relief agencies or to supply humanitarian relief itself.[318] Yet, fundamentally, operations undertaken to eliminate irregular forces threatening either the government or the population are considered combat operations, outside the scope of the peace operations doctrine.[319]

Indian Doctrine

Few developing states have written doctrine for peace operations. India, a country with significant peacekeeping experience, is one of the exceptions. *Indian Army Doctrine* includes basic, paragraph-length descriptions of three "Non-Combat Operations" that could be used to protect civilians in low-threat environments: "Maintenance of Law and Order," "Disaster Relief," and "Humanitarian Assistance." It also includes a short section on "Low-Intensity Conflict Operations and Counter-Insurgency Operations."[320]

A chapter dedicated to UN peacekeeping missions offers a view of basic peacekeeping principles: "consent of the parties involved, international support, unity of C^2 [command and control], impartiality, mutual respect, legitimacy,

---

[316] Ibid., 287.

[317] Ibid., 292.

[318] Ibid., 163, 244, 279, 308, 313ff.

[319] Ibid., 20.

[320] Indian Army, *Indian Army Doctrine*, Part II, Chapter Five, Section 15 (Shimla, India: Headquarters Army Training Command, 18 October 2004), http://indianarmy.nic.in/indianarmydoctrine_2.doc.

credibility and coordination of effort."[321] The doctrine makes a clear distinction between Chapter VI peacekeeping operations and Chapter VII peace enforcement. It also offers that Chapter VI peacekeeping contingents should prepare for tasks "such as security, protection, civic action and logistics," but without more discussion. Chapter VII missions, on the other hand, require a more active military role in which "the tasks (demonstrations, blockade or other operations) and functioning of the contingent would be similar to that while functioning as part of a multi-national force." There is further discussion of ROE, mandates and preparation of forces, but no other references to protecting civilians.

Multinational Doctrine: NATO

For multinational organizations, common doctrine assists their ability to organize and coordinate forces in operations. Of the five major multinational groups willing to lead military missions involving the use of force (and with authority for intervening to protect civilians), none has doctrine designated for operations involving the protection of civilians under imminent threat. As discussed earlier, the UN does not (yet) have official doctrine. The EU, the AU, and ECOWAS are still developing guidance for their deployments. Only NATO has its own fully developed military doctrine for peace operations and other missions. This doctrine is derived from its Member States and reflects a need to balance differing philosophies and interests.

NATO doctrine, *Peace Support Operations*, argues for a clear separation between peacekeeping, and peace enforcement and asserts that any peace support force must be correctly tailored to its operational environment. In other words, a force outfitted for peacekeeping should not attempt peace enforcement. If a peacekeeping force witnessed a loss of local consent and a rapid escalation of violence, for example, the doctrine recommends that the force withdraw or be fully replaced. Given that genocide and ethnic cleansing can emerge suddenly in regions of conflict, NATO doctrine implies that forces may pull out in the face of mass slaughter if reinforcements cannot arrive in time or if political will is lacking. This concept contrasts with that of the British, French, and Canadians, among others, who presume PSOs deploy with all the capacity needed for even the most nightmarish contingency.

The NATO doctrine has no specific section on civilian protection, but recognizes many military tasks required to protect civilians from large-scale abuse. *Peace Support Operations* comes close to addressing requirements for

---

[321] Ibid., Section 16.

coercive protection in its discussion of *Protection of Humanitarian Operations*, as a role for more combat-ready forces:

> [Peace support operations] are increasingly conducted in situations in which there are wide spread and ongoing abuses to basic human rights, ethnic cleansing and genocide. Such abuses frequently occur in collapsed or collapsing states in which the rule of law has ceased to exist. Only a PSF [peace support force] prepared for combat can operate in such an environment, curtail human rights abuses, and create a secure environment in which civilian agencies can redress the underlying causes of the conflict and address the requirements of peace building.[322]

While not detailing how to protect civilians, NATO states that the ROE and mandates are the bottom line for guiding troop behavior (as discussed in Chapter V). The doctrine argues that overly restrictive ROE (and inaction) may be inappropriate, and that military action may be needed in cases of widespread abuse of civilians.[323] NATO doctrine implies that "circumstances of widespread violations of human rights and ethnic cleansing" may require a forceful military response on behalf of civilians' safety and well-being. The doctrine further describes tasks useful for coercive protection operations. These include the imposition of no-fly zones, the forcible separation of belligerent parties, the establishment and supervision of protected or safe areas, and the creation of "safe corridors" for the passage of civilians and aid flows.

NATO's 2001 tactical doctrine, *Peace Support Operations Techniques and Procedures*, also describes relevant missions and tasks. These include *Humanitarian Relief, Restoration of Law and Order Operations, Protection of Humanitarian Operations and Human Rights, Conflict Containment, Establishment of Protected or Safe Area*, and *Guarantee and Denial of Movement Operations*. Few of these tasks make protection an explicit purpose. The section on denial-of-movement operations comes close, however, presuming that a force capable of peace enforcement and escalation may be tasked with preventing "harassment of an unprotected population."[324]

Thus, NATO is cautious about intervening on behalf of civilians. While not tailored for humanitarian intervention missions *per se*, NATO doctrine covers operations from peace support to full combat. In this range, NATO would view protecting civilians from mass violence as a job for military personnel prepared for a hostile environment and for warfighting. Its emphasis is the opposite of

---

[322] NATO Allied Joint Publication, *Peace Support Operations*, AJP-3.4.1 (NATO, Military Agency for Standardisation, July 2001) Chapter 6, para. 0634.

[323] Ibid., 3-5, 3-6.

[324] NATO, *Peace Support Operations Techniques and Procedures*, ATP-3.4.1.1 (NATO, August 2001), para. 0120.

that offered by the UN and other organizations that approach the use of force with great caution. NATO looks toward peacekeeping, and its extension toward peacebuilding and humanitarian operations with care—an understandable stance given its historical roots as a defensive organization. Somewhere between these approaches is a place where the tasks, doctrine, and training for civilian protection—and coercive protection—can be developed more specifically.

ACTION WITHOUT DOCTRINE

Doctrine is still developing for the military missions of the African Union, ECOWAS and the European Union. Within the AU and ECOWAS, few Member States have written national-level doctrine on which to base multinational doctrine, let alone for missions involving civilian protection.

Developing countries in other regions also lack doctrine. Jordan, for example, has significant experience in UN peacekeeping operations and hosts the preeminent peacekeeping training center in the Middle East, yet it does not have official peacekeeping doctrine. Pakistan has highly experienced troops, with service in multiple peace operations including hard missions in Somalia and the DRC. While a top UN troop contributor today, Islamabad has not written doctrine for peace operations. National training is designed to prepare the army for a potential role in peacekeeping, but not specifically in civilian protection.[325]

Experienced troops from developing nations may nevertheless have an understanding of operations from the field—rather than from formalized doctrine and training for peace operations. As one Nigerian officer put it, pointing to his head, doctrine is "up here."[326] In informal surveys of military officers from Eastern Europe, Africa, Asia, and Latin America countries participating in US classroom-based training courses on peace operations, not one said that their national doctrine covered civilian protection in peace operations.[327] Yet many offered that they considered the protection of civilians to be part of their role in peacekeeping missions, if not a central motivation; others offered examples of the challenges they imagined with such a mission mandate.

---

[325] Senior Pakistani Army official, interview with author, May 2005.

[326] Nigerian military officer, ECOWAS Secretariat, interview with author, Abuja, Nigeria, June 2004.

[327] Author discussions with military officers, in seminars run for the US Enhanced International Military Education and Training program, Washington, DC, May 2005, and Newport, RI, July 2005; and seminar, Army War College, Carlisle, Pennsylvania, May 2006. Many represented countries experienced in peace operations: Bangladesh, Bosnia, Bulgaria, Ethiopia, Ghana, India, Italy, Mongolia, Nepal, Rwanda, Romania, Pakistan, Senegal, Ukraine, and the United States.

The African Union

There is little to no written guidance on the conduct of AU-authorized or AU-led missions. The AU Protocol does not discuss doctrine, but suggests that the Commission provide guidelines for the training of the national standby contingents at both the operational and tactical levels, including training guidelines for international humanitarian law and human rights law. Further, the Commission plans to develop and circulate operating procedures to support the standardization of training, doctrines, manuals, and programs for national and regional schools of excellence. It also plans to coordinate the ASF training courses, command and staff exercises, and field training.

The AU will need to develop and provide clear guidance to its forces on the conduct of operations if it is to develop an effective African Standby Force by 2010. The AU is likely to seek outside support from its members and other nations with experience, especially if it is to have effective guidance for humanitarian interventions.[328] Efforts to help the AU develop doctrine are beginning and include support from the United Nations.[329]

ECOWAS

ECOWAS has not had written doctrine for its past deployments of forces; it is working on doctrinal guidance for its operations.[330] The development of doctrine and concepts for the ECOWAS Standby Force (ESF) may be assisted by ECOWAS member states, partner countries such as the United Kingdom, and training centers such as the Kofi Annan International Peacekeeping Training Center (KAIPTC). This regional force may contribute to the African Standby Force but, as mentioned, that effort has yet to produce continent-wide doctrine and is unlikely to start with civilian protection scenarios.[331] According to one ECOWAS advisor involved in this project, he was "not aware of anything that meets the definitions and scenarios" of civilian protection.[332]

ECOWAS has engaged in a process of capacity-building, underway since 2004, that offers a new avenue for the organization to consider the protection of civilians as the potential goal of a mission or as tasks, whether as part of a regional, continental, or UN-led operation.

---

[328] Jakkie Cilliers and Mark Malan, *Progress with the African Standby Force*, Occasional Paper No. 98 (Pretoria: Institute for Security Studies, May 2005).

[329] A/60/19, *Report of the Special Committee on Peacekeeping Operations* para. 141.

[330] ECOWAS Secretariat, interviews with author, Abuja, Nigeria, June 2004; former US advisor to ECOWAS Secretariat, interview with author, March 2006; Malan, *Developing the ECOWAS Civilian Peace Support Operations Structure*. Canada has provided ECOWAS financial support to increase its staff, in part to support development of ECOWAS doctrine.

[331] Advisor, DES-PADS, ECOWAS Secretariat, interviews with author, October 2005.

[332] Ibid., June 2004, October 2005.

The European Union

Like the AU and ECOWAS, the European Union does not yet have official military doctrine. The EU published more detailed guidance on its global security role with EU High Representative Javier Solana's 2003 *A Secure Europe In a Better World: European Security Strategy*. The document addresses emerging threats to EU security and the ways in which the EU can both protect itself and contribute to the global security architecture. Among other issues, it identifies "regional conflicts," "state failure," and "organized crime" as threats to EU security. It recommends tackling these issues through the EU's unique combination of military, humanitarian, and policing capacity.[333] It also argues for developing a "strategic culture that fosters early, rapid, and when necessary, robust intervention," and that the EU engage in preventive efforts "before humanitarian emergencies arise."[334] The document makes no mention of potential EU efforts to halt genocide, ethnic cleansing, or mass killing, although it details statistics on human insecurity in the developing world as part of a general vision of post-Cold War security threats. That the EU could publish such a "security strategy" represents an important step, as the EU seeks to further elucidate the ESDP and its global security "niche." The document shows that the EU is concerned with humanitarian emergencies, human insecurity, and state failure, but does not guide how EU forces might conduct PSOs or protect civilians in practice.

The doctrines of individual EU countries, however, are much more fully developed. Given that most EU Battlegroups will involve only a handful of states, or a single lead nation, effective national doctrine might be all the EU needs. The French-led Battlegroup, for example, could operate under French military doctrine. Nevertheless, if the EU hopes to integrate its military capacity and deploy true multinational battalions and brigades, it will need unified military doctrine.

DOCTRINE AND THE PROTECTION OF CIVILIANS

Is there doctrine for civilian protection? Should there be?

Doctrinal publications identify varied military strategies and tactics for protecting civilians. They are not yet well developed in one place, however, as guidance to military and civilian leadership for peace support operations or for interventions to stop mass violence. UN-led missions directed to "protect civilians" do not have standard direction on how, precisely, peacekeepers should

---

[333] Javier Solana, *A Secure Europe In a Better World: European Security Strategy* (Brussels: adopted by Heads of State and Governments, EU Council, 12 December 2003).
[334] Ibid., 11.

carry that out, which may improve with UN guidance. Nor do other multinational organizations offer their forces such direction.

The lack of linguistic and operational clarity about what "protection" means has important real-world implications for troops deployed today. PSO doctrine generally lacks explicit guidance in key areas—how to stop a belligerent from committing gross human rights abuses, for example, when that action is not a threat to the operation itself or to an important party in the peace process. Such situations are especially difficult when a host government *itself* is a primary source of insecurity. PSOs trying to operate with consent of the parties and impartiality may be ill equipped to deal with intentional, large-scale killing. Thus, missions trying to balance protection tasks with broader political aims may find their goals at odds. The direct targeting of abusive armed groups complicates efforts at political reconciliation, for example, at least in the short term. Political goals and protection goals of PSOs might overlap and be complementary, or they may compete for limited military resources or work against each other.[335] Either way, the goals are not the same. This is exactly why the gap in doctrine matters.

> *Clearer military doctrine on the protection of civilians will help make UN mandates to protect civilians operational, and identify military responsibilities and tasks.*

Clearer military doctrine on the protection of civilians will help make UN mandates to protect civilians operational, and trigger a better set of expected military responsibilities and tasks. It would allow militaries to inform civilian leadership of what is needed to implement specific types of protection operations and improve effective preparation. Doctrine could address the use of force and coercive action in achieving the mission's broader goals, and be clear about the distinction between military interventions explicitly aimed at halting mass violence and those missions where protection is but one of many tasks. Moreover, since developing states and emerging multinational organizations follow the lead of the US, NATO, UK, France and other major militaries in developing their own doctrine, strengthening the doctrine within these major militaries could be used to prepare additional forces, including those that deploy with the EU, the AU, and ECOWAS.

The absence of such doctrine, of course, is a hindrance rather than a death knell for effective peace operations and civilian protection. The relative lack of

---

[335] For examples of each of these scenarios, see Chapter 8 and its study of the DRC and MONUC.

explicit military doctrine on coercive protection tasks does not mean that a well-trained military would be incapable of performing effectively and efficiently. If a mission is told clearly what it is expected to accomplish on the ground, some argue, it can figure out the correct course of action regardless of pre-existing doctrine, provided that troops are sufficiently well-trained and equipped, and that the mission has effective command and control arrangements.

Furthermore, developing civilian protection doctrine should not be difficult. Much current doctrine covers components of likely scenarios, and offers ways for forces to anticipate and respond. Useful guidance is likely to be a matter of arranging and reframing specific military tasks to support operations where the protection of civilians is either a dominant task or the goal of the mission in and of itself. Either way, doctrine should address the use of force, the concepts of protection and the role of military actors in providing physical protection and using coercion. It should also address questions of impartiality, consent, host-nation sovereignty, relationship to civilian leaders and humanitarian actors, and the caveats of "within capabilities" and "area of deployment." The best approach may be to incorporate the protection of civilians within existing doctrine for peace support operations and for other kinds of military interventions. With or without doctrine, the effective training and the deployment of experienced forces might be the most important keys to success—a subject considered next.

—7—
PREPARING FOR THE MISSION: TRAINING

Effective training prepares military personnel for their anticipated missions. It comes in many forms, from classroom learning to live fire practice, strategic gaming to tactical exercises, single service to joint service simulations. Training also differs depending on the levels of command, the force size, the realism of a simulated environment, and the kinds of tasks involved, as well as a nation's doctrine and goals.

Thus, not all training is created equal. Nations provide their forces general training which is standardized and used across mission types, as well as specialized or pre-deployment training which is mission- and force-specific.

At the operational level, doctrine often identifies specific tactics, techniques, procedures, and strategies for a particular mission, which helps establish the kind of training needed. Prior to deployment, force commanders request training packages that they consider most relevant to their next mission. In general, such specialized training increases in importance the more "non-traditional" the mission and where concepts are new to personnel. This instruction may be especially useful for peace support operations, to clarify the rules of engagement and mandates, and to increase preparedness for unfamiliar scenarios.

As doctrine addresses the better known concepts of civilian protection, national training is likely to cover such roles (the *Geneva Conventions concept, humanitarian space concept*).[336] Almost all developed state militaries receive at least rudimentary lessons in their responsibilities to protect civilians as a function of international humanitarian and human rights law, such as the Geneva Conventions. Some nations offer intensive instruction on civil-military operations and cooperation (e.g., CIMIC, CMO) to work with civilian agencies and NGOs in support of the provision of humanitarian relief and assistance, although it is usually only provided to selected national forces. Training for CIMIC and CMO—the primary training most militaries receive on interacting with civilian populations—typically focuses on winning "hearts and minds," not on preventing abusive armed groups from killing non-combatants. Other training

---

[336] Some traditional military training implicitly suggests that civilians will be better off as the result of the greater security that may result from combat operations (the *warfighting concept*) but those training programs are not explored here in depth.

programs also address aspects of civilian protection as part of their larger goals, for NEO missions or the protection of human rights, for example.

Training for peace support operations may address additional military roles for protecting civilians, instructing recruits how to conduct patrols, secure key facilities, handle crowd control, assist disarmament programs, evacuate civilians, and work with the other components of a peace operation. These roles are not always regular features of national military training, however, as some peacekeeping tasks fall closer to policing and establishing civil order.

When a mission or a mission-type lacks doctrine, specific training is also less likely to be available, such as for UN-authorized operations charged to protect civilians. Doctrine is updated periodically, so rapid changes in the nature of military missions may require training to shift *before* new doctrine is formally approved. As current deployments in complex missions blur the line between peacekeeping and warfighting, such a shift may be needed for more robust kinds of civilian protection, and for the preparation of peacekeepers in places like the DRC.[337]

Peace operations often involve both complex tasks and ad hoc force structures, which complicate training. Some military leaders view training for robust peacekeeping and peace enforcement as more demanding than training for warfighting. A 2005 multinational military conference on the impact of peace and stability operations on armed forces found that "the severity of extreme peace support operations can equal, and even exceed, those of much warfighting. The diversity of tasks and their unexpected nature means that training manuals cannot cope with every eventuality."[338] In Iraq, for example, coalition forces saw their situation change dramatically after the first months of occupation. They improvised new techniques and strategies to fit their environment—situations for which they may not have trained before deployment. Moreover, training alone may not result in well-prepared forces. In Africa, for example, it can be hard to train fully formed units—the preferred method for ensuring troops can work together effectively—that then *deploy*

---

[337] The adaptability of a force to its mission also depends on the country and its doctrine. British and French doctrines, for example, aim for rapid adaptation to new types of warfighting/peacekeeping operations.

[338] Peter F. Herrly, *The Impact of Peacekeeping and Stability Operations on the Armed Forces*, Report of an International Conference, 17-18 June 2005, no. 915 (Washington, DC: The Heritage Foundation, 2 December 2005). This report summarizes the proceedings of "The Test of Terrain: The Impact of Stability Operations Upon the Armed Forces," held in Paris on 17–18 June 2005, sponsored by the Strategic Studies Institute of the US Army War College, the Centre d'Études en Sciences Sociales de la Défense (Ministère de la Défense), the Royal United Services Institute, the Association of the US Army, the Förderkreis Deutsches Heer, The Heritage Foundation, and the US Embassy – Paris.

together. Units are sometimes formed specifically for an operation, with individual troops "filled in" to complete a battalion, for example. When these units are deployed as one, they may receive unfamiliar equipment that they are not prepared to operate, creating a "hidden training problem."[339]

Generating consistent and effective training for aspects of civilian protection may be especially challenging. For forces in hostile environments, such a role may require training associated with high-level threats and combat-like situations, training that not all peacekeepers have, or are presumed to need. Training for forces expected to take a role in a UN-led mission into Darfur, Sudan, for example, will need to address how UN forces are to

Without specific doctrine identifying requirements for coercive protection, it is hard to find evidence of training that addresses such missions within multinational organizations or leading peacekeeping troop contributors.

deal with spoilers who threaten civilians. Without specific doctrine identifying requirements for coercive protection, it is hard to find evidence of training that addresses such missions within multinational organizations or leading peacekeeping troop contributors.

Training for peace support operations is expanding, however, with bilateral national programs, NATO exercises, and the development of UN training guidelines, among other initiatives. National training may also shift to meet the requirements of modern operations and revised doctrine—in the US, for example. There are signs of some promising developments. Multinational exercises such as *Cobra Gold* have incorporated more realistic civilian protection scenarios. The UN has developed *Standard Training Modules* (STMs) that detail aspects of civilian protection and touch on coercive protection techniques.

Thus, it is useful to consider what training is broadly available for peace support operations and whether there is evidence of a gap in training that addresses coercive protection.[340] Looking at UN training standards and specific national training for operations provides insight into current preparations to protect civilians. This chapter offers a broad survey of a few training programs that

---

[339] Senior staff, Kofi Annan International Peacekeeping Training Center, interviews with author, Accra, Ghana, June 2004.
[340] Military training is a vast area of practice and experience, and this study is far from a comprehensive review of its many aspects.

touch on civilian protection issues, with a focus on UN, US, multilateral, and bilateral initiatives.

UNITED NATIONS TRAINING

Training for multilateral troop deployments can occur both at the national and multinational levels (e.g., by joint exercises or through multilateral organizations). The training of military personnel for UN-led missions, however, is considered a national responsibility. Countries are urged to provide skilled and capable peacekeepers. Most major troop contributing countries focus their training on good soldiering, preparing forces for multiple environments and achieving a baseline of readiness for missions. UN operations are well served when nations provide solid basic training, including the ability to follow the chain of command and to understand the ROE.

General Approach

The DPKO has traditionally offered very limited training services. Given its restricted authority and capacity, the UN does not provide general training to soldiers. Most training is offered as pre-deployment training by DPKO, for senior staff and troop contributors prior to leaving for their UN mission, augmented with some in-mission and rapid deployment training. The emphasis is on ROE, a central aspect of training but not the whole picture, and countries are not required to participate.[341]

A DPKO survey of over 100 Member States on their use of UN training materials resulted in responses from only thirty-eight countries, with less than ten reporting that they fully used the materials.

With a small staff, DPKO offers teams for "train the trainer" workshops and assistance to regional training centers, and focuses on developing and disseminating training standards for use by troop contributors in their national programs. In the past, the UN has had no guarantee that the personnel offered by nations for peace operations meet basic UN standards, such as speaking the designated mission language.[342] The DPKO now sends assessment teams to identify some training gaps and offers to certify that countries have trained their forces to UN

---

[341] DPKO officials, interviews with author, New York, August 2004, February 2006, and March 2006.

[342] Senior civilian training official, DPKO, interviews with author, February 2006. Language skills are a real challenge; the UN test for mission language skills does not require even a score of fifty percent to pass. Language barriers between UN staff and peacekeepers can undermine effective training efforts.

standards. The UN is also able to provide some training in the field after personnel arrive, which includes instruction by UN agencies beyond the DPKO (reflecting the civilian personnel who work on protection within missions.)[343] Under-prepared peacekeepers could still benefit from extra training. A DPKO survey of over 100 Member States on their use of UN training materials resulted in responses from only thirty-eight countries, with less ten reporting that they fully used the materials.[344]

Traditionally the UN has not coordinated directly with many national training programs or training centers—and had difficulty getting information about what kinds of bilateral training nations receive or offer for peace operations.[345] The United Nations Institute for Training and Research (UNITAR) also supports research, seminars, and a training program run primarily as distance learning, available worldwide with courses in peace operations. UNITAR training modules, however, do not deal directly with civilian protection or interventions for that purpose.[346]

The UN approach to training has changed, however. With the jump in UN peace operations and deployed personnel levels since 2003, Member States recognized the need to improve the coordination and depth of training for these missions, especially as their complexity and demands have grown. In March 2004, the UN Special Committee on Peacekeeping pushed for multiple approaches:

> In the area of training, the Committee supports enhancing the coordination of the DPKO's military, civilian police and civilian training activities, and requests that the Secretary-General report, at the next session, on ways to further improve this coordination, including the feasibility of establishing a single multidimensional training unit... [and] the strengthening of training coordination at United Nations Headquarters. It also fully endorses the establishment of mission training cells and would welcome more detailed information on how these will function. It supports the Department's new focus on providing national and regional peacekeeping training centres with the necessary guidance for training peacekeeping personnel. Also welcome was the introduction of Standardized Generic Training Modules.[347]

---

[343] Training is offered in coordination with Office of the High Commissioner on Human Rights, OCHA, and other UN agencies, especially on issues such as human rights.

[344] Senior civilian training official, DPKO, interviews with author, February 2006.

[345] DPKO, Training and Evaluation Service, interviews with author, August 2004.

[346] Harvey Langholtz, Director, UNITAR Programme of Correspondence Instruction in Peacekeeping Operations, interview with author, June 2004. The 2005 and the 2006 course catalogues reinforce this point. See "Training for Peace Support Operations for UNITAR POCI," www.unitarpoci.org/media/brochure.pdf.

[347] UN General Assembly, Special Committee on Peacekeeping Operations, "UN Faces Major Challenge With 'Almost Unprecedented' Surge In Creation, Expansion Of Peacekeeping Missions, Special Committee Told," GA/PK/180, UN Press Release, 29 March 2004.

In November 2005, DPKO brought military and civilian training together under a new Integrated Training Service (ITS), subsuming the former Training and Evaluation Service (TES). In early 2006, the Special Committee on Peacekeeping affirmed the "high importance" of training efforts in light of the demand for UN peacekeeping.[348] The Committee expressed support for the development of a DPKO training strategy and policy for cooperation with regional and national training centers. It also welcomed the ITS, and urged improvement of UN training standards and their adoption as national training curricula. Further, the Committee encouraged partnerships between countries experienced in peace operations and those newer to the missions. It particularly welcomed the only mandatory pre-deployment training for UN peacekeepers—on prevention of sexual exploitation and abuse and an accompanying Code of Conduct.

UN Standardized Training Modules

Given DPKO's knowledge of what UN missions demand, its recent publication of training standards is an innovative way to help improve the preparation (and evaluation) of future peacekeepers. These training modules are the result of wide consultations between Member States, the UN, participants in peacekeeping operations, and other agencies over many years of seminars and workshops. These materials are still couched as "guidance" that needs to be "complemented by national training material whenever available."[349] Nevertheless, the materials are provided to national and multinational training centers around the world—from Malaysia to Argentina, India to Canada, Ghana to Italy. Many training centers are linked through the International Association of Peacekeeping Training Centers (IAPTC), a network of national institutions, which facilitates better understanding and training efforts, working with the UN to identify training needs internationally.

The training modules come in three levels and set standards for classroom-based training. Beginning in 2002, TES developed *Standardized Generic Training Modules* (SGTMs), or level-one modules, to outline minimum standards for all troops deployed in UN peacekeeping operations. Lessons range from fundamentals ("Introduction to the United Nations," and "Cultural Awareness") to more functional discussions of subjects like logistics and the prevention of sexual exploitation and abuse. The next series, STMs, the level-two and -three modules, are designed respectively for specialized personnel and mission leadership. Together, these modules reflect both the types of tasks for which the

---

[348] A/60/19, *Report of the Special Committee on Peacekeeping Operations.*
[349] UN Department of Peacekeeping Operations, "Standardized Training Generic Modules," Military Division, DPKO, www.un.org/depts/dpko/training/sgtm/sgtm.htm.

UN wants countries to prepare their personnel and the relative priority it assigns to those anticipated roles.

The SGTMs address the need for peacekeepers to observe international humanitarian law and to support humanitarian access. For example, the SGTMs on "Legal Framework for United Nations Peace Operations," "Human Rights in Peacekeeping," and other lessons clearly outline the legal restraints on the use of military force and explain to peacekeepers their obligation to uphold international humanitarian and human rights law. One section of the module states that:

> International humanitarian law is relevant to United Nations peacekeeping because many peace operations are deployed when conflict may still be active or may flare up again. Post-conflict environments may also have characteristics, such as large civilian populations that have been targeted by the warring parties, prisoners of war and other vulnerable groups, to whom the Geneva Conventions would apply. United Nations peacekeepers must always be mindful of existing international standards and norms that govern their daily activities. The Geneva Conventions generally apply in a peacekeeping context.[350]

The module emphasizes the role that many operations play to monitor and promote respect for human rights, a "fundamental obligation" of the UN: "[A]ll peacekeepers should be aware of human rights law and its applicability in their daily tasks. Peacekeepers must never do anything in their official or personal conduct that could be a violation of human rights."[351]

The SGTM on "Civil-Military Coordination" describes ways that peacekeepers and civilian organizations can offer each other support, with the peacekeepers' presence providing security and "an enabling environment that allows others [civilians] to do their job." For instance, peacekeepers can guard relief supplies and refugee camps, share information, escort humanitarian convoys, offer space for humanitarian goods on military trucks, ships, or aircraft, help pitch tents, rebuild local infrastructure, and provide potable water to civilian populations.[352]

An SGTM lesson on the UN Charter, international law, and rules of engagement (in a section on ROE) explains the concept of using force to defend civilians, preferably with a commander's permission and when competent local authorities

---

[350] SGTM 3, "Legal Framework of United Nations Peacekeeping Operations," Military Division, DPKO, www.un.org/depts/dpko/training/sgtm/sgtm.htm.

[351] Ibid.

[352] SGTM 10, "United Nations Civil-Military Coordination," Military Division, DPKO, www.un.org/depts/dpko/training/sgtm/sgtm.htm.

are absent.[353] Likewise, the SGTM on humanitarian assistance instructs troops to fully respect state sovereignty when supporting humanitarian missions—except when the host fails to meet certain key responsibilities. It maintains:

> The only exception [to the norm of non-intervention] is in cases of genocide or other gross human rights abuses or humanitarian disasters where a Government has, in the view of the Security Council lost the ability to appropriately protect and serve its population. In these exceptional cases the Security Council may approve a humanitarian intervention under Chapter VII of the UN Charter... Primary responsibility for the protection and well being of a civilian population rests with the government of the state or authorities that control the territory in which the population is located.[354]

This module acknowledges the fundamental challenge of civilian protection when peacekeepers face situations where a sovereign state has failed a population. The module suggests that one answer is a Council-authorized humanitarian intervention to provide protection, but offers no further details. Likewise, peacekeepers are not given guidance about how to handle their responsibilities in the murky zone of a Chapter VII operation when the state and other actors do not protect civilians from large-scale violence.

UN Standards: Closer to Protection?

A 2005 briefing on the draft STM 3 on humanitarian assistance from a human rights perspective discussed how peacekeeping forces could help protect civilians.[355] The roles cited were those associated with traditional peacekeeping, ranging from monitoring and alerting civilians to risk, providing deterrence by presence, working with humanitarian partners, and reporting human rights violations. The briefing recognized that force might be used, but primarily framed the situation as one in which the room for humanitarian interaction with the military was reduced.

The ITS published the more advanced *Standardized Training Modules 2* and *3* for senior civilian and military mission leadership in March 2006. STM 2 is designed for UN military, police, and key personnel, while STM 3 is targeted at mission leadership. Representing the work of many nations, the modules will continue to be developed and updated to improve guidance to countries on training.

---

[353] SGTM 3 "Legal Framework of United Nations Peacekeeping Operations," Military Division, DPKO, Slide 18, point 1.8, www.un.org/depts/dpko/training/sgtm/sgtm.htm.

[354] SGTM 9, "Humanitarian Assistance," Military Division, DPKO, Slide 6, internal document on file with authors.

[355] Michael Dell'Amico, STM 3, "Humanitarian Assistance: Challenges and Opportunities in an Integrated Mission Context," UNHCR, Geneva, presented in Abuja, 12-22 April 2005.

For this next level of training, an STM 2 module on *Protection of Human Rights by Military Peacekeepers* outlines principles that could help prepare UN peacekeeping personnel for operations with civilian protection mandates—and move toward a greater operational capacity for missions to meet their mandates in hostile environments. The module aims to "address the use of, or the credible threat to use, UN mandated military force to protect human rights and enforce the rule of law."[356] The course outline offers detailed, tactical and operational options to protect human rights and "to anticipate human rights protection tasks...and when resources and mandate may be inadequate to fulfil those tasks."

This STM outline reflects a detailed and innovative draft module prepared by the UN Office of the High Commissioner for Human Rights (OHCHR).[357] The draft guidance, aimed squarely at protecting civilians in non-permissive environments, is clear that at times "protection refers to armed protection." While this module is not intended to prepare troops for "coercive protection" operations, it ably offers training on exactly the questions that peacekeepers have about such missions. The outline explains the compelling rationale for peacekeepers using armed protection. It argues that:

> Use of armed force goes to the very essence, the human rights centre of gravity of UN mandated military forces. Without the inherent capability to project their will by force of arms, every other human rights function of military peacekeepers is weakened, commensurately reducing their value to their peace operations human rights partners.[358]

In other words, protecting civilians using armed force is both worthwhile itself and necessary to support the effectiveness of other, non-coercive human rights efforts.

The distinctive aspect of the module is its discussion of "Armed Protection Tasks" for military forces. The module describes seven techniques that peacekeepers can employ to defend the human rights of civilians:
- *Mission Development*
- *Full Rapid Response when Witnessing Human Rights Violations*
- *Staged Rapid Response to Witnessed Human Rights Violations*

---

[356] Integrated Training Service, "Protection of Human Rights for Military Personnel of Peace Operations," Module 3 of "Human Rights for Military Personnel of Peace Operations," STM 2-1 *United Nations Officers Common Training*, DPKO, as updated February 2006.

[357] Office of the UN High Commissioner for Human Rights, "Protection of Human Rights by Military Peacekeepers," Mil-POHRT Manual, Section C, draft Module 3, UN OHCHR, unpublished and undated draft (number 8). OHCHR has continued to develop this draft module further, one of a package of coordinated modules being developed as guidance on human rights for military personnel of peace operations.

[358] Ibid., slide one.

- *Interposition Operations*
- *Standing Physical Protection of Human Rights Victims*
- *Providing Human Rights Operational Space for Partners*
- *Conflict Containment and Restoration of Law and Order*

The appropriate armed-protection option depends on the nature of the environment, the mission, and the mission's capacity.

The section on *mission development* addresses the need for peacekeepers to adapt their responses as human rights realities change on the ground. It suggests that peacekeepers use a "manoeuvrist approach," allowing field commanders to make tactical decisions based on rapidly changing facts on the ground. If a situation deteriorates unexpectedly, the module argues that peacekeepers must not simply go about business as usual. Even without an explicit mandate to protect civilians under imminent threat, "the implied human rights role of peacekeepers is extensive."[359] At the same time, missions must avoid taking on new tasks beyond the original intent of the mission without the necessary resources and rigorous analysis to avoid "mission creep."[360]

The module teaches that one option is that of *full rapid response*, where a peacekeepers' job is to respond *every time* they witness human rights abuses. Preferably, this response will be unarmed or action will have prevented the abuse from occurring in the first place. The response can involve the use of armed force, if necessary. Peacekeepers should first ensure their own protection and then attempt to end physical violations against others through "inter-positional manoeuvres, or fire, or a combination of both." They will need to conduct incident follow-up and potentially detain violators.[361] If the mission lacks capacity for a preventive response, they should still take *some* action, even if it is just to condemn the violence publicly. The *staged rapid response* option, for example, involves peacekeepers sending "a clear signal to the violators and to the victims" that human rights abuses are illegal.[362]

Interposition operations might be needed to separate parties to a conflict, such as an armed group and a civilian population, or hostile civilian populations. Specific interposition tactics include permanent or recurring presence of troops, cordon-and-search operations, and patrols. They also might involve rapid

---

[359] Ibid., 9.

[360] One US training expert observed that mission creep is really the result of poor planning by those who have not anticipated what a mission requires, such as military planners inexperienced in the requirements of peace and stability operations. US military training expert, interview with author, June 2006.

[361] Office of the UN High Commissioner for Human Rights, "Protection of Human Rights by Military Peacekeepers," 10.

[362] Ibid., 12.

reaction to specific incidents to "reinforce interpositional presence" and "may require the deployment of overwhelming force."[363]

The other protection options, *Standing Physical Protection of Human Rights Victims, Providing Human Rights Operational Space for Partners,* and *Conflict Containment and Restoration of Law and Order,* are relatively well-understood (if not yet effectively implemented) and are not addressed in detail in the module. *Standing Physical Protection,* for example, involves establishing protected areas for civilian populations, such as those established during the war in Bosnia and Herzegovina, where peacekeepers can use traditional techniques of area defense.

Overall, this draft module offers a framework within peacekeeping where personnel can use appropriate, coercive military responses to stop and prevent human rights abuses. It stresses that the principles of minimum use of force, impartiality, and consent do not justify *inaction* in the face of atrocities and, where human rights are violated, "neutrality will certainly run the risk of being immoral, and in situations where international law has created a duty to act, neutrality will be 'illegal.'"[364] Indeed, the module recognizes that impartiality may require a peacekeeper to make clear to hostile forces in the mission area that "protecting the rights of civilians in your AO [area of operations] is the key reason that the UN has sent you to that country. So as to ensure that you fulfil your military duties and to ensure that the UN is not accused of failing in its responsibilities, you consider it your duty to protect the rights of all civilians."[365]

> *This draft module offers a framework within peacekeeping where personnel can use appropriate, coercive military responses to stop and prevent human rights abuses.*

The draft module is unique. It firmly establishes responsibilities for peacekeepers in the context of human rights, and prepares military personnel to consider a range of techniques, including coercion, to protect civilians. Its recognition of the link between human rights and the use of military force goes beyond what is generally in UN guidelines and PSO doctrine to date. Such a module could fill a gap in most guidance for Chapter VII operations and benefit current operations that come close to coercive protection, such as in the DRC.

---

[363] Ibid., 14.
[364] Ibid., 3.
[365] Ibid., slide 19.

Overall, UN training modules do not address how countries should understand the meaning of UN mandates to "protect civilians under imminent threat" or how military forces should prepare to operate in missions with such mandates. While the larger problem is achieving clarity at the policy, conceptual, and doctrinal levels, UN training guidance needs to address this mission role and better support the personnel deploying to such operations today.

MULTINATIONAL & BILATERAL TRAINING INITIATIVES

If UN training efforts for peace support operations are still in their infancy, especially for addressing civilian protection as a coercive action, what other training programs for peace operations, whether strategic, operational, or tactical, address civilian protection? Numerous bilateral and multinational efforts try to increase the capabilities and skills of peacekeepers. Various countries run peace operations training programs for foreign militaries. With too many training programs to survey fully here, it is worth looking at a few examples of these international and national programs.

Overall, UN training modules do not address how countries should understand the meaning of UN mandates to "protect civilians under imminent threat" or how military forces should prepare to operate in missions with such mandates.

For African nations, for example, programs include those of the UK (*British Military Advisory and Training Team*, BMATT), France (*Reinforcement of African Peacekeeping Capacities,* RECAMP) and the US (*African Contingency Operations Training and Assistance* program, ACOTA, and now, *Global Peace Operations Initiative,* GPOI). Knowledgeable military officers from Great Britain, France, and the United States involved in these programs did not think that the training addressed the role for personnel in missions mandated to "protect civilians" within a peace operation or as a mission in itself. Applicable tasks are taught, however, even if a common concept of civilian protection is not.

The US, for example, has not traditionally included coercive use of force as part of its bilateral peacekeeping training programs. The US launched the African Crisis Response Initiative (ACRI) after the 1994 genocide in Rwanda, seeking to prepare African peacekeepers to respond to future crises. ACRI included general tasks that could apply to protection missions (e.g., protect non-combatants, conduct patrols, defend a convoy, and control civilian movement).[366] The 1998

---

[366] US Department of the Army, *African Crisis Response Initiative Program of Instruction May 98* (Fort Bragg, NC: US Department of the Army, Headquarters, 3rd Special Forces Group, 12 May

program set out a goal, characterized under "Protection Skills," to ensure that each trainee unit was "able to protect itself, civilians in its care and the operation. These skills are critical to operational effectiveness."[367] Under human rights training, the manual urges that the goal of the peacekeeping mission is "to ensure the safety and security of the civilian population," but ACRI did not train on the use of lethal force or provide trainees with lethal equipment. The instruction list from ACRI prepared forces for Chapter VI-type missions and stressed "the importance of using minimal necessary force while avoiding collateral damage."[368]

In 2002, the ACOTA program replaced ACRI. ACOTA was designed to include simple shooting instruction and military drills, and could include provision of lethal military equipment. ACOTA has used modular segments based on a DPKO-sanctioned Program of Instruction (POI). This POI covers human rights, refugee protection, force protection, lethal training for combat situations in peace enforcement missions, and includes command and staff training through computer simulations. The instruction also includes practical role-playing exercises emphasizing ROE, mandates, and decision-making in scenarios in which civilians are in harm's way—and those in which a mission mandate changes to Chapter VII.

Under the Global Peace Operations Initiative, announced in 2004, the US aims to help train 75,000 personnel for peacekeeping by 2010, with a specific focus on African forces. GPOI also intends to offer training for lethal operations. While increasing personnel and capacity for peace operations led by the UN and by regional organizations, GPOI does not yet have an explicit component regarding the protection of civilians. GPOI training is based on UN guidelines, previous US training efforts and US doctrine, as well as host-nation training objectives and doctrine. As discussed in the previous section, however, US peace operations doctrine provides few details on approaches for peacekeepers to protect civilians.

Training centers offer another venue for preparing personnel for peace operations. The Lester Pearson Center in Canada, for example, has been a leader in training and education on all aspects of peace operations. No courses, however, are known to have addressed civilian protection specifically.[369] When approached, experts involved with the International Association of Peacekeeping Training Centers were not aware of any training on civilian

---

1998), www2.apan-
info.net/gpoi/documents/ACRI%20Program%20of%20Instruction_May%2098.doc.
[367] Ibid.
[368] Ibid.
[369] Pearson senior staff, interview with author, June 2004.

protection.[370] Newer training centers are expanding to look at the challenges in current peace operations, especially as regional actors become more involved. The Kofi Annan International Peacekeeping Training Center in Ghana, for example, is designed to serve multiple audiences, including ECOWAS, the AU, the UN, and the international community, with a focus on operational issues for civilian and military personnel.[371] The Center hosts a wide range of meetings, including training programs with the UN, RECAMP and IAPTC and sessions to develop the STM series.

Until protection is introduced by a major troop contributor or the UN as a component of training, however, it is unlikely that KAIPTC or other regionally-based training centers will introduce curricula or training scenarios that address civilian protection as a specific component of a PSO or intervention force. These programs suggest the importance of UN standards, which they follow, and demonstrate how a gap in concepts or doctrine can affect the instruction recommended for training.

AT THE NATIONAL LEVEL: THE UNITED STATES

National training programs prepare their forces for the missions they anticipate. The United States, for example, is not a major contributor to UN-led peace operations. It is, however, beginning to focus more on how it prepares American forces for stability and peace operations. The US military trains broadly for offensive, defensive, stability, and support missions, with pressure to cover all the areas required by traditional military missions. The philosophy is that realistic training leads to success in operations. For stability and peace operations, much training has been *ad hoc* prior to deployment.

The US Approach

There has been a fundamental tension within the US over whether current training programs truly prepare American armed forces for complex peace and stability operations — let alone for specific civilian protection tasks. The US has not focused on preparing for peacekeeping missions generally, or developed extensive training programs for these operations. Some officials at military training institutions argue that neither US Army nor joint military training programs are sufficient for likely scenarios for US armed forces deploying to post-conflict environments, and that contingent leaders (i.e., battalion, brigade)

---

[370] This reflects multiple interviews with training experts knowledgeable about IAPTC, which does not have a formal membership. This research did not include a comprehensive review of all the 90-plus participants in IAPTC activities; individual training centers may address civilian protection issues. See the International Association of Peacekeeping Training Centres, www.iaptc.org/about.html.

[371] The Nigerian National War College handles strategic training and the Peacekeeping School in Koulikaro, Mali handles tactical training.

emphasize combat-related tactical training for their soldiers preparing for deployments. One Army training expert suggested that while eighty percent of US military missions are civilian-related, eighty percent of training requested is for combat.[372] As for protecting civilians as a role for forces within stability and peace operations, US military experts offered that they know of little training that squarely addresses civilian protection outside of traditional approaches of international humanitarian law—or as the stabilizing result of going after bad guys in traditional warfighting. As for specific training, one Army expert familiar with US approaches said, "I don't know of any modules that are focused on protection."[373]

This lack of training, in part, goes back to doctrine. "If it is not in doctrine," one US military official pointed out, "they won't teach it."[374] US training is driven by doctrine, in addition to commanders' perception of what they will face on the ground and current training programs. For example, commanders use the Universal Joint Task List (UJTL) as the basis for building joint mission-essential task lists (JMETLs), the common language for identifying tasks and training objectives for specific missions.[375] But within the task lists of the UJTL, there is virtually no discussion of the protection of civilians—except for the evacuation of non-combatant US nationals. The training checklist *does* recognize US military support to those who are expected to protect civilians, describing the assistance to restore order (described as a rule of law question) and assistance to host nations with displaced persons. If no task is identified to protect civilians, then it is likely to be harder to identify how to train personnel. Further, there is little reason to believe it is a presumed task for US service members.

> *There has been a fundamental tension within the US over whether current training programs truly prepare American armed forces for complex peace and stability operations – let alone for specific civilian protection tasks.*

---

[372] Workshop, *Operational Capacities for Civilian Protection Missions*, The Henry L. Stimson Center, Washington, DC, 8 December 2004.

[373] Ibid. The US prepared for an intervention with a training package for Haiti, when General Joseph Kinzer reportedly used the National Simulation Center to train his forces for that mission in the mid-1990s.

[374] Workshop, *Operational Capacities for Civilian Protection Missions*, The Henry L. Stimson Center, Washington, DC, 8 December 2004.

[375] US Department of Defense, *Chairman of the Joint Chiefs of Staff Manual 3500.04B: Universal Joint Task List* (Washington, DC: US Department of Defense, 1 October 1999), www.dtic.mil/doctrine/jel/cjcsd/cjcsm/m3500_4b.pdf; US Department of Defense, *The Joint Training System, A Primer for Senior Leaders* (Washington, DC: US Department of Defense, 1998), 16, www.dtic.mil/doctrine/jel/other_pubs/jtsprim.pdf.

Three major US centers for pre-deployment training provide some scenarios involving civilians: the National Training Center (NTC) at Fort Irwin, California; the Joint Readiness Training Center (JRTC) at Fort Polk, Louisiana; and Hohenfels Combat Maneuver Training Center (CMTC) in Germany. Fort Irwin is seen as focused on traditional combat operations. One NGO participant in a 2004 training session there described it as "a waste of time" since the exercise did not realistically incorporate NGOs and emphasized more force-on-force operations.[376] An Army major who had served in Sarajevo found the NTC training "stifling" in its concentration on heavy forces and felt it did not reflect "the way it works."[377] Hohenfels, which focuses on force maneuver training for all United States Army Europe (USAREUR) Combat Battalions, includes support for NATO training with Germany, France, Canada, and the Netherlands and training for peace operations prior to deployments such as Kosovo. Its training reportedly includes role-playing by civilians.[378] Many consider Fort Polk to be the site most likely to train US troops in realistic scenarios prior to deployment in stability or peace operations.[379] Training, in three-week mission readiness exercises, includes civilians posing as local inhabitants of the future deployment area. One official involved in training by the JRTC, however, stated that the Center's sessions were not realistic enough and did not provide sufficient training for likely peace and stability scenarios.[380]

The US Army's 1998 *Stability and Support Operations Training Support Package* includes a combination of classroom-learning lesson plans and situational training exercises to address ROE and issues such as the use of force.[381] While not an explicit discussion of civilian protection, the sample ROE used in the lessons are from *Operation Restore Hope* (the UN intervention in Somalia in 1992) which allow for the use of deadly force to defend the lives of persons in areas under US control. Training tasks include delivering supplies or humanitarian aid, convoy security, controlling civilian movement, and reacting to civil disturbance.

---

[376] CARE staff person, interview with author, Washington, DC, October 2004.

[377] US Army Major, interview with author, Washington, DC, October 2004.

[378] SFC Richard Hendricks, "COBs: The Civilian Element," *Soldiers Online*, April 1999, www.army.mil/Soldiers/apr1999/features/cob.html. Hendricks writes that civilians "have been used at CMTC since the early 1990s to portray civilian ethnic groups and organizations that Army units might encounter when deployed. The COB's mission is to add realism to situations where units might have to deal with civilian populations while conducting military operations."

[379] Workshop, Operational Capacities for Civilian Protection Missions, The Henry L. Stimson Center, Washington, DC, 8 December 2004.

[380] Ibid.

[381] US Army, Chapter 4. "Rules of Engagement Application," *Stability and Support Operations Training Support Package*, Training Circular 7-98-1, Headquarters, Department of the Army, 5 June 1997, https://atiam.train.army.mil/soldierPortal/atia/adlsc/view/public/11116-1/tc/7-98-1/toc.htm.

Another training expert suggested that there was increased interest in considering the role of US military police, simulations with human factors, and scenarios more reflective of current challenges.[382] Situational examples and the ROE used during the 1992 Los Angeles riots in turn demonstrate the application of and preparation for the use of force when civilians are at risk, which could apply elsewhere. Indeed, one experienced US Army Colonel who helped lead the Army task force in Los Angeles thought it had direct application to peace operations requiring the protection of civilians, perhaps more so than other areas of training and doctrine.[383]

There are signs of change in the US, however.[384] Traditionally, the US military has considered peace operations to be "peripheral" to its wartime mission, while believing that well-trained and disciplined troops make the best peacekeepers.[385] The Pentagon, however, is re-evaluating US preparation for peace and stability operations. The 2005 DoD Directive 3000.05 establishes policy and responsibility for planning, training, and preparing for conducting stability operations, framing them as a core activity of the US armed forces.[386] The Directive offers few specifics, but cites the "immediate goal" of stability operations as providing the local population with security, restoring services, and meeting humanitarian needs. Training will include exercises, games, and as needed, "red-teaming."[387] Likewise, DoD's 2006 Quadrennial Defense Review discusses changes to training for stability and reconstruction operations (though it does not mention protection training specifically).[388] The use of role-playing scenarios at Army training centers (including Fort Irwin and Fort Polk) is producing more realistic training, which could be useful to apply to peace and stability operations, as it has been done for counter-insurgency and preparing US forces for deployments to Iraq.[389] The question is how much the US will invest in more effective training for future stability and peace operations versus continue its focus on traditional warfighting and related operations.

---

[382] Workshop, *Operational Capacities for Civilian Protection Missions*, The Henry L. Stimson Center, Washington, DC, 8 December 2004; US Army officer and participant, interview with author, March 2006.

[383] Ibid.

[384] The US Military Academy at West Point, for instance, developed a class to look at "winning the peace" in a post-conflict scenario to address modern circumstances faced by its graduates.

[385] Lt. Col. Brent Bankus, "Training the Military for Peace Operations: A Past, Present and Future View," in Robert M. Schoenhaus, ed., *Peaceworks 43: Training for Peace and Humanitarian Relief Operations* (Washington, DC: US Institute of Peace, April 2002).

[386] US Department of Defense, Directive 3000.05.

[387] "Red-teaming" refers to training in which personnel play the role of an adversary to identify weaknesses in current operational practices.

[388] US Department of Defense, *Quadrennial Defense Review Report*, 6 February 2006. www.comw.org/qdr/qdr2006.pdf.

[389] Dexter Filkins and John F. Burns, "Mock Iraqi Villages in Mojave Prepare Troops for Battle," *The New York Times*, 1 May 2006; Wells Tower, "Under the God Gun: Battling a Fake Insurgency in the Army's Imitation Iraq," *Harper's Magazine*, 1 January 2006.

Developments in NATO might push the US to reevaluate its training.[390] NATO partners are expected to prepare for non-Article V missions (i.e., peace operations and peacebuilding). The US Joint Forces Command (Norfolk, VA) is developing better scenarios for simulation of likely joint operations and is working on a crisis-response mission task list for operations involving NATO. One Joint Forces official pointed out that the US did not have preparation for such crisis-response missions "in their tool kit."[391] This effort could result in more regularized training for operations likely to involve civilian protection, involving multiple services and countries.

Given the breadth of US training programs, it is likely that some programs will address aspects of protecting civilians, including coercive protection. As discussed in the previous section on doctrine, however, identifying these areas is difficult without a common language or recognition of protection as either central to or the goal of an operation. Even with these challenges, many argue that militaries can train up quickly to meet the situations they will face; the issue is how those situations are defined in advance.

Selected Exercises and Simulations

Exercises and simulations help train military personnel on key skills, aiding them by rehearsing missions and honing their skills for specific situations. One established training series with relevant civilian protection aspects is the US-sponsored *Cobra Gold*, an annual US military multinational exercise developed with Pacific Command (PACOM). In 2005, the exercise was led by the US Marine Corps, and included the United States, Japan, Singapore, Thailand, India, and multiple military, UN, and civilian actors.[392] Those involved in its planning at the US Center for Excellence in Disaster Management and Humanitarian Assistance (Hawaii), which reports to PACOM, said it involved civilian protection scenarios, including military use of force to defend UN

---

[390] NATO has the Working Group on Training and Education for Peace Support Operations (TEPSO), which is designed to help coordinate national training and education programs, to assist with standardization, and to identify new training objectives based on lessons learned. The authors were unable to access information on whether TEPSO addresses training for civilian protection missions.

[391] US official, Joint Forces Command, interview with author, October 2004. This initiative is viewed as especially important by those who believe the US military is still reluctant to accept non-traditional roles.

[392] *Cobra Gold* aims to help simulate and train multinational forces in a contingency operation involving humanitarian aims: "Using a United Nations Chapter VII and NEO scenario, Cobra Gold unites existing bilateral exercises into a regional exercise framework and demonstrates the ability of several nations to rapidly deploy a JTF [Joint Task Force] to conduct joint/combined operation in a Small Scale Contingency." See Center for Excellence in Disaster Management and Humanitarian Affairs, http://coe-dmha.org/cobragold.htm.

mandates and both UN and local personnel.[393] Troops faced a Chapter VII scenario involving a hand-off from an intervention force to a UN force and were required to form a transitional administration. Lessons learned from the Malaysia exercise are slated to be incorporated into the design of *Cobra Gold* 2007, which will be the PACOM-GPOI Capstone Exercise.

The United Kingdom's Peacekeeping Team in the Foreign Commonwealth Office is involved in a series of map-based role-playing exercises known as MapEx. The aim of these exercises is to help implement the recommendations of the Brahimi Report, improve on past operations' capacities, increase interoperability and planning experience, and help create training capacities within participating nations. Past operations include *Blue Pelican* (UK, France, and ECOWAS in Nigeria), *Blue Elephant* (Thailand), *Blue Puma* (Argentina), *Blue Lion* (Senegal), *Blue Tiger* (Bangladesh), and *Blue Jaguar* (Paraguay), with more exercises planned.[394] These exercises simulate complex operations, with civilians at risk and with mandates that mirror those of current UN peace operations.

One simulation model for peace support operations is the Deployable Exercise Support (DEXES). A project of US Southern Command, DEXES is a simulation program designed to support bilingual international training exercises in military operations other than war. DEXES is a computer-based simulation that charts complex factors that influence the success or failure of peace operations. It uses discrete events and player choices to influence a broad set of variables describing social interaction in the host country. Variables include the pace of economic growth, the level of civil unrest, the amount of political participation, and the level of popular support for the peacekeeping forces, among others. An event or player choice that causes a change in one variable will cause changes in other related variables. For example, if a peacekeeping convoy accidentally runs over a civilian, DEXES calculates a slight decrease in popular support for the peacekeeping forces and a potential increase in the perceived bias of the peacekeeping forces. If not addressed, these shifts spur changes in other variables, such as a decrease in political participation and an increase in armed conflict. DEXES includes variables for social conditions such as ethnic distrust, civil unrest, armed conflict, the number of displaced persons, public health conditions such as the daily civilian mortality rate, political conditions including government corruption and competence, economic conditions, and the public opinion of various ethnic groups. DEXES is often

---

[393] John Otte and Sharon McHale, Center for Excellence in Disaster Management and Humanitarian Affairs, interviews with author, October 2004; Otte, interviews with author, January 2006.
[394] Peacekeeping Team, Conflict Issues Group, Foreign Commonwealth Office, UK, interview with author, October 2004.

used during Command Post Exercises in order to simulate the passage of time.[395]

While simulation models such as DEXES can be extremely useful in training for peace support operations, they do suffer from several drawbacks that limit their effectiveness. First, the advanced technology required to run such sophisticated simulations means that significant time is required to master the technical aspects. Most nations do not own and operate simulation technology, so the first several days of a multinational exercise are often spent learning how the technology operates. Second, the high costs of simulation technology make it inaccessible to the majority of countries, particularly developing nations that provide the bulk of contemporary peacekeepers. Finally, almost all simulation expertise is provided by private contractors, further increasing the costs of running exercises.

CHALLENGES: IMPROVING TRAINING FOR PROTECTION OF CIVILIANS

Broadly speaking, there is growing awareness that UN peace operations and other missions need to protect civilians under threat. Current military training efforts address this role primarily in basic, traditional approaches of support to humanitarian action, to rule of law, and in concert with international humanitarian law. There are few signs that training for peacekeepers or national forces has adjusted to address civilian protection more directly as a military role, or to offer guidance to forces deploying under UN mandates to protect civilians. Civilian protection "is on the radar screens," as one US military training expert said, pointing to the UN mandates, but there is "not really" any training to prepare them for upholding these mandates.[396]

Is basic military training with *ad hoc* civilian protection training sufficient to prepare personnel for modern operations mandated to protect civilians? Many UN and military experts argue that protection missions require troops with basic military skills and good command and control in the operation, not specific training for civilian protection. Some countries with little doctrine on peace support operations or coercive protection missions may have well prepared troops nonetheless. Others point out that militaries can train up quickly to meet the situations they will face. The nature of civilian protection offered by

---

[395] For example, a force might train for a particular scenario typical of the early stages of a peace operation. Overnight, DEXES could simulate the passage of months, and present an entirely new scenario the next morning, typical of a later stage of peace operations.

[396] Workshop, *Operational Capacities for Civilian Protection Missions*, The Henry L. Stimson Center, Washington, DC, 8 December 2004.

personnel may depend on the threat facing the mission, and therefore the important issue is the level of intensity at which troops fight and operate, not specialized skills. This view is popular: well-trained troops will generally be better at any mission, even unfamiliar ones, than those who lack basic skills and coherent leadership. Such a point underlies a larger debate about specific training for peace support and stability operations. The other point of view is that training prepares individuals to respond—but that response may be completely inadequate or dangerous if it is applied in the wrong situation. When military personnel are not ready for a situation and have not had realistic training for it, they may respond poorly and be unprepared for unfamiliar missions, such as those required by mandates to protect civilians in a PSO by military forces trained solely for combat.[397]

Specialized training or the development of discrete "civilian protection" training packages is not universally seen as the single answer, however. Many peace operations trainers express dismay at the number of balkanized training packages already circulating through the UN and other institutions. Rather than develop another such package, military planners should place greater emphasis on integrating training for civilian protection into current training for missions where civilians are under threat, and on integrating civilian protection concerns across the mission-planning and training process—whether for peace operations or military interventions. The enduring challenge is using training to address gaps and to generate a common understanding of future missions. Those gaps are hard to address if they are not recognized in the first place.

As peace operations now involve the use of force, experienced military and political leaders of UN missions consider better training for such operations to be critical for peacekeeping forces. Leadership is also vital to a mission's success, yet senior leaders, both civilian and military, may themselves lack training on how to approach the questions of protecting civilians, potentially with the use of force. One DPKO training expert suggested that training could precede civilian protection policy and doctrine if clear, trainable tasks are identified. "You must suss it out," the official suggested, noting that the protection of civilians was intrinsic to tasks for which peacekeepers trained, such as DDR, as well as "common sense" and a "basic" component of human rights work.[398] Such common sense may be insufficient, however, if aspects of the mission are unfamiliar.

At some level, therefore, training that treats the protection of civilians as an explicit goal or the central task of a mission—whether led by the United

---

[397] US military training expert, interview with author, June 2006.

[398] Senior official, Integrated Training Service, DPKO, interview with author, 1 February 2006.

Nations, a lead nation, or a coalition—*is* necessary. While a baseline of well trained forces is required, training for missions involving civilian protection should recognize that the environment and required decision-making are not equivalent either to traditional combat or to traditional peacekeeping scenarios.

With the development of new tools to prepare forces for modern peace and stability operations, there is an opportunity to integrate operational concepts of protection and increase the preparation of today's militaries for the real scenarios they may face. Many of these concepts are suggested in the UN's useful draft module, *Protection of Human Rights by Military Peacekeepers*. The next step should be to expand these limited forays into civilian protection training and to make them a regular feature of the training provided to all troops deploying to regions with civilians at risk. As the UN strengthens its training guidance and other national and other multinational programs expand, these programs should address the roles for military personnel in the

> *At some level, therefore, training that treats the protection of civilians as an explicit goal or the central task of a mission—whether led by the United Nations, a lead nation, or a coalition—is necessary.*

protection of civilians more directly, tackling issues from impartiality to the use of force, from working with humanitarian organizations to providing physical protection in hostile environments. Training should also engage peacekeepers and clarify what is needed—or not needed—in pre-deployment versus general training. Additionally, it should demonstrate to leaders and personnel when a UN mission can no longer offer protection and when, therefore, only an intervening force can offer the kind of physical protection to civilians required. Such an approach would enhance the preparedness of personnel and leaders for current and future operations, especially in the difficult environments where peacekeepers operate today, such as the Democratic Republic of the Congo.

— 8 —
PROTECTING CIVILIANS ON THE GROUND: MONUC AND THE DEMOCRATIC REPUBLIC OF CONGO

I don't think [I feel] guilt. Maybe there could be feelings of impotence, because when you have a gun and know how to use it...it is natural, you want to use it. When you see a group committing such atrocities, you feel rage.

- Lt. Col. Waldemar Fontes,
former executive officer of Uruguayan peacekeepers in the DRC,
discussing his troops' inability to halt atrocities in Bunia in April
and May of 2003[399]

The Democratic Republic of the Congo provides a rich case study of efforts by third-party intervention forces for civilian protection. The deployment of MONUC, the United Nations Organization Mission in the DRC in 1999, the intervention of a French-led EU force in mid-2003, and the continuing MONUC mission demonstrate evolving interpretations of what the charge to "protect civilians" means for peacekeeping forces. MONUC has changed dramatically, developing from a small observer mission with a mandate to protect civilians— but without a capacity to do so—into the UN's largest and most robust operation for which civilian protection is a central purpose.

MONUC also demonstrates multiple concepts of civilian protection: as support to humanitarian space; as a task for UN peacekeepers; and (nearly) as a central goal for military forces. MONUC highlights the challenges for operations that begin under-staffed and ill-equipped, and become widely dispersed across a remote, austere, and volatile region. MONUC further demonstrates issues of protection when peacekeepers operate with differing understandings of their mandate and ROE, with national caveats and varying preparation, with dissimilar views on the use of force, and with mandates that shift from Chapter VI to Chapter VII. Fundamentally, the DRC case illustrates the enormous difficulties of addressing a humanitarian crisis during ongoing civil conflict, where UN forces are drawn into a gray area between peacekeeping and warfighting.

---

[399] "Uruguayan Peacekeepers Faced Trouble in Bunia," *The Wall Street Journal*, 1 October 2003.

The DRC is certainly an extreme environment for peacekeeping—indeed, for trying to protect anyone. The challenges are a violent storm of conflict, geography, poverty, and state failure. The International Rescue Committee has estimated that nearly four million civilians have died as a result of warfare since August 1998, the most devastating death toll in any armed conflict since World War II.[400] The war has engulfed not just the massive DRC, but has crossed its borders into neighboring countries.[401]

> *The DRC is an extreme environment for peacekeeping – indeed, for trying to protect anyone. The challenges are a violent storm of conflict, geography, poverty, and state failure.*

The DRC has few passable roads and little infrastructure, a plethora of exploitable and valuable commodities, multiple rebel groups, influential and difficult neighbors, and a dysfunctional government with limited authority outside the capital. In the east, for example, Rwanda and Uganda have sought control over the boundary areas, exploited the DRC's natural resources, and backed or opposed different armed groups in the country, resulting in much chaos.[402]

In some sense, the DRC may be in the "too hard" category for civilian protection—peacekeepers face an environment where consent is partial, governance is limited, spoilers are rife, and the political commitment to peace is low. One UN official aptly called the DRC mission not peacekeeping but "conflict peacebuilding."[403]

Yet MONUC's experiences illustrate some elements of civilian protection and its requirements. The mission also demonstrates the beginnings of an innovative strategy to integrate differing approaches within an operation, including coercive protection. The question of baseline capacity arises first. A lack of capacity has limited what the UN mission could do to protect people. With ongoing insecurity in the DRC, consent-based, non-interventionist methods of protecting civilians proved largely ineffective, and MONUC initially had insufficient troop

---

[400] Coghlan et al., "Mortality in the Democratic Republic of Congo: a nationwide survey," *Lancet*, 44-51.

[401] The third-largest nation in Africa, the DRC nearly equals Western Europe in size with a 10,730-kilometer border with nine states. Its poor infrastructure requires cross-country travel by air and limits access to remote areas.

[402] UN Security Council, *Report of the Panel of Experts on the Illegal Exploitation of Natural Resources and Other Forms of Wealth of the Democratic Republic of the Congo*, S/2001/357, 12 April 2001.

[403] Fourth GCSP Workshop for Peace Operations, "Pursuing Security in the Post-Conflict Phase," Geneva Center for Security Policy, Geneva, Switzerland, 12-13 June 2005. More civilians have died in the DRC concurrent with a UN peacekeeping operation than in any other country.

strength, equipment, and firepower to engage in coercive protection. Second, MONUC needed conceptual clarity as to the meaning and scope of its protection mandate. Mission leadership did not start with a coherent strategic framework for civilian protection and for how much force the mission should exercise. After years of struggling, MONUC has begun to develop and implement such a framework.

Third is the issue of military willingness and preparedness. Even as MONUC evolved into a Chapter VII operation with more troops and improved military materiel, its forces lacked a common understanding of the mandate and ROE, and consistent willingness to engage in offering physical protection to those at risk. In many cases, troops arrived unaware of the difficult in-country environment, uninformed of their mandate to protect civilians, and unprepared for the tasks ahead. It took years for able, well-trained forces to be deployed in respectable numbers to the DRC's volatile eastern provinces, and to operate with a concept of their protection responsibilities. The EU-authorized *Operation Artemis*, on the other hand, was prepared, willing and able to operate in a hostile environment, and quickly established security in its limited area of operations.

> *MONUC demonstrates the issues that arise when peacekeepers engage in coercive protection, such as compelling armed groups to stop threatening the population.*

Finally, MONUC demonstrates the issues that arise when peacekeepers engage in coercive protection, such as compelling armed groups to stop threatening the population. Some recent MONUC activities fall in a gray area between traditional peacekeeping and "peacemaking," which is more closely associated with warfighting. The mission's robust posture has also complicated other aspects of its work. As MONUC has pushed militia to disarm or join the new Congolese integrated army (the FARDC), the FARDC itself has become a threat to civilians. MONUC's cordon-and-search operations have limited the capacity and movement of armed groups, but have also led to reprisal killings of civilians, reduced NGO willingness to cooperate with the UN mission, and raised accusations of human rights abuses by UN personnel.[404] These are consequences of taking coercive action, and MONUC's experience shows that

---

[404] UN General Assembly, *A Comprehensive Strategy to Eliminate Future Sexual Exploitation and Abuse in United Nations Peacekeeping Operations*, A/59/710, United Nations, 24 March 2005. Tragically, MONUC forces and civilian personnel have threatened civilians and sexually abused and exploited Congolese women and girls, a topic explored in-depth in other analyses.

these issues need to be addressed both in the DRC and for any peacekeeping mission or intervention force.

In such situations, the ability of outside parties with limited resources to protect large numbers of vulnerable civilians remains far from certain. Mission leaders and peacekeepers must be cognizant of the challenges and tradeoffs involved with various protection strategies. This chapter offers a basic history of peacekeeping in the DRC since 1999, analyzes how peacekeepers tried to protect civilians, and evaluates their relative success in doing so. It focuses on mission strategy and preparation—the concepts, mandates, rules of engagement, and training that the operations utilized, or failed to utilize, to protect civilians in the field.

1999-2005: THE UN FORCE AND PEACE IMPLEMENTATION EFFORTS IN THE DRC

On July 10, 1999, the DRC, Angola, Namibia, Rwanda, and Uganda signed the Lusaka Ceasefire Agreement, bringing the war in the DRC to a close, at least on paper. The African-led agreement, facilitated by the Southern African Development Community and President Frederick Chiluba of Zambia, requested a Chapter VII UN peacekeeping force "to ensure implementation of this Agreement; and taking into account the peculiar situation of the DRC, mandate the peacekeeping force to track down all armed groups in the DRC."[405]

This call for a robust peacekeeping force caught the United Nations off guard. The international community was skeptical about the Congolese parties' commitment to peace and aware of the massive difficulties of bringing stability to the DRC. There was a general view that the UN did not "own" the agreement and thus was not responsible for its implementation. "The Congo file started in Africa, not in the United Nations," one diplomat complained. "The Lusaka Agreement called for UN forces. They didn't know what they were writing. The UN wasn't there. The UN came in with a framework that wasn't theirs."[406] Further, recruiting peacekeepers to disarm forces is a tough assignment. "It would be difficult, if not impossible, to identify troop contributing countries willing to contribute contingents to be deployed in eastern DRC for forcible disarmament of groups accused of genocide and other serious crimes against humanity, at least in sufficient numbers and with a sufficiently robust mandate," explained a UN official.[407]

---

[405] *Lusaka Ceasefire Agreement*, 10 July 1999, text available at the US Institute of Peace website, www.usip.org/library/pa/drc/drc_07101999.html.

[406] Clifford Bernath and Anne Edgerton, *MONUC: Flawed Mandate Limits Success* (Washington, DC: Refugees International, May 2003), 5.

[407] Peter Swarbrick, "DDRRR: Political dynamics and linkages," in Malan and Porto, eds., *Challenges of Peace Implementation*, 166. Swarbrick has headed MONUC's DDRRR Division.

Yet many believed the UN could encourage reconciliation and provide relief to the suffering Congolese population. Officials such as Ambassador Richard Holbrooke, the US Permanent Representative to the UN, urged a graduated approach to peacekeeping in the DRC, beginning with a small observation force to report, act as liaisons, and support the negotiations. As the parties demonstrated their commitment to peace, the UN force could expand, reflecting a parallel commitment by the international community.[408]

The Security Council authorized a small deployment of 90 military liaisons in August 1999, and up to 5,537 military personnel in February 2000—far short of the African request for 15,000 to 20,000 troops.[409] MONUC was to deploy in three phases, with the arrival of forces contingent on local actions. In Phase I, a small team liaised with the warring parties and planned for the arrival of military observers. In Phase II, 500 military observers deployed, supported by roughly 5,000 peacekeepers, to monitor and report on the disengagement of the warring parties. In Phase III, MONUC was to embark on a Disarmament, Demobilization, Repatriation, Resettlement and Reintegration program (DDRRR) and oversee the withdrawal of foreign forces. Each phase depended on the parties adhering to the peace process. Later MONUC developed further phases, including the deployment of combat-capable forces in the east.

This approach frustrated many by allowing parties with no interest in peace to set the pace of UN deployment. It also assumed incorrectly that armed groups would disarm voluntarily. The strategy reflected the Council's caution about creating an expensive and controversial peace enforcement mission, especially in such a difficult neighborhood where its permanent five members had few direct national interests. As a result, the UN reacted to events on the ground, rather than shaped them. The Council expanded MONUC's capacity in response to atrocities, rather than to reward progress towards peace.

Even with a Chapter VII clause in its mandate to "protect civilians under imminent threat of physical violence," MONUC initially behaved more like a Chapter VI observer mission, using force only in self defense and doing little to physically protect civilians.[410] In May 2002, soldiers from RCD-Goma (one of the largest Congolese rebel groups, supported by Rwanda) responded to an

---

[408] Others took issue with this approach, arguing that either that UN forces should have come in stronger or that the peace plan should have more squarely addressed the presence of foreign forces.

[409] S/Res/1258, 6 August 1999 and S/Res/1291, 24 February 2000.

[410] The call to "protect civilians under imminent threat of physical violence" was first included in Security Council Resolution 1291 of 24 February 2000. Yet many referred to MONUC as a Chapter VI mission until Council Resolution 1493 in 2003, including MONUC sector leaders. Lawrence Smith, "MONUC's military involvement in the eastern Congo (Maniema and the Kivus)," in Malan and Porto, eds., Challenges of Peace Implementation, 233.

attempted mutiny by massacring civilians in Kisangani, the DRC's third-largest city. MONUC had roughly 1,000 troops and dozens of military observers in the city, but declined to oppose the massacres forcefully or send patrols to deter abuses.[411] The events in Kisangani reportedly led to some of the first discussions in the UN DPKO on the meaning of civilian protection as a military task for MONUC, its implications for ROE, and the suitability and willingness of MONUC contingents to carry out interventions.[412]

Emergency in Ituri

A May 2003 crisis erupted in the Ituri province that significantly impacted MONUC, its mandate, and its willingness to use force. Fighting between the Hema and Lendu tribes began in Ituri in 1999 over a land dispute. The presence of Ugandan forces in the region exacerbated tensions and clashes grew as the conflict in the DRC wore on. In September 2000, the DRC and Uganda signed the Luanda Agreement, which called for the withdrawal of Ugandan forces (the UPDF) from northeastern DRC within three months. The UPDF began to withdraw in late April 2003 and pulled out its 7,000 troops from Ituri in less than two weeks, leaving a dangerous security vacuum.[413]

MONUC was unprepared for the speedy Ugandan exit. Only 712 Uruguayan troops, trained primarily for guard duty, had arrived in Ituri by the time the Ugandans withdrew.[414] Hema and Lendu militias acted quickly, creating chaos. Lendu militias invaded Bunia, murdering Hema and pillaging their houses. The Uruguayan troops tried to set up roadblocks and conduct patrols, but soon abandoned these efforts as futile.[415] The Union of Congolese Patriots (UPC), a Hema militia, retook Bunia a week later and began its own campaign of abuse against the Lendu. More than 400 people were massacred in two weeks.

---

[411] Suliman Baldo and Peter Bouckaert, *War Crimes in Kisangani: The Response of Rwandan-backed Rebels to the May 2002 Mutiny*, No. 6(A) (Human Rights Watch, August 2002), 2.

[412] Former DPKO military planning official, interview with author, 21 May 2006.

[413] Uganda had expressed willingness to keep its forces in Ituri until the UN deployed, but wanted official Security Council recognition of its presence. The Council, however, did not want to set a precedent of authorizing foreign troops on sovereign Congolese soil.

[414] Peacekeeping Best Practices, *Operation Artemis*, 6.

[415] The International Crisis Group (ICG) describes a week of horror: "During that dreadful week, individuals were killed or kidnapped beside the UN compound. MONUC was asked on several occasions to escort or protect Hema individuals out of dangerous locations to more secure areas, and it either failed to do so, or intervened too late. On 10 May, MONUC was informed of the likely assassination of Nyakasanza's parish priest and other Hema clerics. It refused to intervene or even accompany the vicar-general to the parish after the massacre. On 11 May, a man was kidnapped from the MONUC compound. Uruguayan officers were informed but refused to intervene. The person was then executed 100 metres away. On 11 May MONUC refused to escort to its compound nineteen Catholic seminarians who were under death threat and in hiding." International Crisis Group, *Congo Crisis: Military Intervention in Ituri*, Africa Report no. 64 (ICG, 13 June 2003), 12.

MONUC was barely able to protect its own personnel, let alone the population of Bunia.

Despite their small numbers, the Uruguayans in Bunia protected some civilians. When the violence began, around 10,000 people flooded the Bunia airport and about 6,000 went to MONUC sector headquarters.[416] MONUC troops refused to abandon these locations during the crisis, guarding the civilians in their care, facilitating the delivery of food aid and other supplies, and securing the airport to support future use by MONUC and relief organizations. In August 2003, 11,000 civilians remained at the Bunia airport camp. Many of these civilians would surely have perished without protection and support from MONUC.

> *More than 400 people were massacred in two weeks. MONUC was barely able to protect its own personnel, let alone the population of Bunia.*

Operation Artemis and MONUC's Ituri Brigade

In response to a request by Secretary-General Annan, France volunteered to lead an Interim Emergency Multinational Force (IEMF) to establish security in Bunia, provided that other nations offer troops, that the EU lead it, and that the mission be organized under Chapter VII. The resulting *Operation Artemis* deployed under an EU flag with 1,400 troops and a Chapter VII mandate to "contribute to the stabilization of the security conditions and the improvement of the humanitarian situation in Bunia, to ensure the protection of the airport, the internally displaced persons in the camps in Bunia and, if the situation requires it, to contribute to the safety of the civilian population" in "close coordination with MONUC."[417] The IEMF was to serve as a stop-gap, buying time to build up MONUC forces and establish security in Ituri. The first French soldiers arrived in the region on June 6, 2003. The EU force reached its full strength by mid-July, and handed its responsibilities back to MONUC in September 2003.[418]

---

[416] Peacekeeping Best Practices, *Operation Artemis*, 7.

[417] S/Res/1484, 30 May 2003.

[418] Future of Peace Operations program, *Review of European Union Field Operations*, Peace Operations Fact Sheet Series (Washington, DC: The Henry L. Stimson Center, March 2004), 4, www.stimson.org/fopo/?SN=FP20020610372.

The IEMF was authorized to protect IDPs and provide security for civilians only within the town of Bunia. "It is obvious that if we were to go out beyond Bunia to cover the risks in all of Ituri, we would need a much larger force," explained a French Defense Ministry spokesman. "The main thing for us is to set objectives that are realistic and in keeping with the means we have."[419] The force had light armored vehicles, observation helicopters, and French air support from Mirage 2000 fighter jets based in Uganda. It quickly established its authority in Bunia, enforced a "weapons-free zone," and responded aggressively to UPC provocations.[420] One skirmish with the UPC reportedly killed 20 militiamen.[421] The IEMF cut off some weapons shipments into Bunia by monitoring secondary and field airstrips, and running vehicle patrols.

> *During Operation Artemis, the UN rotated new troops into Ituri and the Kivu provinces who were prepared to use force to protect civilians.*

As a sign of the IEMF's success at protecting civilians in its area of operation, thousands of IDPs returned to Bunia from June to August 2003. Improved security also allowed the political process in Ituri to restart. At the same time, at least sixteen massacres reportedly occurred outside Bunia in Ituri during the IEMF's three month deployment.[422]

According to one MONUC official, the Ituri crisis caused a "sea change" in the mission's approach to civilian protection.[423] During *Operation Artemis*, the UN rotated new troops into Ituri and the Kivu provinces who were prepared for the more robust MONUC mandate and to use force to protect civilians. As the IEMF withdrew, the UN organized a brigade-sized force with 4,800 troops, heavy armaments, and combat helicopters. The goal of this new "Ituri Brigade," stated SRSG Ambassador William Lacy Swing, was "to stop the killing and end the violence, the *sine qua non* for all that follows."[424] To prepare for the handover, the Security Council increased MONUC's troop ceiling to 10,800 and authorized it to "take the necessary measures in the areas of deployment of its armed units," and "within its capabilities":

---

[419] "Questions about the 'Artemis' operations in Congo," Joint press briefing by F. Rivasseau and J.F. Bureau, Government of France, 13 June 2003.

[420] Henri Boshoff, "Overview of MONUC's military strategy and concept of operations," in Malan and Porto, eds., *Challenges of Peace Implementation*, 141.

[421] Peacekeeping Best Practices, *Operation Artemis*, 12.

[422] Forum for Early Warning and Early Response (FEWER), *Ituri: Stakes, Actors, Dynamics* (London: FEWER Secretariat, October 2003).

[423] DPKO official, interview with author, 27 November 2005.

[424] William Lacy Swing, "The role of MONUC and the international community in support of the DRC transition," in Malan and Porto, eds., *Challenges of Peace Implementation*, preface, x.

- to protect United Nations personnel, facilities, installations, and equipment;
- to ensure the security and freedom of movement of its personnel, including in particular those engaged in missions of observation, verification, or DDRRR;
- to protect civilians and humanitarian workers under imminent threat of physical violence; and
- to contribute to the improvement of the security conditions in which humanitarian assistance is provided.[425]

The mandate further authorized MONUC to "use all necessary means to fulfil its mandate in the Ituri district and, as it deemed within its capacity, in North and South Kivu." The force was more capable, too. The Ituri Brigade included personnel from Morocco, Bangladesh, Nepal and Pakistan; an Indian aviation unit; and a Bangladeshi and Indonesian engineering unit. Brigadier General Jan Isberg, commander of the Ituri Brigade, confirmed the force's new capacity and attitude towards its role:

> ...[T]he brigade's capacity is enormous. We have all the necessary means—we have helicopters, APCs and the weapons each soldier has. We are capable of countering any attack.... we must act according to our new mandate of Chapter Seven immediately and without hesitation, to be ready to use force when the situation dictates.[426]

The Ituri Brigade established security in Bunia and gradually began to patrol more remote villages, although its impact on security outside Bunia is debatable. In one encounter, a truck full of militia fighters attempted to drive into Bunia, only to be fired upon by a UN surveillance helicopter; three militia members were killed.[427] In another, UN forces found a cache of weapons at UPC political headquarters, and arrested and detained a number of top officials.[428] But some observers criticized the brigade for failing to deal aggressively with armed groups during its first year of deployment. It was not until late 2004 that the brigade truly began to ramp up its use of force.[429]

The increased UN presence in the eastern DRC also improved security for civilians in the Kivus. The new Kivus Brigade conducted high visibility patrols,

---

[425] S/Res/1493, 28 July 2003.

[426] Integrated Regional Information Networks (IRIN), "DRC: EU calls Artemis operation 'a big success,'" Brussels, 17 September 2003; quoted in Boshoff, in Malan and Porto, eds., *Challenges of Peace Implementation*, 142.

[427] Amnesty International, *Ituri: a need for protection, a thirst for justice* (Amnesty International, 21 October 2003), www.amnestyusa.org/icc/document.do?id=71711FE4D330C1C880256DDA00478B0C.

[428] IRIN, "DRC: Six killed as fighting erupts during protest in Bunia," 16 September 2003, www.irinnews.org/report.asp?ReportID=36618&SelectRegion=Great_Lakes&SelectCountry=DRC.

[429] NGO security analyst in the DRC, interview with author, 27 May 2006.

prompting thousands of IDPs to return home. The population in Kindu, for example, grew from about 20,000 in January 2003 to more than 220,000 in August 2003. When MONUC began foot patrols across the Congo River, it received a heroes' welcome and was "showered with leaves and rice as it passed through the crowds."[430] Col. Lawrence Smith, the Kivus brigade commander, concluded, "The mere presence of peacekeepers does have a stabilizing effect on an area that is suffering the aftermath and effects of war."[431] Nevertheless, civilians in such areas remained at risk. "A spin-off from the active patrolling in areas where human rights abuses and violations are rife," explained Smith, "is the decrease in incidents while patrols are operating in the area, and immediately thereafter. The unfortunate truth is, however, that very soon after a patrol has left an area…abuses and violations start again."[432]

Crisis in Bukavu

Security in the Kivus started to deteriorate in late 2003 and early 2004. Tensions grew as the former rebel forces from RCD-Goma began to integrate into the FARDC. The UN announced plans to expand the brigade-sized force in the Kivus to 3,500 troops and to redeploy a battalion of Uruguayans to South Kivu.[433]

In the spring of 2004, a crisis rocked Bukavu, the capital of South Kivu, when mutinous FARDC forces occupied the city for a week. Hundreds of civilians were killed in Bukavu, and to the south in Kamanyola, before the renegade forces withdrew under international pressure. At least 2,000 civilians sought shelter at the MONUC compound and more than 30,000 fled to Burundi and Rwanda.[434] Despite a redeployment of UN troops to the Kivus that had begun months earlier, only 800 UN soldiers were in Bukavu at the time of the crisis.[435] Many Congolese were frustrated with the lack of a forceful UN response to the conflict. Large, violent anti-UN protests occurred in Kinshasa and elsewhere.

---

[430] Smith, "MONUC's military involvement in the eastern Congo," in Malan and Porto, eds., *Challenges of Peace Implementation*, 242.

[431] Ibid., 245.

[432] Ibid., 243-244.

[433] UN Security Council, *Fifteenth Secretary-General Report on MONUC*, S/2004/251, 25 March 2004, para. 33.

[434] UN Security Council, *Third Special Report of the Secretary-General on MONUC*, S/2004/650, 16 August 2004, para. 45.

[435] Philip Roessler and John Prendergast, "Democratic Republic of the Congo: The Case of the United Nations Organization Mission in the Democratic Republic of the Congo (MONUC)," in Durch, ed., *21st Century Peace Operations*, 258. The number of UN troops in Bukavu was based on the tasks and general threat assessment. The area had been fairly calm before the Bukavu crisis. Although Bukavu was a UN Sector Headquarters, the majority of troops were some 15 kilometers outside of town in locations where DDR was planned. Former DPKO military planning official, interview with author, 21 May 2006.

A More Robust MONUC

After the events in Bukavu, the Secretary-General proposed more than doubling MONUC's size, from 10,800 to 23,000 personnel. He requested brigade-sized forces in both North and South Kivu, a new brigade for Katanga and the Kasai provinces, an eastern division headquarters to direct military operations in the Kivus and Ituri, and a "joint mission analysis cell" to improve information analysis.[436] The Security Council approved half the request, raising the force ceiling to 16,700, but eliminated the brigade for Katanga and Kasais. The updated mandate also reiterated the call for MONUC to protect civilians.[437] In

> *From early 2005, MONUC conducted some of the most aggressive actions by blue-helmeted forces in recent memory.*

the months that followed, DPKO made a large-scale effort to shift forces to the eastern DRC, sending almost 5,500 combat-capable troops to the Kivus and Ituri. These troops came mostly from unified Indian and Pakistani brigades and were deployed to North and South Kivu.

From early 2005, MONUC conducted some of the most aggressive actions by blue-helmeted forces in recent memory. SRSG Swing set an April 1 deadline for Ituri militias to hand in their guns. MONUC compelled disarmament of militias through aggressive cordon-and-search operations, intended both to force armed groups to join the DDR program and to pre-empt attacks on local civilians. By June 2005, MONUC had disarmed roughly 15,000 fighters in the region.[438] An ambush by the Nationalist and Integrationist Front (FNI), however, killed nine Bangladeshi peacekeepers in February 2005. In response, UN troops from Nepal, Pakistan, and South Africa, supported by Indian attack helicopters, engaged the FNI in a fierce firefight that left 50 to 60 militia members dead.[439]

The Security Council again strengthened MONUC's mandate to protect civilians in March 2005, providing specific authorization to engage in coercive tactics. It called for MONUC "to ensure the protection of civilians under imminent threat of physical violence, from any armed group, foreign or Congolese," and stressed that "MONUC may use cordon-and-search tactics to prevent attacks on civilians

---

[436] S/2004/650, *Third Special Secretary-General Report on MONUC.*

[437] S/Res/1565, October 2004.

[438] MONUC News Release, "MONUC interventions," MONUC, www.monuc.org/news.aspx?newsID=888, as of 15 April 2006.

[439] The FNI also reportedly used civilians as human shields. UN headquarters was concerned by the number of dead militia; DRC community leaders accused MONUC of reprisals for past attacks on UN personnel. IRIN, "DRC: UN Troops Killed 50 Militiamen in Self-Defence, Annan Says," 4 March 2005, www.irinnews.org/report.asp?ReportID=45923&SelectRegion=Great_Lakes; NGO security analyst of the DRC, interview with author, May 2006.

and disrupt the military capability of illegal armed groups that continue to use violence in those areas."[440]

MONUC's 3,700-strong Pakistani brigade in South Kivu, which included personnel with recent experience fighting insurgents along the Afghan-Pakistan border, engaged in active, coercive efforts to protect civilians. *Operation Safe Path*, for example, sought to ensure safe passage for civilians though the Kahuzi-Biega park. *Operation Lake Watch* attempted to provide security on Lake Kivu. *Operations Night Flash* and *Good Night* involved night patrols and radio communication to respond to militia attacks on villages in Walungu and urban centers.[441] *Operation Night Flash* was particularly novel. The mission organized village defense committees to alert peacekeepers of imminent attacks, reportedly through banging pots and blowing whistles.[442] A 50-troop strong Pakistani Rapid Reaction Force remained on high alert throughout the night in nearby Kanyola, ready to respond to disturbances with light personal weapons, mortars, night vision glasses, and available aerial cover.[443] The strategy allowed the Pakistanis to provide a security presence to the Walungu territory's 524 separate villages.

The Pakistanis also aggressively pursued the FDLR (*Forces Démocratiques de Libération du Rwanda*), Hutu rebels with links to the 1994 Rwandan genocide who operate in eastern Congo. Alongside Guatemalan Special Forces, the Pakistani peacekeepers delivered an ultimatum and then helicoptered to FDLR camps deep in the bush, dispersed the militia, and burned their camps.[444] One MONUC official counted the destruction of thirteen to sixteen such camps as of October 2005.[445] The Pakistani brigade commander, General Shujaat Ali Khan, appeared eager for more robust operations and willing to forcibly disarm the FDLR if the UN mandated such activity.[446] General Patrick Cammaert, MONUC Eastern Division commander, expressed similar views about using force against remaining militia groups: "The sooner we can engage them the

---

[440] S/Res/1592, 30 March 2005. One analyst argued that earlier mandates implicitly allowed for "cordon-and-search" operations, and that the new mandate's emphasis on this particular coercive tactic could actually inhibit use of other tactics. Former ICG analyst, interview with author, 28 May 2006.

[441] Yulu Kabamba and Tom Tshibangu, "Weekly Press Briefing of 18 January 2006," MONUC, 19 January 2006, www.monuc.org/news.aspx?newsID=9666.

[442] Keith Harmon Snow, *Operation Iron Fist: UN Troops Chase Down Child Soldiers in Congo's Forgotten War; Hutu Militias as Pawn in Great Game for Central Africa's Mineral Wealth*, Special to World War 4 Report, 1 August 2005, www.ww4report.com/node/848.

[443] James Traub, "The Congo Case," *The New York Times Magazine*, 3 July 2005; Joelle Sabella, "Operation Night Flash: Hope is Born Again in Kanyola," *MONUC News*, 15 April 2005.

[444] The ultimatum to the FDLR gave them sufficient warning to move their forces and equipment before the UN operations began. NGO security analyst in the DRC, interview with author, 27 May 2006.

[445] Traub, "The Congo Case."

[446] Ibid.

better."[447] Although MONUC decreased the FDLR's freedom of movement, the group remained in eastern Congo and was not successfully disarmed.

By early 2006, MONUC was focused on preparing for elections in the DRC, initially scheduled for June 2006 but postponed until the end of July. The EU agreed to deploy a 1,250-person force for four months to help maintain security during the elections, with troops primarily from France and Germany.[448]

ANALYSIS OF CIVILIAN PROTECTION

Analyzing MONUC's efforts to protect civilians requires understanding the nature of civilian vulnerability in the DRC. Of the nearly four million who have died there since 1998, most perished from preventable and treatable diseases hastened by the mass displacement of civilians fleeing militias. About two percent of these deaths resulted directly from violence.[449] Death rates from disease and malnutrition are significantly higher where militia groups are active, such as the Kivus. Where militias no longer operate and civilian displacement has abated, morality rates have declined roughly to their pre-war level.[450] Thus, insecurity is central to the cause of the crisis, even as disease and malnutrition claim more lives than direct violence. "The number one humanitarian problem is security," explained a senior MONUC official in 2005.[451]

Reducing this insecurity is no easy task, however. For peacekeepers, it is not simply a matter of demonstrating presence or patrolling a ceasefire line. Rebel groups in the DRC exhibit little of the predictable behavior associated with a concern for victory in a traditional sense. Instead, armed groups set up camp in civilian population centers and support themselves through pillage and extortion. Rather than fight a stronger group, they may flee, bringing violence, rape, looting, kidnappings, and death to another population center.

The multiple dimensions of civilian vulnerability in the DRC have led to a continuum of responses. Humanitarian groups have provided invaluable food, shelter, and health services to vulnerable civilian populations, alleviating

---

[447] Bryan Mealer, "U.N. Peacekeepers, Struggling to Pacify Congo, Turn to Warlike Methods," *Associated Press*, 17 June 2005.

[448] "Germany Says EU Force to Stay in DR Congo Till New Government in Place," Agence France Presse, 31 March 2006.

[449] International Rescue Committee, "The Lancet Publishes IRC Mortality Study from DR Congo."

[450] The IRC found, for example: "If the effects of insecurity and violence in Congo's eastern provinces were removed entirely, mortality would reduce to almost normal levels. Such was the case in Kisangani-Ville, where the arrival of peacekeepers helped quell fighting, allowing the IRC and its partners to rehabilitate basic health care, water and sanitation services. Crude mortality rates subsequently declined by 79 percent and excess mortality was eliminated." International Rescue Committee, "IRC Study Reveals 31,000 Die Monthly in Congo Conflict and 3.8 Million Died in Past Six Years. When Will the World Pay Attention?" IRC, 9 December 2004.

[451] MONUC official, interview with author, 27 October 2005.

immediate suffering and saving lives. UN civilian and police leaders have mediated political negotiations, promoted the rule of law, and worked to reduce government corruption. Peacekeeping forces have in turn provided presence, conducted patrols, supported disarmament and reintegration of former fighters, and used force against armed groups to compel disarmament and prevent attacks on civilians.

In an environment like the DRC, however, the use of coercive action requires a baseline of military capacity, a clear concept of the mission objectives, effective preparation, and a willingness among both mission and contingent leadership to use force. For many years, these requirements were missing from MONUC. By 2005, as it overcame these shortcomings, MONUC faced new complications brought on by its increased use of force. Thus, sufficient capacity, effective preparation, and a sound strategy alone are not a guarantee of success at protecting civilians in such environments, but are, rather, the basis for making it possible.

Baseline Capacity

From the start, the UN leadership had few illusions about MONUC's basic capabilities and its ability to protect civilians. Not only were there too few troops to offer comprehensive security in a large country like the DRC, the mission was hampered by slow deployments, inadequate funding, poor transportation, and insufficient supplies. Most mission forces came from developing states such as Uruguay, Tunisia, Senegal, Bolivia, Morocco, and Ghana. MONUC staff recognized that they lacked sufficient training, equipment, and preparation to challenge abusive and determined armed groups. SRSG Amos Namanga Ngongi, for example, cautioned that "full protection" was impossible. He urged a narrower view of what the operation could do:

> [C]learly it is understood that MONUC does not have the capacity to be able to ensure full protection of the civilian population in the DRC—that's not possible. But clearly MONUC has the responsibility and the mandate to be able to protect those whose lives are in imminent danger, especially in the areas in which MONUC is fully deployed, like Kisangani.... We can take dissuasive action, rather than proactive protection. We don't have the troops or the equipment for that. But that's no excuse for not coming to the rescue of people whose lives are in danger.[452]

Here, although Ngongi never elaborates on the meaning of "dissuasive action," he clearly envisions a reactive stance for MONUC rather than one of going after militias. Nevertheless, he suggests the peacekeeping force should act when "lives are in danger."

---

[452] Bernath and Edgerton, *MONUC*, 9.

In his June 2002 report to the Security Council, the Secretary-General echoed caution, even for the idea that MONUC could respond adequately to civilians at risk. He directly linked the expectations for the peacekeeping force to its capacity to intervene:

> MONUC troops currently deployed in the Democratic Republic of the Congo are not equipped, trained or configured to intervene rapidly to assist those in need of such protection. If MONUC is to take the steps necessary to enable it to protect more effectively civilians under imminent threat of physical violence, it will be necessary for the Security Council to consider adjusting the strength of MONUC with a view to reconfiguring and re-equipping contingents considerably to permit them to intervene more actively.[453]

A senior DPKO military officer took this analysis a step further, raising basic concern for the safety and protection of the UN force *itself*:

> The troop strength in MONUC is a drop in the bucket. You say 'Why not send troops with MILOBS (Military Observers) and security officers?' What if those troops are attacked? We can't get troops from Kinshasa or other places for hours or days. You can't send in troops without plans for helping them if they run into problems. That's basic military strategy. All they are trained or equipped or manned to do is protect their bases and equipment.[454]

Thus, without a baseline of sufficient and capable troops and firepower, MONUC was initially expected to be a mostly static mission, focused on defending and protecting itself and, at best, reacting when civilians came under threat, rather than preventing such threats in the first place. Not until 2003 and the Ituri brigade did this approach change, and even then, MONUC continued to struggle with what level of physical protection it could offer to civilians.

Willingness and Preparedness

In addition to limited operational capacity, MONUC troop contingents were not initially prepared to implement their civilian protection mandate. When DPKO asked the Uruguayan battalion (URABATT) to redeploy to Bunia in April 2003, for example, it specified only limited duties for the forces, such as guarding UN assets and personnel—without mention of civilian protection.[455] Further, those Uruguayan troops were trained primarily for guard duty, and few had seen combat. Lt. Col. Waldemar Fontes, the Uruguayan executive officer in 2003, was in the difficult position of leading troops who expected a benign environment into a conflict zone:

---

[453] UN Security Council, *Eleventh Report of the Secretary-General on the United Nations Organization Mission in the Democratic Republic of the Congo*, S/2002/621, 5 June 2002.
[454] Bernath and Edgerton, *MONUC*, 9-10.
[455] Peacekeeping Best Practices, *Operation Artemis*, 7.

The mission changed. We realized that this was not the task we had originally been sent for. If we knew this was going to happen, first, the personnel we would have sent would have been different. Second, the ammunition and the kind of weaponry would have been different. We would have brought more ammunition! We would have brought more offensive weapons, maybe grenades, rocket launchers, sniper guns—weapons more suited to launch offensive operations. The battalion that we had was dedicated to static operations, guarding fixed positions... [The troops] were not prepared psychologically for this because they came to Congo expecting to be on guard duty.[456]

Prior to the Ituri crisis, most UN troops were not equipped, trained, or organized effectively to intervene to protect civilians. MONUC contingents deployed with varying understandings of their role. Some believed they were only to protect the UN mission and the civilians in their immediate area. Others believed they would only conduct Chapter VI operations. These judgments reflected their interpretation of the UN mandate, their MOU and any national guidance provided. In some cases, as with Uruguay, national guidance contradicted UN expectations.[457]

The expectations of some MONUC contingents in Ituri contrasts with the preparedness of the IEMF to protect civilians. According to a UN study[458] and reports from former UN staff, the strengths of the IEMF included:

- The use of the airport in Entebbe, Uganda, only 40 minutes from Bunia, which allowed for the deployment of effective air assets and substantial operational support;
- The use of overflights to monitor the situation on the ground and intimidate would-be spoilers;
- The deployment of 150 French and 70 to 80 Swedish Special Forces to target and counter militia threats, even outside the force's area of operations;
- The use of mostly French speaking forces, which allowed for better communication in the mission, with the population and for collection of human intelligence;
- The use of satellites to monitor militia movements and intercept cellular phone communications;
- An emphasis on supplying information to the public, to promote positive local perceptions of the operation;
- Quality medical capacity, including a doctor in each IEMF company;[459] and
- Effective cooperation and information exchange with both UN forces and NGOs on the ground.[460]

---

[456] "Uruguayan Peacekeepers Faced Trouble in Bunia," *The Wall Street Journal*, 1 October 2003. If Uruguay had anticipated what happened in Bunia, it might not have sent troops in the first place.

[457] Former DPKO military planning official, interview with author, 21 May 2006.

[458] Peacekeeping Best Practices, *Operation Artemis.*

[459] Although medical capacity was intended primarily to support the force, some capacity was used, when appropriate, to address local needs. Former DPKO military planning official, interview with author, 21 May 2006.

The IEMF personnel's common language with the DRC population was helpful. "They could yell 'Stop, or I'll shoot!' and people could understand them," pointed out one MONUC official.[461] The attitude of the force was another factor. "They were very aggressive, and would shoot to kill.... The people in Bunia *did* feel that these people [the IEMF] were there to protect them. And if someone did something wrong, they'd be shot."[462]

Following the crisis in Ituri, DPKO began a concerted effort to better prepare MONUC forces, particularly those deploying to the east. One UN official reported that reviewing the mission mandate with a troop contributor prior to deployment improved its forces' effectiveness significantly. For example, MONUC flew three staff to Nepal to conduct pre-deployment training for Nepalese military officers shortly after the Ituri crisis. The UN trainers discussed both the broad situation on the ground—such as the large number of child soldiers and the use of rape as a weapon of war—and useful capacities for troops stationed there, such as supplies to deal with civilian medical emergencies. "The Nepalese said [the training] was very helpful," recalled one trainer. "They said it changed what they brought. They took more doctors, more medical supplies, and some more women."[463] DPKO reportedly conducted similar briefings during the expansion of MONUC from 2003 to 2005.[464] MONUC also conducted "induction courses" for all troops and civilian personnel shortly after they arrived in the DRC, with briefings on child protection, human rights, and the humanitarian situation, among other issues.[465]

Conceptual Clarity

Generating and preparing well-equipped troops is only part of the challenge, however. Decisions about strategy are also important. For example, the crisis in Ituri resulted from a clear strategic disconnect between the Security Council and MONUC: the Council pressured the Ugandan forces to withdraw from Ituri before sufficient peacekeepers had arrived to replace them. Moreover, the UN Secretariat had warned for years that foreign troop withdrawal would result in instability. As early as 2001, the Secretary-General had argued that "the UN should examine what it can do to help prepare for the situation, which may

---

[460] Peacekeeping Best Practices, *Operation Artemis*, 13-14.

[461] Former Chief, MONUC Humanitarian Affairs Section, interview with author, 1 February 2006.

[462] Ibid.

[463] Ibid.

[464] In October 2003, for example, two DPKO planners traveled to Morocco to brief its army leadership on the new MONUC operational concept so their forces could be reorganized and equipped for a Chapter VII operation in the eastern DRC. Former DPKO military planning official, interview with author, February 2005 and May 2006. The Nepalese experience fighting the insurgents at home is also cited as a basis for their relative effectiveness in the DRC. Former ICG analyst, interview with author, 27 May 2006.

[465] Former Chief, MONUC Humanitarian Affairs Section, interview with author, 1 February 2006.

develop in the DRC following the withdrawal of foreign forces, which are now responsible for the security of the civilian population under their control."[466] Likewise, he anticipated that the rising number of peacekeepers in the DRC could create public expectations for civilian protection.[467] The Secretary-General expressed concern in September 2002 that more forces might result in calls for "all concerned urgently to address the security situation."[468] Thus, even as the UN leadership anticipated the challenges in Ituri and recognized that MONUC would be expected to protect civilians, the Security Council failed to support a positive strategy to meet these challenges.

The crisis in Bukavu demonstrated a similar strategic disconnect. Unlike in Ituri, UN forces in Bukavu had firepower that might have allowed them to protect the city if ordered to do so. MONUC's response, however, appeared plagued by internal confusion and disagreement on basic strategy. A DPKO report found that MONUC Force Commanders in the eastern DRC correctly identified the mutinous forces as hostile to the transitional government and recommended that MONUC oppose them forcefully, but senior civilian leadership in Kinshasa and New York overruled these commanders.[469] The UN force in Bukavu had no back-up if the conflict grew beyond its control, some feared.[470] Once the crisis erupted, the chain of command appeared to break down at least once *within* MONUC as well, when Deputy Force Commander serving as Sector Commander General Jan Isberg ordered the Uruguayan contingent to protect the airport but the Uruguayans handed it over without a fight.[471]

Beginning in 2005, MONUC began to address this strategic deficit. The mission attempted to integrate the diverse international actors in the DRC around a joint concept of civilian protection—an "umbrella framework" for civilian protection relevant to *all* actors' activities. The impetus behind the effort probably began much earlier, albeit in an *ad hoc*, informal manner. After the Ituri crisis, MONUC's humanitarian affairs officers realized that they had an important role to play beyond observing and reporting on the catastrophe. With the arrival of 16,000 IDPs at its doorstep in Bunia, "MONUC had to start protecting civilians;

---

[466] UN Security Council, *Seventh report of the Secretary-General on MONUC*, S/2001/373, 17 April 2001, para. 118.

[467] UN Security Council, *Eleventh report of the Secretary-General on MONUC*, S/2002/621, 5 June 2002, para. 71.

[468] UN Security Council, *Special Report of the Secretary-General*, S/2002/1005, para. 61, as cited in Peacekeeping Best Practices, *Operation Artemis*, 5, 8.

[469] Peacekeeping Best Practices Unit, *MONUC and the Bukavu Crisis 2004*, Best Practices Unit, DPKO, on file with authors, March 2005; NGO security analyst in the DRC, interview with author, 27 May 2006.

[470] Former DPKO military planning official, interview with author, May 2006.

[471] International Crisis Group, *The Congo's Transition Is Failing: Crisis in the Kivus*, Africa Report No. 91 (ICG, 30 March 2005), 24.

they had no choice," argued one MONUC humanitarian official.[472] Humanitarian officers began to act as conduits between military and humanitarian actors on the ground, and to promote cooperation towards the overarching goal of "protection." MONUC began to serve as an important "force multiplier" for relief organizations with limited resources, linking the mission components. One former MONUC official gave an example: "Let's say Oxfam has $100,000 to feed and shelter civilians in Sector A. You [MONUC] have a plane. Now you can get Oxfam there and they can do more. To me, that's protection. That's protecting the humanitarian environment."[473] According to this officer, MONUC embraced new tasks to protect civilians and expand humanitarian space, by "initiating" humanitarian access (rather than just accepting it), "challenging military contingents to take on their responsibilities, conducting joint assessments, providing military protection to humanitarian convoys, physically taking civilians out of danger, demining, and establishing field hospitals."[474]

Building off of these efforts, MONUC worked with UN agencies, NGOs, and MONUC military, police, and civilian sections in "joint protection working groups" at key flashpoints in the DRC (such as North and South Kivu, Ituri, Katanga, Kindu and Kinshasa) during 2005.[475] The first joint protection working group was established in North Kivu to address civilian protection in the Masisi territory. It took a straightforward approach: first, assessing the major threats to civilian physical security; second, determining strategies for addressing these threats; and, third, implementing these strategies. The North Kivu working group identified twenty-six major types of threats to civilians—including rape, violence in IDP camps, killings, executions, and disappearances—and determined a variety of strategies to address them, such as eliminating impunity among FARDC forces through judicial reform and improving MONUC's deterrent military presence.

According to MONUC Deputy SRSG Ross Mountain, the working groups were designed so all actors would realize the larger purpose of their activities, see how these activities fit within the mission goal to protect civilians, and divide

---

[472] Former Chief, MONUC Humanitarian Affairs Section, interview with author, 27 November 2005.
[473] Ibid.
[474] Ibid.
[475] Mark Cutts and Ann-Marie Linde, "Mission to the DRC," InterAgency Internal Displacement Division (IDD), 12-20 May 2005, www.reliefweb.int/idp/docs/reports/2005/DRC%20mission%20report%2012-20%20May%202005.pdf.

tasks effectively based on organizational *competencies*.[476] By early 2006, MONUC's protection framework was still developing and few details were sufficiently public to assess its effectiveness. The general principles included:

- A focus on *physical* violence against civilians;
- A comprehensive approach based on mutual cooperation and involving all the major international actors on the ground, including both legal/political and field-based actors;
- A recognition of the need for a division of labor in the field among military and humanitarian actors, to preserve humanitarian space;
- Effective coordination and exchange of information between military and humanitarian actors, where appropriate;
- More proactive efforts to *compel* the provision of humanitarian space where it cannot be secured by negotiation alone, through the threat and/or use of military force.[477]

Along with its joint protection framework, MONUC developed a more active military strategy to protect civilians, including "field protection activities" to be conducted by military, human rights, and humanitarian actors. Military protection activities include removal of threats against civilians by "a cordon-and-search operation and/or disarmament of individuals threatening civilian population;" the establishment of "buffer zones between combatants" and safe areas "with adequate military protection;" utilization of an "area domination" strategy through frequent patrols, overflights, and "mobile temporary operations bases;" escorting humanitarian and human rights actors to areas; and evacuating populations out of danger zones.[478]

Rather than defend a limited group of civilians at a particular site—an IDP camp or a UN base—some MONUC contingents began to attempt to protect civilians from violence within broad geographic areas under their control.[479] MONUC now is trying to provide wider security for dispersed civilian populations, in contrast to earlier efforts to protect only those civilians who fled directly into its care. Even after a Bangladeshi contingent was ambushed by armed groups in Ituri in February 2005, the Security Council applauded the more forward-leaning peacekeeping approach, commending "the dedication of MONUC's personnel, who operate in particularly hazardous conditions. [The Council] welcomes the action of MONUC against the militia groups responsible for these

---

[476] Mountain, also the MONUC Resident Coordinator and Humanitarian Coordinator, has played a leadership role in the integrated approach to protecting civilians across military and humanitarian sectors.

[477] MONUC official, interview with author, 30 January 2006.

[478] MONUC, internal documents, August 2005.

[479] MONUC official, interview with author, 27 October 2005.

killings and MONUC's continued robust action in pursuit of its mandate."[480] Yet for many MONUC contingents, coercive protection is not a primary focus.[481]

Challenges of Coercive Protection

Not all observers approve of MONUC's increased use of force. The medical relief group, Médecins sans Frontières, argued that even with MONUC's cordon-and-search activities to disarm militia groups, there was "nothing new in Ituri" as of August 2005. MSF found no general decrease in the number of its consultations for sexual violence from June 2003 to June 2005.[482] Armed groups still preyed on civilians nearly everywhere in Ituri except Bunia; humanitarian access outside of Bunia was almost nonexistent; and MSF withdrew from Bunia following the kidnapping of two of its employees in June 2005.[483]

Similarly, one former MONUC humanitarian official argued that the mission's forceful disarming of combatants in the eastern DRC contradicts its mandate to protect civilians and facilitate humanitarian access. MONUC's tactics have led to reprisal killings against civilians—a Congolese militia claimed that it conducted three civilian massacres in retaliation for MONUC actions.[484] MONUC efforts to root out militia and push them farther into the bush can result in increased population displacement as militia destabilize new areas. Further, by using force against particular groups, MONUC may find that aid organizations reduce their cooperation if they fear they will lose access to vulnerable populations and endanger the safety of their unarmed workers. When MONUC uses the same vehicles to transport soldiers as it does IDPs, or torches FDLR camps deep in the Congolese forest, these actions may have a direct, negative impact on local perceptions and humanitarian access. In such cases, assistance groups may limit their cooperation with the mission, information-sharing, and use of MONUC transport.[485]

MONUC efforts to work with the FARDC are similarly fraught. By 2005, various MONUC officials emphasized, the most serious threats to civilians came from the integrated FARDC, which suffers from poor discipline and

---

[480] UN Security Council, *Statement by the President of the Security Council*, S/PRST/2005/10, 2 March 2005. Nine Bangladeshi peacekeepers were killed during the incident.

[481] The Pakistanis are reportedly the only contingent aggressively attempting to expand the geographic area under their control.

[482] Médecins sans Frontières, *Nothing New in Ituri*, 9.

[483] Ibid., 3.

[484] MONUC official, interview with author, 27 October 2005.

[485] Views offered by former MONUC humanitarian official, interview with author, 27 November 2005.

oversight.[486] The same fighters who preyed on civilians as militia now behave similarly as "official" soldiers in the new Congolese military. Thus, civilian protection issues in the DRC are directly linked to those of good governance, public finance, and security sector reform. One way to reduce atrocities against civilians may be to ensure that military salaries are paid, so that the FARDC soldiers refrain from brutal methods of extortion.[487] The UN has attempted to address FARDC abuses by providing training to select FARDC commanders on humanitarian principles and the protection of civilians. In May 2006, UN agencies led training for forty-five FARDC officers in Bunia on international legal norms, addressing issues including children in conflict and the role of armed forces in protecting women and children from sexual violence.[488]

CONCLUSION AND LESSONS LEARNED

This case demonstrates the dilemmas for UN-led forces tasked to protect civilians without having all the tools to do it. The experience of MONUC and *Operation Artemis* also highlights the impact of concepts of operation, capacity, mandates and ROE, doctrine, and training on peace operations directed to protect civilians. MONUC's experience further identifies standard questions for future military missions: the definitions of vicinity and capacity, the integration of actors, clarity on the use of force and the role of peacekeepers in providing broad security in lieu of a state's responsibility—and the operational concept of protection. Given the continuing trend to direct military forces to protect civilians, these key areas deserve further consideration.

First, UN missions with a mandate "to protect civilians under imminent threat" require a *baseline capacity*, coupled with the authority and expectation that peacekeepers will act. Without these parameters, most UN forces will find that mandates to protect civilians lie outside their capacity—undermining the meaning of the mandate. Capacity is especially important where conflict continues and where parties to a peace agreement provide only partial consent to a UN or multinational peacekeeping force. In general, well-armed and experienced troops in sufficient numbers *may* be able to provide security for vulnerable populations in a challenging region; poorly trained troops in insufficient numbers with limited supplies are unlikely to provide more than presence—if that. Quality information and a clear chain of command are also essential, as the tragic events in Ituri and Bukavu demonstrate.

---

[486] "U.N., groups push for report on alleged massacre," *Associated Press*, 2 February 2006.
[487] MONUC official, interview with author, 27 November 2005.
[488] UN Department of Public Information/OCHA, "FARDC Commanders Receive Training in Humanitarian Principles," MONUC, 17 May 2006, www.monuc.org/News.aspx?newsId=11075.

Second, for multinational missions such as MONUC and *Operation Artemis*, political and military leaders need to provide *conceptual clarity* about how the operation should approach protecting civilians. Ideally, this strategy should be consistently understood throughout the leadership of the mission, by the troop contingents, and within the Security Council. After struggling for years, MONUC had a clearer concept by 2005. The mission operated more in accordance with its Chapter VII mandate. Peacekeepers conducted cordon-and-search operations and worked with local populations to identify spoilers to the peace. MONUC leadership began to use the goal of protection as an organizing tool to integrate civilian and military roles. A new mission strategy attempted to address civilian vulnerability across the board, from human rights monitoring and reporting, to the provision of humanitarian space, to coercive physical protection. No single concept defined the mission's civilian protection efforts; rather, the mission embraced multiple ideas and strategies.

Third, MONUC's experience demonstrates the need for *well prepared* and *willing peacekeepers*. Guidance to forces about their role in providing protection to civilians is best given at the start, through pre-deployment training and in-country or on-the-ground mission briefings. Contributing countries would benefit from having doctrine for such missions. At the least, TCCs should understand that their troops may be asked to use force, especially if deployed with a civilian protection mandate to volatile regions. Likewise, countries offering contingents for Chapter VII missions need to be clear about how national constraints on their personnel could contradict the mission's tasks and goals.

Fourth, missions authorized with robust civilian protection mandates need to understand the level of force to be used to achieve their goals, and whether they are *coercive protection* operations. As demonstrated in the DRC, mission leaders must navigate tough, inevitable choices about protecting civilians in hostile environments. The strategy of protection should be based on an understanding of the causes of civilian insecurity and the best remedy for the environment. Traditional strategies of supporting humanitarian space and conducting peacekeeping tasks can fall far short of protecting civilians, such as in the DRC where irregular armed groups have operated with impunity. Protecting civilians may require blocking the capacity of armed groups to wreak violence, and potentially using military force to defeat or disarm them. Such actions risk a counterinsurgency-like response if the armed groups refuse to stand down. A well-led UN force could undertake that approach, if UN Members States were willing to provide the capacity and personnel prepared for the environment.

Finally, as recognized in UN mandates, the role of peace operations in providing protection is always balanced by its relationship with the sovereign country in which they operate. In most UN operations, that government maintains primary responsibility for the welfare of its people. When a state is on the verge of failure or recovering from a conflict, like the DRC, the division between its responsibilities and those of a UN peace operation are blurred. The UN must continuously balance between taking responsibility for protecting the Congolese populace, offering support to the political process, and cooperating with the government.

Operating in that gray area between traditional peacekeeping and an intervention force suggested by *The Responsibility to Protect* is the central problem in protecting civilians, however. Protection is just one of many goals for the UN mission in the DRC, where the line between peacekeeping and peacemaking is not clear.

As long as forces are sent to protect civilians, they will require leadership to offer a strategy for protection. The innovative continuum approach to civilian protection in the DRC is a start at recognizing how differing concepts of protection can work together effectively. But that approach is not a substitute for a strategy for military forces and for preparing troops with their own concepts, doctrine, training and leadership for these kinds of operations. The Security Council and nations that support peacekeeping missions are on notice that such missions are in urgent need of conceptual clarity and better tools to prepare and support those sent to strengthen peace. MONUC's experience in the DRC shows that these issues need to be addressed both there and for any future peacekeeping mission or intervention force directed to offer protection.

— 9 —
CONCLUSION:
FILLING GAPS, LOOKING FORWARD

...[S]overeign states have a responsibility to protect their own citizens from avoidable catastrophe...when they are unwilling or unable to do so, that responsibility must be borne by the broader community of states.[489]

Ambitions to protect citizens from mass violence and genocide are energizing international debate over state sovereignty and its responsibilities. When nations fail to provide safety to their population on a large-scale, then the international community weighs when and how to step in. As urged by *The Responsibility to Protect*, there is a growing call to embrace responsible sovereignty and to intervene when lives are on the line. Indeed, nations dramatically endorsed the basic concept of a "responsibility to protect" at the UN World Summit in 2005.

The idea of protection has developed from a long history of concern for civilians caught in conflict. Emerging from the failures to stop genocide and mass killing in the 1990s, the international community debated the merits and risks of military interventions and focused on improving peace operations and humanitarian efforts. UN Secretary-General Kofi Annan challenged critics of "humanitarian intervention" to square international respect for state sovereignty with the desire to prevent a future Rwanda or Srebrenica. In 2000, the *Brahimi Report* argued for clearer guidance and adequate resources for peace operations, but warned of a "potentially large mismatch between desired objective and resources available" for peacekeepers to extend protection to civilians.[490] The ICISS panel took the question further, offering *The Responsibility to Protect*, a challenge to an uncertain world soon after September 11, 2001.

Debates about humanitarian action and military intervention are still in the news, as third parties deploy to foreign soil in efforts to secure peace and, increasingly, to protect civilians. From Afghanistan to Haiti, from the Democratic Republic of Congo to Timor-Leste, from Kosovo to Burundi, large numbers of forces serve

---

[489] ICISS, *The Responsibility to Protect*, viii.
[490] A/55/305-S/2000/809, 21 August 2000, 11.

worldwide in peace and stability operations under varied flags. Over 70,000 uniformed personnel are deployed in UN missions alone, and the growing participation of troops in operations led by NATO, the European Union, the African Union, and ECOWAS further swell the ranks of peacekeepers.

Lively discussions of a "responsibility to protect" and of various protection strategies bode well for closing the protection gap recognized in the 1990s. The 2006 US National Security Strategy, for example, declares that "(w)here perpetrators of mass killing defy all attempts at peaceful intervention, armed interventions may be required."[491] Headlines call for militaries to help protect vulnerable populations in post-conflict environments or to intercede in ongoing violence. This attention offers evidence that a new norm may move from the realm of dialogue to one with practical applications for modern forces.

WHY IT MATTERS

Interpretations of the "responsibility to protect" can spiral off in innumerable directions. Debates over civilian protection have proliferated, framing discussions of the role of international organizations, of their capacity to lead operations, and of specific missions such as AMIS in Darfur and *Operation Artemis* in the DRC. Reducing civilian vulnerability has also animated a broad "protection" agenda within humanitarian organizations and agencies, marshalling resources and driving new strategies ranging from conflict prevention to addressing the "inner emotional life" of a refugee, for example. UN reports and resolutions have further declared concern for the protection of civilians. NGOs frame policy recommendations around meeting the "responsibility to protect" and urge it as a rationale for multiple strategies to reduce vulnerability for civilians in conflicts.

There are two main hazards with so many approaches to protection. First, as more actions are cast as supporting the "responsibility to protect," its meaning is diluted. This broad base may increase the overall capacity to reduce threats to civilians, but weaken focus on the ICISS argument for intervention in the face of the worst violence: mass killing, genocide, and ethnic cleansing. The powerful argument of the report is that nations *must act* when extreme violence endangers civilian populations. That kind of intervention is rarely offered and is likely to require advance thinking and planning.

Second, debates over a "responsibility to protect" norm may distract the international community from addressing the practical, immediate challenges within current operations. Certainly the world's governments have fallen short

---

[491] *The National Security Strategy of the United States of America*, March 2006, 16-17.

of fully endorsing a "responsibility to protect" and adopting criteria for the Security Council to trigger an intervention. Nations have merely acknowledged it as grounds for responding to mass violence. But at one level the basic argument about whether to send forces to protect civilians is over; troops have already been sent, and sent in large numbers, under mandates to "protect civilians under imminent threat." While debates over sovereignty and responsibility continue in capitals around the world, more than 55,000 troops serve in six UN-led operations in volatile environs, with mandates to protect civilians, but without guarantee of the capacity to meet that mandate.

Since 1999, missions led by the UN, the EU, the AU, and ECOWAS have been directly charged to "protect civilians." The Security Council has made this directive a regular feature of Chapter VII mandates for operations, and in April 2006, the Council again reaffirmed the role of peacekeepers to ensure aspects of civilian protection and its inclusion in UN mandates. The requirement is likely to continue as the UN deploys troops at unprecedented levels and plans for new missions. NATO, the EU, the AU and ECOWAS have expanded their ability to organize and lead missions, primarily as peace support operations, and have some capacity to intervene in cases of mass violence and genocide. While not sent to halt genocide, peace operations approach the idea at the heart of the ICISS report: using armed personnel to protect civilians from violence.

What, then, does it mean for militaries assigned such a role? The protection of civilians is an implicit job of peacekeeping forces, but it has not been the traditional goal of peace operations. While balancing the broader political goals of the mission, peacekeepers have tried various strategies and tactics of protection: patrolling, escorting humanitarian supplies, supporting the disarmament and demobilization of local fighters, responding to violent militias, working with government forces, and trying to provide broad security. They also offer support to elections, to establish the rule of law, and to build local and national government capacity to provide its population with security. In the DRC, for example, peacekeepers have tried to strengthen peace in a region where millions have perished. The large UN force of 18,000 includes some highly skilled contingents with combat experience operating in regions such as Ituri, where violence is especially high. The mission is using force to protect civilians under imminent threat, with a stance more aggressive than other UN missions with similar mandates.

But operations such as MONUC are not authorized, designed or equipped as humanitarian or military interventions. They operate in a gray zone between more traditional peacekeeping missions and military interventions, navigating questions of sovereignty, consent, impartiality, and mission goals. Many face situations that are hazardous for peacekeepers and civilians alike. Missions are challenged to protect civilians in difficult environments where a state's capacity may be severely limited, but where the mission must respect its sovereignty. Two issues arise: first, who is responsible for protection, and second, who can provide it? The peacekeeping force is neither fully responsible nor fully capable; neither is the state. Navigating partial responsibility, with limited means, can lead to unclear goals for peace operations and their military forces. The offer of protection is undercut by the inability of outside forces to deliver it.

In the future, militaries may be asked to conduct operations for which protection *is* the central aim. With the growing argument that military forces should play a leading role in providing physical security for civilian populations threatened by genocide and ethnic cleansing, the unaddressed operational aspects of such missions take on increased, urgent importance. Thousands of military personnel already work in environments where civilians are at great risk or could be. These uniformed personnel too often operate without sufficient capacity, clear guidance and doctrine, adequate training and leadership, and a concept of their mission to uphold their mandates to "protect civilians." They and the international community are not well-served by this stance. Neither is the local population that hopes to find security with the deployment of such personnel.

TRANSLATING IDEAS INTO CAPACITY

This study began as an investigation of preparedness for operations to protect civilians from mass violence and genocide. Surprisingly, there was little information about preparation for military interventions to protect civilians—or for addressing protection as a role for armed forces serving in peace and stability operations. This study considered the many concepts of protection, the role of military forces, and the primary tools used to prepare personnel for missions that might address civilian protection.

Competing Concepts

Fundamentally, every mission needs an approach to protecting civilians, whether for a UN-led peace operation or for a military intervention force authorized to halt a genocide. It is not sufficient to deploy forces and hope they figure out an effective protection strategy once they arrive. The concept should support both a strategic framework for the mission and tactical guidance to troops on the ground.

There are multiple, contradictory concepts of what the protection of civilians means for modern operations, reflecting the divergent views of military and civilian leaders, NGOs, and international organizations. Even experienced military officers and humanitarian leaders can be confused. It is no surprise then that mandates from the Security Council do not translate easily into operational terms. Six concepts of protection with implications for a military role stand out:

- Protecting civilians can be conceived of as a *legal obligation* of military actors to abide by international humanitarian and human rights law during the conduct of war.
- Protection may be seen as the natural outcome of *traditional warfighting* through the defeat of a defined enemy.
- Protection may be viewed as a job for humanitarian organizations aided through the provision of broad security and *"humanitarian space"* by military forces.
- Protection may be considered the result of the *operational design* of assistance by relief agencies to reduce the vulnerability of civilians to physical risk.
- Protection may be viewed as a *set of tasks* for those deployed in complex peace operations or other interventions, potentially involving the use of force to deter or respond to belligerent attacks on vulnerable populations.
- Protection may be the *primary mission goal*, where the operation is designed specifically to halt mass killing in the immediate term, as stipulated in *The Responsibility to Protect*.

Military actors are familiar with some of these concepts of protection, such as their obligations under international law and the Geneva Conventions. Most forces recognize security as the result of defeating an enemy, a longer-term means of providing protection. Those experienced in stability and peace operations understand the concept of humanitarian space and their role in supporting assistance strategies. Common tasks such as patrolling are well known roles that help reduce civilian insecurity, for example. Within a mission, military contingents can also balance these varied concepts of protection.

In general, however, the ideas originating in the humanitarian community about protection do not transfer automatically to military operations. "Civilian protection" and "protection" are not terms widely used in military publications. Operationally, military and civilian leaders may face a proliferation of approaches to protection but lack a common language to discuss them. These communities employ different means to achieve their goals and have different understandings of what protection means. Clarifying the divergent approaches, how they fit together, and when each is appropriate could improve peace operations.

NATO, the EU, the AU, and ECOWAS are the organizations most likely to intervene militarily on behalf of civilians. None has an institutional concept of civilian protection for their military missions, however. Reflecting its civilian leadership and humanitarian orientation, the UN has focused more on non-coercive forms of protection—legal, humanitarian, and political—than on military roles or the use of force to offer protection. The United Nations has developed an umbrella approach, giving room to varied concepts of civilian protection across agencies and within operations. Despite UN mandates, recognition of the role for UN peacekeepers has been slower. The Secretary-General and the Security Council have nonetheless made more explicit reference to their roles within the last year.

To plan and lead a mission, however, military and civilian leaders need a clear concept of operation, identifiable goals, a desired end-state and a realistic means to get there. These needs raise an important distinction between military missions designed to halt mass killing and military roles in peace operations with civilian protection mandates. The former type of mission crosses the sovereignty threshold identified by *The Responsibility to Protect*, where a desire for consent, impartiality, and limited use of force take a back seat to the immediate goal of saving lives. Unlikely to be led by the United Nations, such a military intervention may look very little like peacekeeping, and more like combat.

In more stable environments with less, or localized violence against civilians, a peace operation with protection as a mandated task might be appropriate. This type of peace operation has numerous incarnations, including UN operations authorized under Chapter VII as well as the AU mission in Darfur. Peace operations are not primarily designed to protect civilians, however; they aim to provide security and promote long-term stability through support to local governance capacity. Most can intervene in specific instances if civilians become threatened, but the focus is on carrying out their tasks in support of peacebuilding, humanitarian assistance, and the rule of law.

Efforts to "operationalize" the "responsibility to protect" should therefore address both types of missions: full-scale "responsibility to protect" military interventions and peace operations with protection mandates. A different name is needed for missions that deploy in hostile environments with a willingness to use force to save civilians who are threatened by large-scale violence. When civilians face immediate physical threats, the decision to use force for their protection may shift the operation to a *coercive protection* mission.

Moving to Coercive Protection

"Coercive protection" tries to capture the strategy of using or threatening to use force to protect civilians. Such missions can be consistent with a UN Chapter VII mandate, but can come close to the approach of a military intervention, testing the principles of traditional peacekeeping. In circumstances of large-scale violence or genocide, modifying a peace operation is inadequate for upholding protection mandates. In those situations, forces need to have a clear goal of protecting civilians, with that objective driving their strategy and tactics. Full-scale interventions to protect civilians are likely to occur only in extreme cases and only for a limited time. They could involve significant force and war-like tactics to eliminate the capacity of the killers or to halt violence quickly. Yet such interventions are not traditional warfighting operations, since the goal is not to defeat a designated enemy—although that may be a strategy—but to stop violence against a civilian population.

Clarifying the mission goal is therefore crucial. Most military thinkers and planners insist on defining a military mission first, and then the strategy, tactics, and procedures to accomplish it. By identifying protection of civilians as the operation's goal, military leaders will draft a strategy to achieve it, just like any other mission assigned to them. As military personnel serve worldwide in peace and stability operations with mandates to protect civilians, they too require guidance and preparation for their role in providing physical protection for civilians, and, if needed, to intervene forcefully to save lives. Issues involve the right level of force, of consent and of potential escalation; whether to take action or to react; to whom and where to offer protection; and how to transition to a follow-on peace operation. Such questions should be considered prior to deployments to help prepare those leading and participating in the mission.

Willing Actors and Operational Capacities

So who can act? The UN, NATO, the EU, the African Union, and ECOWAS have the most capacity to mount interventions under their own authority. While none has explicitly endorsed the concept of a "responsibility to protect" as a basis for its actions, each organization could intervene to halt mass killings, genocide, or ethnic cleansing. Each can also launch peace operations where protection is a task or the goal of its mission. Indeed, except for NATO, each organization has *already* deployed forces under mandates explicitly to protect civilians, with the standard caveats. These organizations can also authorize coalitions of the willing, which offer another avenue for organizing and leading operations to intervene on behalf of civilians.

These organizations are developing more operational capacities. NATO has the most robust military force and is working on the NATO Response Force, which will boast 25,000 troops rapidly available for deployment. The European Union is developing its rapid reaction force and its new Battlegroups model; the African Union is establishing the African Standby Force and working with African subregional organizations; and ECOWAS is organizing its own regional standby force.

The baseline capacity required to stop mass violence against civilians, however, is not clear. Missions always benefit from trained, equipped, and capable military forces with strong leadership. Few studies offer specific, detailed designs for an intervention force to protect civilians in conflict. Without agreement on precise components for such missions, it is best to judge these groups as somewhat capable, depending on the requirements of a particular operation.

It is still wise to heed the warning of the *Brahimi Report*: "If an operation is given a mandate to protect civilians, therefore, it also must be given the specific resources needed to carry out that mandate."[492] Peace operations that include civilian protection and enforcement activities, for example, require sufficient equipment and support to conduct civilian protection within the frameworks of their missions—and help prevent break-out of larger-scale killing. UN operations can lack such robust capacity. The AU has led two peace operations and ECOWAS has deployed multiple times in West Africa, but neither organization has the headquarters support and operational capacity of NATO or Western militaries, or the United Nations. Most missions led by the EU itself tend not to involve robust forces and Chapter VII authorization. Thus, the organizations most likely to deploy with a mandate to protect civilians are either not designed to lead military interventions (i.e., the UN), or are not yet prepared to organize and manage complex peace operations (i.e., the AU and ECOWAS).

Pushing for protection mandates regardless of capacity could have perverse effects. If forces cannot implement them, they will erode the credibility of peacekeeping as an enterprise. They may also raise civilians' hopes and alter their behavior, leaving them vulnerable to attacks from which the UN and other organizations cannot or will not protect them. This has been seen not only in Rwanda and in the former Yugoslavia, but also in the DRC, where active MONUC patrolling gave the appearance of security but did not materialize into coercive protection in Bukavu and elsewhere until 2005. Thus, if capacity and coordination are not forthcoming, the Security Council and leading nations should at least be candid about matching expectations with mandates.

Mandates and Rules of Engagement

Political and military leaders use mandates and ROE to guide their choices about the design of an operation, its level of force, and instruction to personnel about their role. For UN-authorized interventions, the mission's mandate and ROE are derived from Security Council resolutions, but there is little evidence that either the Secretary-General or the Security Council establishes the operational

---

[492] *Report of the Panel on United Nations Peace Operations*, A/55/305, S/2000/809, para. 63.

meaning of language such as "protect civilians under imminent threat." In turn, the political leadership for a new mission or intervention is unlikely to have direct guidance about what is expected in terms of protecting civilians. Thus, moving from the Council's call for protection to an understanding of how individual peacekeepers should provide protection is not a clear path.

Since its first such mandate for UNAMSIL, the Security Council has strengthened Chapter VII mandates and ROE to be more explicit in allowing and directing peacekeepers to protect civilians. Earlier operations had been authorized to promote a "secure and stable environment," to protect personnel associated with the UN or UN-authorized missions, or to establish "humanitarian areas" or "safe areas." These mandates usually cast the use of force as a response to attacks; peacekeepers did not expect to use force robustly, and the Council did little to push them. With the adoption of "protect civilians" language for nearly a dozen missions, a new standard is being set. In addition to UN operations, similar direction is in mandates for those led by regional organizations and coalitions, including AMIS, the ECOWAS intervention in Côte d'Ivoire, the French-led force in Côte d'Ivoire, and the EU-authorized *Operation Artemis* in the DRC.

Mandates and ROE allow, but do not require, that personnel take certain actions. UN mandates have reoccurring caveats: that forces should protect civilians "without prejudice to the responsibilities" of the host government and to do so "within capabilities" and "within area of deployment" of the authorized force. These conditions offer plenty of room for interpretation by mission leaders, planners, troop contingents, and the nations that send the forces for each mission, allowing for divergent views and implementation. The doctrine and the training of forces also impact how they understand their role and their ROE.

For example, critics of the AU in Darfur called for a strengthened AMIS mandate to protect civilians. The mandate was clarified in 2006 to take all necessary steps "to ensure a more forceful protection of the civilian population" and no longer referred to the Government of Sudan as responsible for the protection of civilians.[493] Yet AMIS still lacked capacity, mobility, leadership, and a desire to take a more active stance. As a result, attacks against civilians continued. The letter of the mandate may be less important than its interpretation by mission leaders and instructions given to the peacekeepers on the ground. When missions with protection mandates do use force they also face criticism, as seen in Haiti and the DRC. UN operations in those countries have been accused both of being too passive in protecting civilians and of using too much force and endangering citizens.

---

[493] AU Peace and Security Council, Communiqué of the 46th Ordinary Session, 10 March 2006.

The willingness to use force is a question for every level of a mission. Within UN-led operations, this starts with the authorizing body (i.e., the United Nations) and runs through the political leadership to the force commander, to the leaders of individual sectors and troop contingents, and finally, to those in the field. Troop contingents from various nations can certainly interpret the same mandate and ROE differently. For missions not led by the UN, NATO, or nations with advanced militaries, mission-wide rules of engagement for forces may not exist. Willingness is further affected by the actors' perception of the risks and level of force protection; the ability to do other tasks as part of the mission; the training and operational capacity of troop contingents; and the direction of the military leadership. Lacking a common understanding of the purpose and ROE of a mission is, unfortunately, familiar territory.

Especially in operations where consent is partial, the mission needs a clear concept of civilian protection and use of force. More than one officer pointed out the need to project the idea that the mission is going to "do something." Without common doctrine for UN missions, the translation of Council mandates into ROE varies widely, especially for missions with Chapter VII authority where force is directly used to compel compliance or protect individuals. The issues with mandate and ROE interpretation can be addressed by military doctrine and training for missions, which help clarify for leadership and for personnel how the mission concept translates on the ground.

Doctrine and Training

Doctrine and training prepare forces for operations. Militaries use doctrine to help translate concepts into action and to support missions at the strategic, operational and tactical levels. Policy decisions, however, always shape how doctrine is applied.

Most civilian-led multinational organizations, however, do not have formal doctrine. Although resolutions began to call for peace operations to "protect civilians" more than six years ago, the UN is just starting to prepare guidance on this directive. For the first time, the UN is developing doctrine for peace operations, which should assist troop contributing countries and mission leaders. The EU, AU, and ECOWAS also lack formal doctrine and are moving to write it for their missions. Only NATO has well-established doctrine for its operations.

The United Kingdom and Canada identify the protection of civilians as a potential goal of a military operation, as suggested by *The Responsibility to Protect*, but offer no specific operational guidance to that end. Other countries with extensive peace support operations doctrine, such as the United States, France and the Netherlands, make no direct reference to this concept as a mission goal, except in the context of other operations, such as for non-combatant evacuations. These nations make important distinctions in their approach to peace support operations about Chapter VII, the role of forces in working with civilian populations, and in strategies for civilians at risk. But their doctrine offers less guidance for operations directed to support physical protection to civilians.

Most peace operations doctrine approaches the protection question cautiously and without identifying specific tactics for stopping *génocidaires*. There are good reasons for this, as the fundamental principles of such missions run counter to robust, coercive civilian protection. Peace support operations are expected to be impartial; to use force to uphold their mandate, but not to defeat a party to a conflict, regardless of its abhorrent behavior. They focus on managing consent and providing support to a political agreement, not taking sides. In general, nations with doctrine specifically for peace support operations treat the protection of civilians as an obligation of forces under international humanitarian law, as support to the rule of law and humanitarian efforts, and more broadly as part of civil-military relations. Where doctrine addresses how peace support operations should consider the use of force, there is little that discusses the use of coercive action to protect a civilian population.

This doctrinal gap arises partly from the lack of a common terminology to identify missions and tasks "triggered" by a mandate to protect civilians. There are certainly areas within existing doctrine that apply to such roles, as seen in doctrine for counterinsurgency, peace support, peace enforcement, peacekeeping, operations other than war, humanitarian assistance, non-combatant evacuation, small wars, military policing, and civil-military cooperation. These doctrine encompass traditional military and humanitarian concepts of protection: as an obligation of warfighting, as observance of international humanitarian and human rights law, and as support to the provision of humanitarian space. Some peace operations doctrine also provides limited lists of military tasks for protecting civilians. There are a few areas where doctrine identifies coercive tactics to protect civilians, but they are not categorized as such. Thus, there is basic preparation for peace operations involving the use of force and for combat missions with tasks applicable to protecting civilians. But arriving at more active types of civilian protection through peace support operations doctrine will require a shift in traditional interpretations of mandates and an exercise in leadership not often found in peace operations.

Almost no doctrine, however, addresses the concept of civilian protection as the *goal* of a military mission. Skilled militaries could conduct operations mandated to protect civilians—and get much of it right—even without explicit doctrine on coercive protection tasks. If a mission is clear about what to accomplish on the ground, a force can figure out a strategy and course of action, provided that troops are sufficiently well-trained and equipped, and that the mission has effective command and control arrangements. Yet the lack of doctrine means that there is less preparation for the mission and its tasks, which can reduce the effectiveness of the mission.

Where doctrine addresses civilian protection, national training is also likely to cover military roles, such as operating within the Geneva Conventions, or providing support to rule of law and to humanitarian space. Some forces have national instruction on working with civilian agencies and NGOs, but this training does not address preventing armed groups from using violence against non-combatants. Training programs also cover civilian protection as part of operations for evacuating civilians from foreign countries, for instance, and teach likely tasks, such as conducting patrols and securing facilities; assisting disarmament programs and crowd control; and helping support other components of a peace operation. Some of these roles fall close to policing and establishing civil order.

Coercive protection is not well-defined or a priority within most military training programs. When there are rapid changes in the nature of military missions, training may need to shift *before* new doctrine is formally approved. As complex operations blur lines between peacekeeping and warfighting, such a shift is needed for more robust kinds of civilian protection and to prepare peacekeepers for missions in places like the DRC.

Overall, UN training modules do not yet address how countries should understand mandates to "protect civilians under imminent threat" or how military forces should prepare for missions with such mandates. The United Nations has developed more training standards for peace operations, and is developing guidance on civilian protection which builds on traditional roles for peacekeepers to support human rights, the rule of law, and international humanitarian principles. Draft modules rightfully stress that the principles of minimum use of force, impartiality, and consent do not justify *inaction* in the face of atrocities. Further, there is a beginning effort to address a military peacekeeping role in defending human rights, including the potential use of coercive techniques to protect civilians. This approach to human rights and military actions goes beyond what is found in most UN guidelines to date for protecting civilians, as well as within much doctrine for peace support operations.

Training efforts like this approach can fill a gap in guidance for operations that may use coercive protection. Without explicit guidance in key areas—how to stop a belligerent from committing gross human rights abuses, for example—missions trying to balance protection with broader political aims may find their goals at odds. Training that treats the protection of civilians as an explicit goal or as the central task of a mission—whether led by the United Nations, a lead nation, or a coalition—*is* necessary and should be a regular feature of training provided to troops deploying to regions with civilians at risk.

As countries and multinational organizations develop new and revised doctrine and training for peace and stability operations, there is an opportunity to better address these areas. Until a major troop contributor or the UN develops these tools, however, it is unlikely that regionally-based training centers will introduce curricula or scenarios that address civilian protection as a specific component of a peace operations or intervention force. This suggests the importance of UN standards and demonstrates how a gap in concepts or doctrine can affect training instruction.

Lessons from MONUC and the DRC

In the DRC, mission leaders have tried to navigate tough, inevitable choices about protecting civilians in a hostile environment. MONUC had authority *on paper* to protect civilian lives since 2000, but *in practice* mission personnel took years to adjust their understanding of the mission and its goals. Different contingents interpreted their mandates in contradictory ways. Some forces and their leaders were not even aware of their mandates with Chapter VII authority to protect civilians. MONUC began to develop a more aggressive stance to protect civilians in the DRC after the Ituri crisis of 2003 and *Operation Artemis*. Even then, with more robust ROE, the lack of a unified conception of MONUC's mandate and responsibilities continued to cause internal confusion and lead to a failure to protect civilians.

In the DRC, the stark contrast between the UN's mandate to protect civilians and its inability to respond to violence in Kisangani, Bunia, and Bukavu eventually led to troop increases for MONUC—to a level far higher than anyone could have predicted in 1999 when almost *no* political will existed for peacekeepers in the DRC. It also led to a change in MONUC's approach and its willingness to use force. After struggling for years, MONUC had developed a clearer approach to protection by 2005. The military component acted more in accordance with its Chapter VII mandate; peacekeepers conducted cordon-and-search operations and worked locally to identify spoilers to the peace. Peacekeepers also faced the repercussions of using aggressive tactics, as militia retaliated violently against the UN forces.

A distinct approach to protecting civilians has emerged from the MONUC mission. Driven by the leadership on the ground, MONUC has used its civilian protection mandate to integrate the varied civilian agencies with the military peacekeeping roles. Rather than pick one approach to protect civilians, MONUC leaders ask representatives of its military and civilian components what they can do, today, for protection purposes. The result is a more coherent, mission-wide strategy for increasing protection. While that approach alone does not address the role of military forces in providing physical protection, it helps integrate the role of military actors with that of civilian agencies.

The DRC case demonstrates serious dilemmas for UN peacekeepers tasked to protect civilians without having all the tools to do it. The success of a shift in strategy is still being assessed. The MONUC operation continues to demonstrate both creative approaches to a military role in providing protection and the difficulties faced by outside actors in providing protection. The experiences of MONUC and *Operation Artemis* highlight the impact of concepts of operation, capacity, mandates and ROE, doctrine, and training on peace operations directed to protect civilians. MONUC's experience also offers standard questions for future military missions: the definitions of vicinity and capacity, the integration of actors, clarity on the use of force and the role of peacekeepers in providing broad security in lieu of a state's responsibility—and the operational concept of protection. Given the trend of military forces being sent on missions to protect civilians, these critical areas deserve deeper consideration.

MAKING THE MANDATE POSSIBLE: GAPS AND OPPORTUNITIES

In debates over the "responsibility to protect," critics and advocates often end their discussion at whether or not to "send in the troops." Yet that is where more attention is needed: Which troops should be sent to do what job? What are the goals and concept of such missions? Will forces be asked to stop marauding militia or to bolster the government to do its job? What kinds of mandate, ROE, doctrine, and training should guide armed services in this area? Such questions may puzzle military and civilian actors in operations in the DRC, Haiti, Sudan, and elsewhere. These issues deserve as much attention as do debates over future interventions.

Protecting civilians is *not* an impossible mandate. Success requires that forces understand their mission's goal, know their own role toward achieving that goal, and be prepared to serve that role. Military leaders can organize operations to achieve goals asked of them, but need political leaders to describe the ends in clear terms. Basic characteristics for successful missions are easy to identify: a baseline capacity, a concept of the operation, authority and willingness to act, and well-prepared and trained military personnel prepared to offer coercive protection as needed. Thus, a mandate that is possible may still be hard to achieve.

Civilian protection mandates can lay bare the gaps between the reality on the ground and the capacity of the UN or other organizations to impact it. Where military forces are directed to provide physical security and protection to civilians that role needs support. Those roles may require deterring or dissuading bad actors from using violence—or to defeat abusive armed groups and employ tactics closer to traditional warfighting. These missions need more than just enough troops, but a well-coordinated and commanded force, strong leadership, and other tools of military engagement. Organizations including the UN need to be entrusted with sufficient capacity to be effective. Where protection mandates require the use of force and the lead organization is *not* able to implement them, mandates should be recast to reflect what is possible. Mandates need to offer more than an appearance that something is being done to address civilian suffering.

Understanding Gaps

Multinational organizations and nations offer little evidence of preparing their forces to intervene in genocide or to stop mass violence as part of a stability or peace operation. Why is that so?

First, the gap in Western doctrine and training suggests that more developed militaries are not concerned with civilian protection. This may not be as cold-hearted as it sounds, but reflect what military leaders traditionally see as force requirements for their defensive and warfighting roles. NATO and coalition operations are not often deployed with mandates to provide protection to civilians, with exceptions such as the French-led mission *Operation Licorne* in Côte d'Ivoire. NATO and the coalition forces in Iraq and Afghanistan, for example, are concerned with the civilian population, but have roles to provide security and stability and assist the governments, rather than protect civilians *per se*. Most EU-led missions have not involved the use of force or protection mandates, with the exception of *Operation Artemis*. The AU and ECOWAS do have protection aims, but rely on African nations to support their missions.

Western militaries also provide few personnel to UN-led missions. Of the more than 100 countries supplying upwards of 70,000 uniformed personnel to UN operations each month, the top contributors are developing states, traditionally nations with less military capacity, doctrine, and training. The US, UK, Canada and France, for example, provide less than a thousand military personnel, combined. As a result, their contingents are not often asked to protect civilians—and their leaders are not queried as to what such a mandate means. Thus, these nations are less likely to design their doctrine, training, simulations and gaming to address protection roles for their national military forces.

Yet Western countries with well-developed forces and sophisticated doctrine— the US, the UK, and France, for instance—serve on the UN Security Council and vote for UN mandates. They debate UN peace operations; provide funding, leaders and military equipment to these missions; and support their success politically. Along with other nations, they have participated in discussions of the "responsibility to protect," received reports on protecting civilians from the Secretary-General and been given regular briefings on the humanitarian costs of conflict and on civilian populations at risk worldwide. There is no lack of information about the problem or the concept of protection.

Thus, there is a second view of what hinders developing tools to prepare forces for protection missions: Nations do not see the mandates to protect civilians as having an operational role for their military forces. One officer suggested that interest in protection was a fad and would disappear in a few years.[494] Further, protection is associated with humanitarian efforts. The language of protection has deep roots within the humanitarian community, which has an extensive protection agenda. Civilian relief agencies and human rights organizations desire Security Council mandates with civilian protection to facilitate their engagement with UN peacekeeping operations in the field.

Such endeavors may create field-based strategies for better civilian-military roles in joint efforts for protection. But that approach is not itself an answer to what, actually, is the appropriate military role in protecting civilians under threat of physical violence. Most approaches to protection used by the humanitarian and human rights community do not address the role of military forces. Their strategies are related to, but different than, those associated with military roles in peace operations or as intervention forces to halt genocide.

There is a third reason for this gap: It is hard work to identify the proper role for military actors to protect civilians, and thus, to develop doctrine, training, and related guidance. As established with UN mandates, peace operations must balance their provision of protection with the role of the government where they operate. For most UN operations, the sovereign power holds primary responsibility for the welfare of its people. In weak states or in ones recovering from war, such as the DRC, the division of responsibilities can be unclear. The UN continuously maneuvers between offering support to the political process,

---

[494] US Army Colonel (retired) with extensive peacekeeping experience, interview with author, Newport, RI, July 2005.

cooperating with the government, and taking responsibility for protecting the local populace. Even when there is conceptual clarity within mission leadership, when troops are well-organized and well-equipped, and when forces are ready and prepared to use force, the "right" approach may be elusive for military forces and their leaders.

Finally, there is an argument that specialized preparation is unnecessary for operations mandated to protect civilians or for full-scale military interventions to stop genocide. Experienced military officers are unlikely to view a humanitarian intervention as a completely new mission or one for which they are ill-prepared. Rather, they argue that protection just requires organizing existing capabilities to achieve that goal. On the strategic level, this argument makes sense and recommends using military leaders' insights into organizing future missions. As an immediate response to large scale violence, however, traditional warfighting and other military operations are not designed to halt violence against civilians. There is little to suggest that many nations have conducted missions to protect civilians; that lessons from these missions are integrated in current doctrine and training; and thus, that modern forces appreciate how to protect civilians during an operation.

Likewise, there is an argument that the tasks needed to halt mass violence are familiar to military forces. Some countries train for tasks that are both well-known military roles, such as patrolling, protecting a perimeter, and engaging armed actors, and for tasks more associated with policing and other missions, such as engaging with local populations. Yet many militaries do not receive such training and deploy to operations prepared more for securing a physical area than preventing violence against a dispersed population.

If a concept of protection—such as coercive protection—was imbedded in the doctrine, training and other tools used to prepare militaries for their role, however, troops could take on such missions or tasks without much question—and then face the normal problems of any military operating in a conflict or post-conflict environment. Alternatively, if personnel recruited for missions with civilian protection mandates were given a working concept regarding their operational role in protection, they could determine how to draw on and apply their existing doctrine and training to the situation. Yet neither means of preparing for missions is evident. Guidance on protecting civilians focuses more on traditional, permissive, and low-threat post-conflict environments, and on the requirements of international humanitarian law. Multinational forces are often prepared to work with NGOs, support civilian order, provide security to refugees and IDPs, offer support to elections and conduct preventive patrols. More explicit guidance for contingencies that approach or cross the threshold identified by the ICISS—namely genocide, ethnic cleansing, and mass killing—is not easily identified. Without a clearer link to tools used to prepare military and peacekeeping forces for a "civilian protection" role, there is a large gap in the preparedness of many militaries and their leaders to carry out such missions.

Looking Forward

The international community expects military forces to protect civilians both today and in the future. A shift is needed to meet this expectation. The development of tools to prepare forces for missions, however, often relies on Western militaries to take the lead. For guidelines, regional training centers and multinational organizations—including the UN, NATO, the AU, the EU and ECOWAS—usually turn to existing national doctrine, training, ROE, and other tools in developing their own. Likewise, national training programs for foreign forces usually mirror a nation's own guidance for operations. Therefore, the tools developed by major militaries or multinational organizations for civilian protection missions can help prepare and support forces in other national or multinational missions.

There is a clear opportunity today to develop those tools and improve capabilities to halt mass violence against non-combatants. As Iraq and Afghanistan suffer from continued instability, NATO and Western militaries feel the strain on their capacity to undertake complex missions and look for better strategies to establish security in failed or failing states. The United Nations is under stress as it attempts to manage its growing force of peacekeepers in large, complex missions with explicit "protect civilians" mandates. Driven by new contingencies worldwide, other nations and multinational organizations are re-evaluating how they deploy troops and conduct missions. The UN, for its part, is developing more doctrine and training guidance. The EU, the AU, and ECOWAS are improving their capacity and evaluating their resources for future missions.

Protection should be on the agenda. While Darfur and Iraq, Haiti and the DRC are each troubling environments for civilians, for example, they suggest different strategies for military forces concerned with protecting civilians. The questions raised by this study are a starting point to consider the requirements of missions with protection mandates: Is protection the central mission goal or one of many tasks of the mission? What are the concepts of protection being used by the mission leadership and personnel? What is the military's role, therefore, and what basic capacities will forces need? What do military forces need to understand about the mandate, their ROE and calibrating the use of force? What doctrine and training should guide their approach? What is the longer-term strategy for protection?

The current environment may be a unique moment, where creative dialogue on the means of intervention is energized and where new approaches are more welcome. That opportunity should be seized. First, recent operations should be examined in greater depth to identify successful strategies and to develop knowledge of what works—and what does not. The deep experience within military and civilian circles should also be tapped. Many countries have provided troops for peace and stability operations, ranging from well-developed Western forces serving under NATO, to leading UN troop contributing countries from Asia and Africa, to nations newer to such missions within the EU and the AU. Each of these nations has much to offer.

Second, the lessons and analysis drawn from the field and headquarters should be thoroughly tested. They should be incorporated into scenarios with military and civilian leaders in gaming exercises and simulations. These efforts can identify guidance for future Chapter VII missions by nations, coalitions and multinational organizations.

The impact of the varied definitions of protection within the military, peacekeeping, and humanitarian communities should also be assessed. This review could lead to better understanding within and between these communities about concepts of civilian protection and development of terminology recognizable within military circles. In the future, more effective communication could ensure that all parties understand their responsibilities, the nature of the mission, and the types of situations they may encounter on the ground.

Third, from these testing efforts, doctrine and training can be improved. The UN can help develop and define a working concept of the protection of civilians for those leading or deploying with its peace operations. By building on its recently developed training standards, the UN could strengthen approaches to civilian protection within its Standardized Training Module series for peacekeepers, as well as in other civilian, police and military training programs. UN and national guidance should also address questions of impartiality, consent, host nation sovereignty, relations with civilian leaders and humanitarian actors, and the caveats of "within capabilities" and "area of deployment." Civilian leaders would benefit from training in ROE and mandates, since they often direct missions involving peacekeepers and should understand the grounds for the legitimate use of force. National and regional organizations and many bilateral and multinational training programs could adapt these guidelines for their own programs.

Efforts to develop guidance could bear fruit immediately for pre-deployment training for troops. Guidance can also be incorporated into tactics, techniques, and procedures, which frequently precede formal doctrine and training. Military leaders could also better inform civilian leaders of what they require for specific types of protection operations and to improve preparation.

In the long-term, the role of military actors in providing physical protection should be integrated with existing doctrine for peace support operations and for other kinds of military interventions. Developing draft doctrine could spur useful discussion among multinational organizations and with nations revising their own doctrine. Doctrine should address coercive action in achieving the mission's broader goals and distinguish between military interventions explicitly aimed at halting mass violence and those missions where protection is but one of many tasks. As nations revise their doctrine, they could better identify military responsibilities and tasks for operations mandated to protect civilians. In turn, guidance should be included in more general training programs to align with revised doctrine. As major militaries address protection with doctrine, training and other guidance, there will be multiple benefits both for their own forces and for those that deploy with multinational organizations and coalitions.

This approach is an important part of operationalizing the "responsibility to protect," and what the UN, NATO, the EU, the AU and ECOWAS require to develop more capacity for interventions and for modern peace and stability operations.

*   *   *

Today, millions of citizens live in conflict zones, facing lives disrupted and terrorized by violence. Whereas past failures to act against mass killing have horrified and shamed the world, countries have begun to step up and take some action. The idea of protecting civilians from mass violence has prompted important debate and gained increased acceptance. While no outside parties can prevent all violence against another nation's citizens, they can take action when other diplomatic, political and humanitarian efforts fail and where violence threatens to reach extreme levels.

The instinct to embrace a "responsibility to protect" is fundamentally a moral one. Nations are right to call for countries to stand up to their sovereign responsibilities and to shield citizens from mass violence and killings. No nation should shy from that position. Those who are realists and schooled in pragmatic thinking, however, rightfully question how such a norm will work, and if it is embraced, how it will be carried out.

This study tries to narrow the space between those ideals and reality. As states acknowledge a "responsibility to protect" and presuppose a distinct military role for protecting civilians, multinational organizations and national militaries need to be ready and better prepared for such roles. That goal cannot be put into practice without identifying the capabilities and the tools to act. This study suggests a starting point to support that exercise. Serious, sustained efforts are needed to take these concepts further and move aspirations for protecting civilians from rhetoric to action; from debate to knowledge; from a desire to protect to a deliberate strategy of protection. As the capacity to protect is strengthened, the right question for nations will be whether they are meeting their responsibilities, both to their own citizens and those of other lands. That worthy goal should drive wise preparation, in hopes that the responsibility to protect will one day no longer be debated and that every nation will provide for its own people.

ANNEX 1: UN SECURITY COUNCIL RESOLUTIONS FOR MISSIONS INVOLVING ASPECTS OF CIVILIAN PROTECTION

This chart reviews Security Council resolutions providing mandates that involve or imply protection of civilians for missions led by the United Nations, multinational forces, or individual countries. Section I covers mandates with direct reference to civilian protection in Council resolutions. The second section looks at selected missions with implicit or possible civilian protection components and their Council resolutions. Both sections of the chart identify the conflict area and mission name, cite relevant UN Security Council resolutions, identify Chapter VII citations by the Council, excerpt specific language from UN resolutions, and identify mission force levels and the troop contributing countries. This chart can be used in a variety of ways: to identify which missions have explicit and implicit requirements for civilian protection; to compare the specific language of mission mandates involving the protection of civilians; to determine which countries regularly contribute troops to such operations; to look at the evolution of UN resolutions; and to compare the force size of various civilian protection missions.

The UN Security Council did not explicitly direct peacekeepers to "protect civilians" or carry out missions for the "protection of civilians" in mandates prior to 1999. In earlier mandates, resolutions identified tasks or goals implying protection, such as the creation of "safe zones" and the maintenance of "public safety" and a "secure environment," which imply authority to provide some level of protection to the civilian population. Selections here include excerpts indicating the authority to use force to uphold UN mandates, which impacts how missions intervene on civilians' behalf. In trying to capture all civilian protection-mandated missions from 1960 to April 2006, this chart looks at operations where peacekeeping forces are authorized to take action in potentially hostile environments for civilian protection. This chart does not look at more indirect mission activities that help provide protection to civilians over time (e.g., demobilization, disarmament and reintegration activities; ceasefire monitoring; and human rights assistance). It addresses language relating to the actions of peacekeepers themselves, not other actors such as parties to the conflict or national governments. Section II includes a range of missions, including those in hostile environments such as Bosnia-Herzegovina, Somalia, and Rwanda, where civilian populations were under serious threat. Other missions in Section II, such as Operation Alba in Albania, the UN Mission in the Central African Republic, and the UN Mission in Haiti, took place in more benign environments or lacked clear Chapter VII authorization, and are included in order to provide grounds for comparing resolution language.

CHART KEY

Data is from the United Nations unless stipulated otherwise.

Conflict Area: Names the country or location of the mission.
Mission Name: Lists the name referenced by the United Nations or used by the lead state or organization.
UNSC Resolution: Lists major Security Council resolutions relevant to the mission (except those extending the mission without change).
Mission Type: Identifies citation of Chapter VII authority under the UN Charter and the mission leadership, e.g., the UN, multilateral organization, multinational force, or lead nation.
Selected Language From UN Mandates: Excerpts sections from UN Security Council resolutions for operation mandates, focusing on the phrases "protect civilians" or "protection of civilians" or excerpts implying potential civilian protection, such as language stipulating creation of "safe zones," "public safety," and a "secure environment" that imply authority to provide some level of protection to the civilian population. Selections also include language that indicates the missions' authority to use force. In a few cases, such as the mandates for AMIS, IFOR, and SFOR, some language is not from Security Council resolutions, and the alternate source is specified.
Mission Strength: Identifies either the maximum number of troops authorized by the UN resolution or troops deployed at a specific time.
Troop Contributing Countries: Includes all the countries that have contributed civilian police, military observers, or actual troops to the mission.

I.			UN Security Council Resolutions for Missions with Direct Reference to the Protection of Civilians		
Conflict Area	Mission Name	Relevant UNSC Resolutions	Mission Type	Selected Language From UN Mandates	Mission Strength *authorized or reported[1]*	Troop Contributing Countries *Nation of force commander in italics[2]*

Conflict Area	Mission Name	Relevant UNSC Resolutions	Mission Type	Selected Language From UN Mandates	Mission Strength *authorized or reported[1]*	Troop Contributing Countries *Nation of force commander in italics[2]*
Burundi	United Nations Operation in Burundi (ONUB)	1545 (2004)	UN-led Chapter VII	**Resolution 1545:** ...5. Authorizes ONUB to use all **necessary means to carry out the following mandate, within its capacity and in the areas where its armed units are deployed,** and in coordination with humanitarian and development communities: ... – to contribute to the creation of the necessary security conditions for the provision of humanitarian assistance, and facilitate the voluntary return of refugees and internally displaced persons, – **without prejudice to the responsibility of the transitional Government of Burundi, to protect civilians under imminent threat of physical violence,** – to ensure the protection of United Nations personnel, facilities, installations and equipment, as well as the security and freedom of movement of ONUB's personnel, and to coordinate and conduct, as appropriate, mine action activities in support of its mandate....	**Authorized strength:** 5,650 military personnel, including 200 military observers, 120 civilian police personnel, 434 international civilian personnel, 170 United Nations Volunteers and 446 local civilian staff (S/2004/210/Add.1).	**Contributors of military personnel:** Algeria, Bangladesh, Belgium, Benin, Bolivia, Burkina Faso, Chad, China, Egypt, Ethiopia, Gambia, Ghana, Guatemala, Guinea, India, Jordan, Kenya, Kyrgyzstan, Malawi, Malaysia, Mali, Mozambique, Namibia, Nepal, Niger, Nigeria, Pakistan, Paraguay, Peru, Philippines, Portugal, Republic of Korea, Romania, Russia, Senegal, Serbia and Montenegro, *South Africa,* Spain, Sri Lanka, Thailand, Togo, Tunisia, Uruguay, Yemen, and Zambia. **Contributors of police personnel:** Benin, Burkina Faso, Cameroon, Chad, Guinea, Madagascar, Mali, Niger, Nigeria, and Senegal.
Côte d'Ivoire	United Nations Operation in Côte d'Ivoire (UNOCI)	1528 (2004) 1609 (2005)	UN-led Chapter VII	**Resolution 1528:** ...6. Decides that the mandate of UNOCI ...shall be the following: (i) To protect United Nations personnel, installations and equipment, provide the security and freedom of movement of United Nations personnel and, **without prejudice to the responsibility of the Government of National Reconciliation, to protect civilians under imminent threat of physical violence, within its capabilities and its areas of deployment....** **Resolution 1609:** ...2. ... *Support for humanitarian assistance* (o) To facilitate the free flow of people, goods and humanitarian assistance, inter alia, by helping to establish the necessary security conditions and taking into account the special needs of vulnerable groups, especially women, children and elderly people.... (It also includes language identical to Res. 1528 above)	**Authorized strength:** Up to 7,090 military personnel and up to 725 police officers, including three formed police units, and the necessary additional civilian personnel (S/RES/1609, 2005).	**Contributors of military personnel:** Bangladesh, Benin, Bolivia, Brazil, Chad, China, Croatia, Dominican Republic, Ecuador, El Salvador, France, Gambia, Ghana, Guatemala, Guinea, India, Ireland, Jordan, Kenya, Moldova, Morocco, Namibia, Nepal, Niger, Nigeria, Pakistan, Paraguay, Peru, Philippines, Poland, Romania, Russian Federation, Senegal, Serbia and Montenegro, Togo, Tunisia, Uganda, Uruguay, Yemen, and Zambia. **Contributors of police personnel:** Bangladesh, Benin, Cameroon, Canada, Central African Republic, Chad, Djibouti, El Salvador, France, Ghana, India, Jordan, Lebanon, Madagascar, Niger, Nigeria, Philippines, Portugal, Senegal, Sri Lanka, Togo, Turkey, Uruguay, Vanuatu, and Yemen.

I. UN Security Council Resolutions for Missions with Direct Reference to the Protection of Civilians

Conflict Area	Mission Name	Relevant UNSC Resolutions	Mission Type	Selected Language From UN Mandates	Mission Strength *authorized or reported*[1]	Troop Contributing Countries *Nation of force commander in italics*[2]
Côte d'Ivoire	Operation Licorne	1464 (2003), 1528 (2004), 1609 (2005)	UN-authorized Chapter VII (France)	**Resolution 1464:** …9. [A]uthorizes Member States participating in the ECOWAS forces in accordance with Chapter VIII together with the French forces supporting them **to take the necessary steps** to guarantee the security and freedom of movement of their personnel and **to ensure, without prejudice to the responsibilities of the Government of National Reconciliation, the protection of civilians immediately threatened with physical violence within their zones of operation, using the means available to them.…** **Resolution 1528:** 16. Authorizes…the French forces to use all necessary means in order to support UNOCI in accordance with the agreement to be reached between UNOCI and the French authorities, and in particular to: – Contribute to the general security of the area of activity of the international forces, – Intervene at the request of UNOCI in support of its elements whose security may be threatened, – Intervene against belligerent actions, if the security conditions so require, outside the areas directly controlled by UNOCI, – **Help to protect civilians, in the deployment areas of their units.…**	**Reported strength:** 4000 troops.[3]	*France*
Côte d'Ivoire	ECOWAS Mission in Côte d'Ivoire (ECOMICI)	1464 (2003)	UN-authorized Chapter VII (Economic Community of West African States)	**Resolution 1464:** …9. [A]uthorizes Member States participating in the ECOWAS forces in accordance with Chapter VIII together with the French forces supporting them **to take the necessary steps** to guarantee the security and freedom of movement of their personnel and **to ensure, without prejudice to the responsibilities of the Government of National Reconciliation, the protection of civilians immediately threatened with physical violence within their zones of operation, using the means available to them.…**	**Reported strength:** 1,369 military personnel.[4]	Benin, Ghana, Niger, *Senegal*, and Togo.[5]

Conflict Area	Mission Name	Relevant UNSC Resolutions	Mission Type	Selected Language From UN Mandates	Mission Strength authorized or reported[1]	Troop Contributing Countries Nation of force commander in italics[2]
Democratic Republic of Congo	United Nations Mission in the Democratic Republic of Congo (MONUC)	1258 (1999), 1279 (1999), 1291 (2000), 1355 (2001), 1376 (2001), 1417 (2002), 1445 (2002), 1468 (2003), 1493 (2003), 1501 (2003), 1565 (2004), 1592 (2005)	UN-led Chapter VI from 1999 to 2003, with a Chapter VII clause added in 2000; full Chapter VII from 2003 to present	**Resolution 1291:** ...8. Acting under Chapter VII of the Charter of the United Nations, decides that MONUC may take the necessary action, **in the areas of deployment of its infantry battalions and as it deems it within its capabilities,** to protect United Nations and co-located JMC personnel, facilities, installations and equipment, ensure the security and freedom of movement of its personnel, and **protect civilians under imminent threat of physical violence....** **Resolution 1493:** ...25. Authorizes MONUC to take the necessary measures **in the areas of deployment of its armed units, and as it deems it within its capabilities:** – to protect United Nations personnel, facilities, installations and equipment; – to ensure the security and freedom of movement of its personnel, including in particular those engaged in missions of observation, verification or DDRRR; **– to protect civilians and humanitarian workers under imminent threat of physical violence;** – and to contribute to the improvement of the security conditions in which humanitarian assistance is provided; 26. Authorizes MONUC to use all necessary means to fulfil its mandate in the Ituri district and, as it deems it within its capabilities, in North and South Kivu.... **Resolution 1565:** .... 4. Decides that MONUC will have the following mandate: (a) to deploy and maintain a presence in the key areas of potential volatility in order to promote the re-establishment of confidence, to discourage violence, in particular by deterring the use of force to threaten the political process, and to allow United Nations personnel to operate freely, particularly in the Eastern part of the Democratic Republic of the Congo, (b) **to ensure the protection of civilians, including humanitarian personnel, under imminent threat of physical violence,** (c) to ensure the protection of United Nations personnel, facilities, installations and equipment, (d) to ensure the security and freedom of movement of its personnel, ...6. Authorizes MONUC to use all **necessary means, within its capacity and in the areas where its armed units are deployed,** to carry out the tasks listed in paragraph 4, subparagraphs (a) to (g) above....	**Authorized maximum strength:** 16,700 Military personnel, 475 Police personnel. In addition, on 6 September 2005, the Security Council authorized a temporary increase of 841 personnel in the strength of the Mission; and on 28 October 2005, the Security Council authorized a temporary increase of 300 personnel in its military strength for the period of the elections.	**Contributors of military personnel:** Algeria, Bangladesh, Belgium, Benin, Bolivia, Bosnia and Herzegovina, Burkina Faso, Cameroon, Canada, China, Czech Republic, Denmark, Egypt, France, Ghana, Guatemala, India, Indonesia, Ireland, Jordan, Kenya, Malawi, Malaysia, Mali, Mongolia, Morocco, Mozambique, Nepal, Netherlands, Niger, Nigeria, Pakistan, Paraguay, Peru, Poland, Romania, Russian Federation, Senegal, Serbia and Montenegro, South Africa, Spain, Sri Lanka, Sweden, Switzerland, Tunisia, Ukraine, United Kingdom, Uruguay, and Zambia. **Contributors of police personnel:** Argentina, Bangladesh, Benin, Burkina Faso, Cameroon, Central African Republic, Chad, Côte d'Ivoire, Egypt, France, Guinea, India, Jordan, Madagascar, Mali, Niger, Nigeria, Romania, Russian Federation, Senegal, Sweden, Turkey, Vanuatu, and Yemen.

Conflict Area	Mission Name	Relevant UNSC Resolutions	Mission Type	Selected Language From UN Mandates	Mission Strength *authorized or reported[1]*	Troop Contributing Countries *Nation of force commander in italics[2]*
Democratic Republic of Congo	Operation Artemis	1484 (2003), 1501 (2003)	UN-authorized Chapter VII (European Union)	**Resolution 1592:** ... 7. *Emphasizing* that MONUC is **authorized to use all necessary means, within its capabilities and in the areas where its armed units are deployed,** to deter any attempt at the use of force to threaten the political process and **to ensure the protection of civilians under imminent threat of physical violence, from any armed group, foreign or Congolese,** in particular the ex-FAR and Interahamwé, *encourages* MONUC in this regard to continue to make full use of its mandate under Resolution 1565 in the eastern part of the Democratic Republic of the Congo, and **stresses that, in accordance with its mandate, MONUC may use cordon and search tactics to prevent attacks on civilians and disrupt the military capability of illegal armed groups that continue to use violence in those areas....** **Resolution 1484:** ...1. *Authorizes* the deployment until 1 September 2003 of an Interim Emergency Multinational Force in Bunia in close coordination with MONUC, in particular its contingent currently deployed in the town, to contribute to the stabilization of the security conditions and the improvement of the humanitarian situation in Bunia, **to ensure the protection of the airport, the internally displaced persons in the camps in Bunia and, if the situation requires it, to contribute to the safety of the civilian population, United Nations personnel and the humanitarian presence in the town....**	**Reported strength:** 1,800 troops.[6]	Belgium, Brazil, Canada, *France* (lead nation), Germany, Greece, South Africa, Sweden, and the United Kingdom.[7]
Haiti	United Nations Stabilization Mission in Haiti (MINUSTAH)	1542 (2004)	UN-led Chapter VII	**Resolution 1542:** ...7. *Acting* under Chapter VII of the Charter of the United Nations with regard to Section I below, *decides* that MINUSTAH shall have the following mandate: I. Secure and Stable Environment: (a) in support of the Transitional Government, to ensure a secure and stable environment within which the constitutional and political process in Haiti can take place; ...(e) to protect United Nations personnel, facilities, installations and equipment and to ensure the security and freedom of movement of its personnel, taking into account the primary responsibility of the Transitional Government in that regard; **(f) to protect civilians under imminent threat of physical violence, within its capabilities and areas of deployment, without prejudice to the responsibilities of the Transitional Government and of police authorities...**	**Authorized strength:** 6,700 military personnel; 1,622 civilian police, 548 international civilian personnel, 154 United Nations volunteers and 995 local civilian staff.	**Contributors of military personnel:** Argentina, Bolivia, *Brazil*, Canada, Chile, Croatia, Ecuador, France, Guatemala, Jordan, Malaysia, Morocco, Nepal, Paraguay, Peru, Philippines, Spain, Sri Lanka, United States, Uruguay, and Yemen. **Contributors of police personnel:** Benin, Bosnia and Herzegovina, Brazil, Burkina Faso, Cameroon, Canada, Chad, Chile, China, Egypt, El Salvador, France, Ghana, Guinea, Jordan, Mali, Mauritius, Nepal, Niger, Nigeria, Pakistan, Philippines, Romania, Russia, Senegal, Sierra Leone, Spain, Togo, Turkey, United States, Uruguay, Vanuatu, Yemen, and Zambia.

Conflict Area	Mission Name	Relevant UNSC Resolutions	Mission Type	Selected Language From UN Mandates	Mission Strength *authorized or reported[1]*	Troop Contributing Countries *Nation of force commander in italics[2]*
Liberia	**United Nations Mission in Liberia (UNMIL)**	1408 (2003), 1458 (2003), 1478 (2003), 1497 (2003), 1509 (2003), 1521 (2003), 1532 (2004), 1549 (2004), 1638 (2005), 1683 (2005)	UN-led Chapter VII	**Resolution 1509:** ….3. Decides that UNMIL shall have the following mandate: …**Protection of United Nations Staff, Facilities and Civilians:** (i) to protect United Nations personnel, facilities, installations and equipment, ensure the security and freedom of movement of its personnel and, **without prejudice to the efforts of the government, to protect civilians under imminent threat of physical violence, within its capabilities.**…	**Authorized strength:** Up to 15,000 military personnel, including up to 250 military observers and 160 staff officers, and up to 1,115 civilian police officers.	**Contributors of military personnel:** Bangladesh, Benin, Bolivia, Brazil, Bulgaria, China, Croatia, Czech Republic, Denmark, Ecuador, Egypt, El Salvador, Ethiopia, Finland, France, Gambia, Germany, Ghana, Indonesia, Ireland, Jordan, Kenya, Kyrgyzstan, Malawi, Malaysia, Mali, Moldova, Namibia, Nepal, Niger, *Nigeria*, Pakistan, Paraguay, Peru, Philippines, Poland, Republic of Korea, Romania, Russian Federation, Senegal, Serbia and Montenegro, Sierra Leone, Sweden, Togo, Ukraine, United Kingdom, United States, and Zambia. **Contributors of police personnel:** Argentina, Bangladesh, Bosnia and Herzegovina, China, Czech Republic, El Salvador, Fiji, Gambia, Germany, Ghana, Jamaica, Jordan, Kenya, Kyrgyzstan, Malawi, Namibia, Nepal, Niger, Nigeria, Norway, Pakistan, Philippines, Poland, Russian Federation, Samoa, Senegal, Serbia and Montenegro, Sri Lanka, Sweden, Turkey, Uganda, Ukraine, United States, Uruguay, Yemen, Zambia, and Zimbabwe.

Conflict Area	Mission Name	Relevant UNSC Resolutions	Mission Type	Selected Language From UN Mandates	Mission Strength *authorized or reported*[1]	Troop Contributing Countries *Nation of force commander in italics*[2]
Sierra Leone	**United Nations Mission in Sierra Leone (UNAMSIL)**	1270 (1999), 1289 (2000), 1299 (2000), 1313 (2000), 1346 (2001), 1470 (2003), 1492 (2003), 1508 (2003), 1537 (2004), 1562 (2004)	UN-led Chapter VI with a Chapter VII clause added in 1999; expanded in 2000 to full Chapter VII	**Resolution 1270:** …14. Acting under Chapter VII of the Charter of the United Nations, decides that in the discharge of its mandate UNAMSIL may take the necessary action to ensure the security and freedom of movement of its personnel and, **within its capabilities and areas of deployment, to afford protection to civilians under imminent threat of physical violence, taking into account the responsibilities of the Government of Sierra Leone and ECOMOG.**… **Resolution 1289:** …10. Acting under Chapter VII of the Charter of the United Nations, decides further that the mandate of UNAMSIL shall be revised to include the following additional tasks, to be performed by UNAMSIL within its capabilities and areas of deployment and in the light of conditions on the ground: (a) To provide security at key locations and Government buildings, in particular in Freetown, important intersections and major airports, including Lungi airport; (b) To facilitate the free flow of people, goods and humanitarian assistance along specified thoroughfares; (c) To provide security in and at all sites of the disarmament, demobilization and reintegration programme;… authorizes UNAMSIL to take the necessary action to fulfil the additional tasks set out above, and **affirms that, in the discharge of its mandate, UNAMSIL may take the necessary action to ensure the security and freedom of movement of its personnel and, within its capabilities and areas of deployment, to afford protection to civilians under imminent threat of physical violence, taking into account the responsibilities of the Government of Sierra Leone.**…	**Authorized strength:** (maximum): 17,500 military personnel, including 260 military observers (S/RES/1346) and up to 170 civilian police personnel (S/RES/1436).	**Contributors of military personnel:** Bangladesh, Bolivia, China, Croatia, Egypt, Gambia, Germany, Ghana, Guinea, India, Indonesia, Jordan, Kenya, Kyrgyzstan, Malawi, Malaysia, Nepal, Nigeria, Norway, *Pakistan*, Russian Federation, Slovakia, Sweden, Tanzania, Ukraine, United Kingdom, Uruguay and Zambia. **Contributors of civilian police:** Australia, Bangladesh, Cameroon, Canada, Gambia, Ghana, India, Jordan, Kenya, Malawi, Malaysia, Mauritius, Namibia, Nepal, Niger, Nigeria, Norway, Pakistan, Russia, Senegal, Sri Lanka, Sweden, Tanzania, Turkey, United Kingdom, United States, Zambia, and Zimbabwe.
Darfur, Sudan	**African Mission in the Sudan (AMIS)**	1502 (2003), 1547 (2004), 1556 (2004), 1564 (2004)	UN-recognized Chapter VII (African Union)	**Resolution 1564:** …*Acting* under Chapter VII of the United Nations Charter ….2. *Welcomes and supports the* intention of the African Union to enhance and augment its monitoring mission in the Darfur region of Sudan, and encourages the undertaking of proactive monitoring.… **African Union – Communiqué of the Seventeenth Meeting of the Peace and Security Council (20 October 2004):** …4. Decides that the enhanced AMIS shall be deployed…to perform the following mandate: …to contribute to a secure environment for the delivery of humanitarian relief and, beyond that, the return of IDPs	**Authorized strength:** a total of 6,171 military personnel, with an appropriate civilian component, including up to 1,560 civilian police personnel (Communiqué of the 28th Meeting of the AU Peace and Security Council, 28 April 2005).	Rwanda, Nigeria, Senegal, Gambia, Chad, Kenya, and South Africa (as of 20 October 2005).

Conflict Area	Mission Name	Relevant UNSC Resolutions	Mission Type	Selected Language From UN Mandates	Mission Strength *authorized or reported*[1]	Troop Contributing Countries *Nation of force commander in italics*[2]
				and refugees to their homes, in order to assist in increasing the level of compliance of all Parties with the Humanitarian Ceasefire Agreement and to contribute to the improvement of the security situation throughout Darfur; ...6. Decides that, within the framework of its mandate as spelt out in paragraph 4 above, AMIS shall, inter alia, perform the following tasks: ...**Protect civilians whom it encounters under imminent threat and in the immediate vicinity, within resources and capability, it being understood that the protection of the civilian population is the responsibility of the GoS**.... **African Union – Communiqué of the Forty-Sixth Meeting of the Peace and Security Council (10 March 2006):** ...3. Decides to extend the mandate of AMIS...to undertake the following: contribute to the improvement of the general security situation, provide a secure environment for the delivery of humanitarian assistance and the return of IDP and refugees, and **contribute to the protection of the civilian population in Darfur**...4. b) In order to improve the security, humanitarian and human rights situation, Council: i) Requests the Commission to immediately **take all necessary steps** for the consistent, flexible, broad and robust interpretation of the mandate provided for in paragraph 3 above and the tasks deriving thereof ...in order to ensure a **more forceful protection of the civilian population.**		

		I.		UN Security Council Resolutions for Missions with Direct Reference to the Protection of Civilians		
Conflict Area	Mission Name	Relevant UNSC Resolutions	Mission Type	Selected Language From UN Mandates	Mission Strength *authorized or reported[1]*	Troop Contributing Countries *Nation of force commander in italics[2]*
Sudan	United Nations Mission in the Sudan (UNMIS)	1590 (2005)	UN-led Chapter VII	**Resolution 1590:** 4. … (a)…(ix) To ensure an adequate human rights presence, capacity, and expertise within UNMIS to carry out human rights promotion, **civilian protection,** and monitoring activities; …(d) To contribute towards international efforts to protect and promote human rights in Sudan, as well as to **coordinate international efforts towards the protection of civilians with particular attention to vulnerable groups including internally displaced persons, returning refugees, and women and children, within UNMIS's capabilities and in close cooperation with other United Nations agencies, related organizations, and non-governmental organizations;** …16. *Acting under Chapter VII of the Charter of the United Nations,* (i) Decides that **UNMIS is authorized to take the necessary action, in the areas of deployment of its forces and as it deems within its capabilities,** to protect United Nations personnel, facilities, installations, and equipment, ensure the security and freedom of movement of United Nations personnel, humanitarian workers, joint assessment mechanism and assessment and evaluation commission personnel, and, **without prejudice to the responsibility of the Government of Sudan, to protect civilians under imminent threat of physical violence;**	**Authorized strength:** Up to 10,000 military personnel including some 750 military observers. **Proposed strength:** 715 police, 1,018 international civilian staff, 2,623 national staff and 214 United Nations Volunteers.	**Contributors of military personnel:** Australia, Austria, Bangladesh, Belgium, Benin, Bolivia, Brazil, Burkina Faso, Cambodia, Canada, China, Croatia, Denmark, Ecuador, Egypt, El Salvador, Fiji, Finland, Gabon, Germany, Greece, Guatemala, Guinea, *India,* Indonesia, Italy, Jordan, Kenya, Kyrgyzstan, Malawi, Malaysia, Mali, Moldova, Mongolia, Mozambique, Namibia, Nepal, New Zealand, Nigeria, Norway, Pakistan, Paraguay, Peru, Philippines, Poland, Republic of Korea, Romania, Russia, Rwanda, Sri Lanka, Sweden, Switzerland, Tanzania, Thailand, Turkey, Uganda, Ukraine, United Kingdom, Yemen, Zambia, and Zimbabwe. **Contributors of police personnel:** Argentina, Bangladesh, Brazil, China, El Salvador, Fiji, Finland, Ghana, India, Jamaica, Jordan, Kenya, Kyrgyzstan, Namibia, Nepal, Nigeria, Norway, Pakistan, Philippines, Russia, Samoa, Sri Lanka, Sweden, Tanzania, Turkey, Uganda, Ukraine, United States, Zambia, and Zimbabwe.

II. Selected UN Resolutions for Missions With Implications for Protection of Civilians

Conflict Area	Mission Name	Relevant UNSC Resolutions	Mission Type	Selected Language From UN Mandates	Mission Strength *authorized or reported[1]*	Troop Contributing Countries *Nation of force commander in italics[2]*
Afghanistan	International Security Assistance Force (ISAF)	1386 (2001), 1413 (2002); 1444 (2002); 1510 (2003)	UN-authorized Chapter VII (NATO)	**Resolution 1386**: …1. Authorizes, as envisaged in Annex 1 to the Bonn Agreement, the establishment for 6 months of an International Security Assistance Force **to assist the Afghan Interim Authority in the maintenance of security in Kabul and its surrounding areas,** so that the Afghan Interim Authority as well as the personnel of the United Nations can operate in a secure environment; …3. Authorizes the Member States participating in the International Security Assistance Force to take all necessary measures to fulfill its mandate…. **Resolution 1510**: …Authorizes expansion of the mandate of the International Security Assistance Force to allow it, as resources permit, to support the Afghan Transitional Authority and its successors in **the maintenance of security in areas of Afghanistan outside of Kabul and its environs,** so that the **Afghan Authorities** as well as **the personnel of the United Nations and other international civilian personnel engaged,** in particular, in reconstruction and humanitarian efforts, **can operate in a secure environment, and to provide security assistance for the performance of other tasks in support of the Bonn Agreement**….	**Reported strength:** 9,000 troops.[8]	Albania, Austria, Azerbaijan, Belgium, Bulgaria, Canada, Croatia, Czech Republic, Denmark, Estonia, Finland, France, Former Yugoslav Republic of Macedonia, Germany, Greece, Hungary, Iceland, Ireland, Italy, Latvia, Lithuania, Luxembourg, Netherlands, New Zealand, Norway, Poland, Portugal, Romania, Slovakia, Slovenia, Spain, Sweden, Switzerland, Turkey, United Kingdom, and the United States.[9]
Albania	Operation Alba	1101 (1997)	UN-authorized Chapter VII (Multi-national Force)	**Resolution 1101**: …2. Welcomes the offer made by certain Member States to establish a temporary and limited **multinational protection force to facilitate the safe and prompt delivery of humanitarian assistance,** and **to help create a secure environment for the** missions of international organizations in Albania, including those providing humanitarian assistance.… 4. Authorizes the Member States participating in the multinational protection force to conduct the operation in a neutral and impartial way to achieve the objectives set out …above and, acting under Chapter VII of the Charter of the United Nations, further authorizes…Member States **to ensure the security and freedom of movement of the personnel of the said multinational protection force.**…	**Reported strength:** 6,000 troops.[10]	Italy (lead nation), Greece, France, Italy, Portugal, Romania, Slovenia, Spain, and Turkey; slight participation from Austria, Denmark, and Belgium.[11]

II. Selected UN Resolutions for Missions With Implications for Protection of Civilians

Conflict Area	Mission Name	Relevant UNSC Resolutions	Mission Type	Selected Language From UN Mandates	Mission Strength *authorized or reported[1]*	Troop Contributing Countries *Nation of force commander in italics[2]*
Bosnia-Herzegovina /Croatia /Macedonia	United Nations Protection Force (UNPROFOR)	**Selected resolutions:[12]** 743 (1992); 749 (1992); 758 (1992); 761 (1992), 770 (1992), 771 (1992), 776 (1992), 779 (1992), 781 (1992), 786 (1992), 795 (1992), 815 (1993), 816 (1993), 819 (1993), 824 (1993), 836 (1993), 844 (1993), 900 (1994), 908 (1994), 914 (1994), 941 (1994), 958 (1994), 959 (1994), 982 (1995), 998 (1995), 1004 (1995)	UN-led Chapter VI prior to 1993, and Chapter VII after Resolution 815 (1993)	**Resolution 824:** ...3. Declares that the capital city of the Republic of Bosnia and Herzegovina, Sarajevo, and other such threatened areas, in particular the towns of Tuzla, Zepa, Gorazde, Bihac, as well as Srebrenica, and their surroundings should be treated as **safe areas** by all the parties concerned and should be free from armed attacks and from any other hostile act.... **Resolution 836:** ...5. Decides to extend to that end the mandate of UNPROFOR in order to enable it, in the safe areas referred to in Resolution 824 (1993), **to deter attacks against the safe areas**, to monitor the cease-fire, to promote the withdrawal of military or paramilitary units other than those of the Government of the Republic of Bosnia and Herzegovina and to occupy some key points on the ground, in addition to participating in the delivery of humanitarian relief to the population as provided for in Resolution 776 (1992) of 14 September 1992; 6. Affirms that these safe areas are a temporary measure and that the primary objective remains to reverse the consequences of the use of force and to allow all persons displaced from their homes in the Republic of Bosnia and Herzegovina to return to their homes in peace, beginning, inter-alia, with the prompt implementation of the provisions of the Vance-Owen Plan in areas where those have been agreed by the parties directly concerned; ...9. Authorizes UNPROFOR, in addition to the mandate defined in Resolutions 770 (1992) of 13 August 1992 and 776 (1992), in carrying out the mandate defined in paragraph 5 above, **acting in self-defence, to take the necessary measures, including the use of force, in reply to bombardments against the safe areas by any of the parties or to armed incursion into them or in the event of any deliberate obstruction in or around those areas to the freedom of movement of UNPROFOR or of protected humanitarian convoys.**...	**Reported strength:** (March 1995): 38,599 military personnel, 684 military observers, 803 civilian police, 2,017 international staff, and 2,615 local staff.[13]	Bangladesh, Belgium, Canada, Denmark, *France, India,* Pakistan, *Sweden,* and the United Kingdom among the top contributors; 37 countries total.[14]

II. Selected UN Resolutions for Missions With Implications for Protection of Civilians

Conflict Area	Mission Name	Relevant UNSC Resolutions	Mission Type	Selected Language From UN Mandates	Mission Strength *authorized or reported*[1]	Troop Contributing Countries *Nation of force commander in italics*[2]
Bosnia-Herzegovina	Implemen-tation Force (IFOR)/ Stabilization Force (SFOR)	1031(1995), 1088 (1996)	UN-authorized Chapter VII (NATO)	**Resolution 1031:** 14. Authorizes the Member States acting through or in cooperation with the organization referred to in Annex 1-A of the Peace Agreement to establish a multinational implementation force (IFOR) under unified command and control in order to fulfil the role specified in Annex 1-A and Annex 2 of the Peace Agreement; 15. Authorizes the Member States acting under paragraph 14 above to take **all necessary measures to effect the implementation of and to ensure compliance with Annex 1-A of the Peace Agreement**. stresses that the parties shall be held equally responsible for compliance with that Annex, and shall be equally subject to such **enforcement action** by IFOR as may be necessary to ensure implementation of that Annex and the protection of IFOR, and takes note that the parties have consented to IFOR's taking such measures, ...17. Authorizes Member States to take all necessary measures, at the request of IFOR, either in defence of IFOR or to assist the force in carrying out its mission, and recognizes the right of the force to take all necessary measures to defend itself from attack or threat of attack.... **The General Framework Agreement, Annex 1A: Article VI:** Deployment of the Implementation Force, ...3. The Parties understand and agree that the IFOR shall have the right to fulfill its supporting tasks, within the limits of its assigned principal tasks and available resources, and on request, which include the following: a. to help create secure conditions for the conduct by others of other tasks associated with the peace settlement, including free and fair elections; b. to assist the movement of organizations in the accomplishment of humanitarian missions; **c. to assist the UNHCR and other international organiza-tions in their humanitarian missions;** d. to observe and prevent interference with the movement of civilian populations, refugees, and displaced persons, and **to respond appropriately to deliberate violence to life and person;** and, e. to monitor the clearing of minefields and obstacles....	**IFOR reported strength:** [15] 60,000 troops. **SFOR reported strength:** [16] 34,000 troops.	**IFOR troop contributing countries:** All NATO nations with armed forces. NATO also invited 16 non-NATO countries to participate: Austria, Czech Republic, Estonia, Finland, Hungary, Latvia, Lithuania, Poland, Romania, Russia, Slovakia, Sweden, and Ukraine (all Partnership for Peace countries) plus, Egypt, Pakistan, and Malaysia.[17] **SFOR troop contributing countries (1997/98 & 2000/01):** (NATO) Australia, Belgium, Canada, Denmark, France, Germany, Greece, Italy, Luxembourg, Netherlands, Norway, Portugal, Spain, Turkey, United Kingdom, and the United States; (non-NATO) Albania, Austria, Czech Republic, Estonia, Egypt, Finland, Jordan, Hungary, Latvia, Lithuania, Malaysia, Morocco, New Zealand, Poland, Romania, South Africa, Russia, Sweden, and Ukraine.[18]

II. Selected UN Resolutions for Missions With Implications for Protection of Civilians

Conflict Area	Mission Name	Relevant UNSC Resolutions	Mission Type	Selected Language From UN Mandates	Mission Strength *authorized or reported[1]*	Troop Contributing Countries *Nation of force commander in italics[2]*
Burundi	African Union Mission in Burundi (AMIB)	1375 (2001)	Endorsed by UN Security Council after AU deployment, implicit Chapter VI (African Union)	**Resolution 1375:** ...4. Endorses the efforts of the Government of South Africa and other member States to support the implementation of the Arusha Agreement, and strongly supports in this regard the establishment of an interim multinational security presence in Burundi, at the request of its Government, to protect returning political leaders and train an all-Burundian protection force....To secure identified assembly and disengagement areas; **To provide VIP protection for designated returning leader;** To facilitate **safe passage** for the parties during planned movement to the designated assembly areas. *Note: According to the Institute for Security Studies (Pretoria), the AU mandate for AMIB included monitoring, DDR, facilitating the delivery of humanitarian assistance and other tasks, but no explicit mention of civilian protection. The mission's rules of engagement, however, allowed for the use of force to protect civilians "under imminent threat of physical violence." [19]*	**Authorized strength:** 3,500 troops.[20]	Ethiopia, Mozambique, *South Africa*.[21]
Central African Republic	United Nations Mission in the Central African Republic (MINURCA)	1159 (1998), 1182 (1998), 2001 (1998), 1230 (1999), 1271 (1999)	UN-led Chapter VI	**Resolution 1159:** ...10. Decides that, taking into account the recommendations of the Secretary-General in his report of 23 February 1998, MINURCA shall have the following initial mandate: (a) **To assist in maintaining and enhancing security and stability, including freedom of movement, in Bangui and the immediate vicinity of the city;** (b) To assist the national security forces in **maintaining law and order and in protecting key installations in Bangui;** ...(d) To ensure security and freedom of movement of United Nations personnel and the safety and security of United Nations property;. ...13. Affirms that MINURCA may be required to take action to ensure security and freedom of movement of its personnel in the discharge of its mandate.... **Resolution 1182:** ...4. Recognizes that MINURCA, in implementing its mandate, may conduct limited-duration reconnaissance missions outside Bangui, and other tasks involving the security of United Nations personnel in accordance with paragraph 10 of Resolution 1159 (1998)....	**Reported strength:** 1,350 troops and military support personnel and 24 civilian police, supported by international and local civilian staff.[22]	**Contributors of military personnel:** Benin, Burkina Faso, Cameroon, Canada, Chad, Côte d'Ivoire, Egypt, France, *Gabon*, Mali, Portugal, Senegal, Togo, and Tunisia.

II. Selected UN Resolutions for Missions With Implications for Protection of Civilians

Conflict Area	Mission Name	Relevant UNSC Resolutions	Mission Type	Selected Language From UN Mandates	Mission Strength *authorized or reported[1]*	Troop Contributing Countries *Nation of force commander in italics[2]*
Congo	**United Nations Operation in the Congo (ONUC)**	143 (1960), 145 (1960), 146 (1960), 161 (1961), 169 (1961)	UN-led operation (Chapter VII not specified, but well-known that force was used)	**Resolution 143:** ...2. Decides to authorize the Secretary-General to take the necessary steps, in consultation with the Government of the Republic of the Congo, to provide the Government with such military assistance as may be necessary until, through the efforts of the Congolese Government with the technical assistance of the United Nations, the national security forces may be able, in the opinion of the Government, to meet fully their tasks.... **Resolution 161:** ...1. Urges that the United Nations take immediately all appropriate measures **to prevent the occurrence of civil war in the Congo,** including arrangements for cease-fires, the halting of all military operations, the prevention of clashes, and the use of force, if necessary, in the last resort....	**Reported strength:** (maximum): 19,828 troops, supported by international civilian and locally recruited staff.[23]	Argentina, Austria, Brazil, Burma, Canada, Ceylon, Denmark, Ethiopia, Ghana, Guinea, India, Indonesia, Iran, Ireland, Italy, Liberia, Malaya, Federation of Mali, Morocco, Netherlands, Nigeria, Norway, Pakistan, Philippines, Sierra Leone, Sudan, Sweden, Tunisia, United Arab Republic, and Yugoslavia.[24]
Georgia	**United Nations Observer Mission in Georgia (UNOMIG)**	858 (1993), 881 (1993), 937 (1994), 1077 (1996), 1494 (2003)	UN-led Chapter VI	**Resolution 1494:** ...17. *Endorses* the recommendations by the Secretary-General in his report of 21 July 2003 (S/2003/751, para. 30) that a civilian police component of 20 officers be added to UNOMIG, to strengthen its capacity to carry out its mandate and in particular **contribute to the creation of conditions conducive to the safe and dignified return of internally displaced persons and refugees...**	**Reported strength:** 131 total uniformed personnel, including 120 military observers and 11 police.	**Contributors of military personnel:** Albania, Austria, Bangladesh, Croatia, Czech Republic, Denmark, Egypt, France, Germany, Greece, Hungary, Indonesia, Jordan, Pakistan, Poland, Republic of Korea, Romania, Russian Federation, Sweden, Switzerland, Turkey, Ukraine, United Kingdom, United States, and Uruguay. **Contributors of police personnel:** Germany, Hungary, Poland, Russian Federation, and Switzerland.

II. Selected UN Resolutions for Missions With Implications for Protection of Civilians

Conflict Area	Mission Name	Relevant UNSC Resolutions	Mission Type	Selected Language From UN Mandates	Mission Strength *authorized or reported*[1]	Troop Contributing Countries *Nation of force commander in italics*[2]
Haiti	**Operation Uphold Democracy**	940 (1994)	UN-authorized Chapter VII (Multi-national Force)	**Resolution 940:** ...4. Acting under Chapter VII of the Charter of the United Nations, authorizes Member States to form a multinational force under unified command and control and, in this framework, to use all necessary means to facilitate the departure from Haiti of the military leadership, consistent with the Governors Island Agreement, the prompt return of the legitimately elected President and the restoration of the legitimate authorities of the Government of Haiti, and **to establish and maintain a secure and stable environment** that will permit implementation of the Governors Island Agreement, on the understanding that the cost of implementing this temporary operation will be borne by the participating Member States; ...16. Emphasizes the necessity that, inter alia: (a) All appropriate steps be taken **to ensure the security and safety of the operations and personnel engaged in such operations;** and (b) The security and safety arrangements undertaken extend to **all persons engaged in the operations....**	**Reported strength:** 22,000 troops.[25]	United States (lead nation providing 20,000 troops), and 12 other countries.[26]
Haiti	**United Nations Mission in Haiti (UNMIH)**	867 (1993), 940 (1994), 975 (1995), 1048 (1996)	UN-led Chapter VI	**Resolution 940:** .... 9. Decides to revise and extend the mandate of the United Nations Mission in Haiti (UNMIH) for a period of six months to assist the democratic Government of Haiti in fulfilling its responsibilities in connection with: (a) **sustaining the secure and stable environment** established during the multinational phase and **protecting international personnel and key installations....**	**Reported strength** (maximum): 6,065 troops and military support personnel, and 847 civilian police, supported by international and local civilian staff.	**Contributors of military and civilian police personnel:** Algeria, Antigua and Barbuda, Argentina, Austria, Bahamas, Bangladesh, Barbados, Belize, Benin, *Canada,* Djibouti, France, Guatemala, Guinea Bissau, Guyana, Honduras, India, Ireland, Jamaica, Jordan, Mali, Nepal, Netherlands, New Zealand, Pakistan, Philippines, Russian Federation, Saint Kitts and Nevis, Saint Lucia, Suriname, Togo, Trinidad and Tobago, Tunisia, and the *United States.*

II. Selected UN Resolutions for Missions With Implications for Protection of Civilians

Conflict Area	Mission Name	Relevant UNSC Resolutions	Mission Type	Selected Language From UN Mandates	Mission Strength *authorized or reported[1]*	Troop Contributing Countries, *Nation of force commander in italics[2]*
Haiti	**Multinational Interim Force (Operation Secure Tomorrow)**	1529 (2004)	UN-authorized Chapter VII (Multinational Force)	**Resolution 1529:** ...2. *Authorizes* the immediate deployment of a Multinational Interim Force for a period of not more than three months from adoption of this resolution: (a) **To contribute to a secure and stable environment in the Haitian capital and elsewhere in the country,** as appropriate and as circumstances permit, in order to support the Haitian President's request for international assistance to support the constitutional political process under way in Haiti; (b) To facilitate the provision of humanitarian assistance and the access of international humanitarian workers to the Haitian people in need; (c) To facilitate the provision of international assistance to the Haitian police and the Haitian Coast Guard in order **to establish and maintain public safety and law and order and to promote and protect human rights....**	**Reported strength:** 3,300 troops.[27]	United States (lead nation), Canada, Chile, and France.[28]
Northern Iraq	**Operation Provide Comfort I/II, Operation Safe Haven**	678 (1990), 687 (1991), 688 (1991)	Unclear UN authorization (United States & Multinational Force)	**Resolution 688:** ...1. Condemns the repression of the Iraqi civilian population in many parts of Iraq, including most recently in Kurdish populated areas, the consequences of which threaten international peace and security in the region; 2. Demands that Iraq, as a contribution to remove the threat to international peace and security in the region, immediately end this repression and express the hope in the same context that an open dialogue will take place to ensure that the human and political rights of all Iraqi citizens are respected; 3. Insists that Iraq allow immediate access by international humanitarian organizations to all those in need of assistance in all parts of Iraq and to make available all necessary facilities for their operations.... 6. Appeals to all Member States and to all humanitarian organizations to contribute to these humanitarian relief efforts....	**Reported strength:** 13,000 troops (US, Provide Comfort) and 5,000 troops (US, Safe Haven).[29]	United States (lead nation), United Kingdom, France, Turkey, and nine other nations.[30]
Kosovo	**Kosovo Force (KFOR)**	1160 (1998), 1199(1998), 1203(1998), 1239(1999), 1244(1999)	NATO bombing campaign not authorized by UN; follow-on UN-authorized Chapter VII peace operation (NATO)	**Resolution 1244:** ...9. Decides that the responsibilities of the international security presence to be deployed and acting in Kosovo will include: ...(c) **Establishing a secure environment in which refugees and displaced persons can return home in safety, the international civil presence can operate, a transitional administration can be established, and humanitarian aid can be delivered;** (d) **Ensuring public safety and order until the international civil presence can take responsibility for this task;** ... (h) Ensuring **the protection and freedom of movement of itself, the international civil presence, and other international organizations....**	**Authorized strength:** 50,000 troops.[31]	Argentina, Armenia, Austria, Azerbaijan, Belgium, Bulgaria, Canada, Czech Republic, Denmark, Estonia, Finland, France, Georgia, Germany, Greece, Hungary, Ireland, Italy, Latvia, Lithuania, Luxembourg, Mongolia, Morocco, Netherlands, Norway, Poland, Portugal, Romania, Slovakia, Slovenia, Spain, Sweden, Switzerland, Turkey, Ukraine, United Kingdom, and the United States.[32]

II. Selected UN Resolutions for Missions With Implications for Protection of Civilians

Conflict Area	Mission Name	Relevant UNSC Resolutions	Mission Type	Selected Language From UN Mandates	Mission Strength *authorized or reported[1]*	Troop Contributing Countries *Nation of force commander in italics[2]*
Kosovo	United Nations Mission in Kosovo (UNMIK)	1160 (1998), 1199 (1998), 1203 (1999), 1207 (1999), 1239 (1999), 1244(1999)	UN-led Chapter VII civilian operation	**Resolution 1244:** …11. Decides that the main responsibilities of the international civil presence will include: (i) **Maintaining civil law and order**, including establishing local police forces and meanwhile through the deployment of international police personnel to serve in Kosovo; (j) **Protecting and promoting human rights;** (k) **Assuring the safe and unimpeded return of all refugees and displaced persons to**…Kosovo….	n/a	n/a
Liberia	ECOWAS Mission in Liberia (ECOMIL)	1497 (2003)	UN-authorized Chapter VII (Economic Community of West African States)	**Resolution 1497:** …1. Authorizes Member States to establish a Multinational Force in Liberia to support the implementation of the 17 June 2003 ceasefire agreement, including establishing conditions for initial stages of disarmament, demobilization and reintegration activities, **to help establish and maintain security in the period after the departure of the current President and the installation of a successor authority,** taking into account the agreements to be reached by the Liberian parties, and to secure the environment for the delivery of humanitarian assistance, and to prepare for the introduction of a longer-term United Nations stabilization force to relieve the Multinational Force…. *Note: The mandate for the ceasefire monitoring group laid out in the June 2003 ceasefire agreement includes tasks such as monitoring, DDR, and security for VIPs, but no explicit mention of civilian protection.*	**Reported strength:**[33] 3,600 troops.	Benin, Gambia, Ghana, Guinea-Bissau, Mali, *Nigeria*, Senegal, and Togo.[34]

II. Selected UN Resolutions for Missions With Implications for Protection of Civilians

Conflict Area	Mission Name	Relevant UNSC Resolutions	Mission Type	Selected Language From UN Mandates	Mission Strength authorized or reported[1]	Troop Contributing Countries Nation of force commander in italics[2]
Rwanda	United Nations Mission for Rwanda (UNAMIR)	812 (1993), 846 (1993), 872 (1993), 891 (1993), 893 (1994), 909 (1994), 912 (1994), 918 (1994), 925 (1994), 929 (1994), 935 (1994), 965 (1994), 977 (1995), 978 (1995), 989 (1995), 997 (1995), 1005 (1995), 1011 (1995), 1013 (1995), 1028 (1995), 1029 (1995), 1047 (1996), 1050 (1996), 1053 (1996)	UN-led Chapter VI; Chapter VII arms embargo after Resolution 918 (1994)	**Resolution 912:** ...8. Decides, in the light of the current situation in Rwanda, to adjust the mandate of UNAMIR as follows:... (c) To monitor and report on developments in Rwanda, **including the safety and security of the civilians who sought refuge with UNAMIR....** **Resolution 918:** ...3. Decides to expand UNAMIR's mandate under Resolution 912 (1994) to include the following additional responsibilities within the limits of the resources available to it: (a) **To contribute to the security and protection of displaced persons, refugees and civilians at risk in Rwanda, including through the establishment and maintenance, where feasible, of secure humanitarian areas;** (b) To provide security and support for the distribution of relief supplies and humanitarian relief operations; 4. Recognizes that **UNAMIR may be required to take action in self-defence against persons or groups who threaten protected sites and populations,** United Nations and other humanitarian personnel or the means of delivery and distribution of humanitarian relief.... **Resolution 925:** ...4. Reaffirms that UNAMIR, in addition to continuing to act as an intermediary between the parties in an attempt to secure their agreement to a cease-fire, will: (a) Contribute to the **security and protection of displaced persons, refugees and civilians at risk in Rwanda including through the establishment and maintenance, where feasible, of secure humanitarian areas;** (b) Provide security and support for the distribution of relief supplies and humanitarian relief operations....	**Authorized strength:** (maximum, 17 May 1994 to 8 June 1995): 5,500 military personnel, including approximately 5,200 troops and military support personnel, 320 military observers, and 90 civilian police.[35]	**Contributors of military and civilian police personnel:** Argentina, Australia, Austria, Bangladesh, Belgium, Brazil, *Canada*, Chad, Congo, Djibouti, Egypt, Ethiopia, Fiji, Germany, Ghana, Guinea, Guinea Bissau, Guyana, *India*, Jordan, Kenya, Malawi, Mali, Netherlands, Niger, Nigeria, Pakistan, Poland, Romania, Russian Federation, Senegal, Slovak Republic, Spain, Switzerland, Togo, Tunisia, United Kingdom, Uruguay, Zambia, and Zimbabwe.

II. Selected UN Resolutions for Missions With Implications for Protection of Civilians

Conflict Area	Mission Name	Relevant UNSC Resolutions	Mission Type	Selected Language From UN Mandates	Mission Strength *authorized or reported[1]*	Troop Contributing Countries *Nation of force commander in italics[2]*
Rwanda	**Operation Turquoise**	929 (1994)	UN-authorized Chapter VII (France)	**Resolution 929:** ...2. Welcomes also the offer by Member States (S/1994/734) to cooperate with the Secretary-General in order to achieve the objectives of the United Nations in Rwanda through the establishment of a temporary operation under national command and control aimed at **contributing, in an impartial way, to the security and protection of displaced persons, refugees and civilians at risk in Rwanda,** on the understanding that the costs of implementing the offer will be borne by the Member States concerned; 3. Acting under Chapter VII of the Charter of the United Nations, authorizes the Member States cooperating with the Secretary-General to conduct the operation referred to in paragraph 2 above **using all necessary means** to achieve the humanitarian objectives set out in subparagraphs 4 (a) and (b) of Resolution 925 (1994).... **Resolution 925:** 4.... (a) **Contribute to the security and protection of displaced persons, refugees and civilians at risk in Rwanda, including through the establishment and maintenance, where feasible, of secure humanitarian areas;** and (b) Provide security and support for the distribution of relief supplies and humanitarian relief operations....	**Reported strength:** 2,500.[36]	France (lead nation), Senegal.[37]
Somalia	**Unified Task Force (UNITAF)/ Operation Restore Hope**	794(1992)	UN-authorized Chapter VII (Multi-national Force)	**Resolution 794:** ...10. Acting under Chapter VII of the Charter of the United Nations, authorizes the Secretary-General and Member States cooperating to implement the offer referred to in paragraph 8 above to **use all necessary means to establish as soon as possible a secure environment for humanitarian relief operations in Somalia....**	**Reported strength** (peak): 30,000 US military personnel and 10,000 personnel from 24 other states.[38]	Australia, Belgium, Botswana, Canada, Egypt, France, Germany, Greece, India, Italy, Kuwait, Morocco, New Zealand, Nigeria, Norway, Pakistan, Saudi Arabia, Sweden, Tunisia, Turkey, United Arab Emirates, United Kingdom, *United States* (lead nation), and Zimbabwe.[39]

				II. Selected UN Resolutions for Missions With Implications for Protection of Civilians		
Conflict Area	Mission Name	Relevant UNSC Resolutions	Mission Type	Selected Language From UN Mandates	Mission Strength *authorized or reported[1]*	Troop Contributing Countries *Nation of force commander in italics[2]*
Somalia	**United Nations Operation in Somalia II (UNOSOM II)**	814 (1993), 837 (1993), 865 (1993), 878 (1993), 885 (1993), 886 (1993), 897 (1994), 923 (1994), 946 (1994), 953 (1994), 954 (1994)	UN-led Chapter VII	**Resolution 814:** *This resolution establishes UNOSOM II's mandate according to the Report of the Secretary General of 3 March 1993. According to the UN, this report authorized UNOSOM II to "take appropriate action, including enforcement measures, to establish throughout Somalia a secure environment for humanitarian assistance."[40]* **Resolution 837:** …Reaffirms that the Secretary-General is authorized under Resolution 814 (1993) to **take all necessary measures** against all those responsible for the armed attacks referred to in paragraph 1 above, including against those responsible for publicly inciting such attacks, to **establish the effective authority of UNOSOM II throughout Somalia**, including to secure the investigation of their actions and their arrest and detention for prosecution, trial and punishment.…	**Authorized strength:** (maximum): 28,000 military and civilian police personnel; 2,800 international and local civilian staff.	Australia, Bangladesh, Belgium, Botswana, Canada, Egypt, France, Germany, Ghana, Greece, India, Indonesia, Ireland, Italy, Kuwait, *Malaysia*, Morocco, Nepal, Netherlands, New Zealand, Nigeria, Norway, Pakistan, Philippines, Republic of Korea, Romania, Saudi Arabia, Sweden, Tunisia, *Turkey*, United Arab Emirates, United States, Zambia, and Zimbabwe.
Timor Leste	**International Force for East Timor (INTERFET)**	1264 (1999)	UN-authorized Chapter VII (Multi-national Force)	**Resolution 1264:** …2. Emphasizes the urgent need for coordinated humanitarian assistance and the importance of allowing full, safe and unimpeded access by humanitarian organizations and **calls upon all parties to cooperate with such organizations so as to ensure the protection of civilians at risk, the safe return of refugees and displaced persons and the effective delivery of humanitarian aid;** 3. Authorizes the establishment of a multinational force under a unified command structure, pursuant to the request of the Government of Indonesia conveyed to the Secretary-General on 12 September 1999, with the following tasks: **to restore peace and security in East Timor,** to protect and support UNAMET in carrying out its tasks and, within force capabilities, to facilitate humanitarian assistance operations, and authorizes the States participating in the multinational force to take all necessary measures to fulfil this mandate.…	**Reported strength:** As of March 2000, two brigades numbering approximately 9,000 troops.[41]	Includes *Australia* (lead nation), Brazil, Brunei, Canada, Denmark, Egypt, Fiji, France, Germany, Ireland, Italy, Jordan, Kenya, Malaysia, Mozambique, Nepal, New Zealand, Norway, Philippines, Portugal, Republic of Korea, Singapore, Sweden, Thailand, United Kingdom, and the United States.[42]

II. Selected UN Resolutions for Missions With Implications for Protection of Civilians						
Conflict Area	Mission Name	Relevant UNSC Resolutions	Mission Type	Selected Language From UN Mandates	Mission Strength *authorized or reported[1]*	Troop Contributing Countries *Nation of force commander in italics[2]*
Timor Leste	United Nations Transitional Administration in East Timor (UNTAET)	1272 (1999), 1319 (2000), 1338 (2001), 1392 (2002)	UN-led Chapter VII	**Resolution 1272 (1999):** ...Decides to establish, in accordance with the report of the Secretary-General, a United Nations Transitional Administration in East Timor (UNTAET), which will be endowed with overall responsibility for the administration of East Timor and is empowered to exercise all legislative and executive authority, including the administration of justice; 2. Decides also that the mandate of UNTAET shall consist of the following elements: (a) **To provide security and maintain law and order throughout the territory of East Timor**; ...(d) To ensure the coordination and delivery of humanitarian assistance, rehabilitation and development assistance.... **Resolution 1319:** ...6. **Underlines that UNTAET should respond robustly to the militia threat in East Timor,** consistent with its Resolution 1272 (1999) of 22 October 1999....	**Authorized strength:** (maximum): Military 9,150 troops and 1,640 civilian police.	**Contributors of military personnel:** Australia, Bangladesh, Bolivia, Brazil, Chile, Denmark, Egypt, Fiji, Ireland, Japan, Jordan, Kenya, Malaysia, Nepal, New Zealand, Norway, Pakistan, Philippines, Portugal, Republic of Korea, Russian Federation, Singapore, Slovakia, Sweden, *Thailand,* Turkey, United Kingdom, United States, and Uruguay. **Contributors of civilian police personnel:** Argentina, Australia, Austria, Bangladesh, Benin, Bosnia & Herzegovina, Brazil, Canada, China, Egypt, Gambia, Ghana, Jordan, Kenya, Malaysia, Mozambique, Namibia, Nepal, Niger, Nigeria, Norway, Pakistan, Philippines, Portugal, Russian Federation, Samoa, Senegal, Singapore, Slovenia, Spain, Sri Lanka, Sweden, Thailand, Turkey, Ukraine, United Kingdom, United States, Vanuatu, and Zimbabwe.

[1] Unless otherwise noted, figures in this column come from the UN Department of Peacekeeping Operations (DPKO) website, mission "Facts and Figures" pages, www.un.org/depts/dpko, as of 6 April 2006.

[2] Unless otherwise noted, information in this column comes from the DPKO website, mission "Facts and Figures" pages, www.un.org/depts/dpko, as of 6 April 2006.

[3] US Department of State, "Background Note: Côte d'Ivoire," www.state.gov/r/pa/ei/bgn/2846.htm, as of 11 April 2006.

[4] Ifeoha Azikiwe, "Ivorien Crisis: One Year of ECOWAS Diplomatic Initiative," *This Day* Online, 16 November 2004, www.thisdayonline.com/archive/2003/11/12/20031112dip01.htm.

[5] Ibid.

[6] The Henry L. Stimson Center, "Review of European Union Field Operations," Factsheet, Future of Peace Operations project, March 2004, www.stimson.org/fopo/pdf/Factsheet_EUFieldOperations.pdf.

[7] Ibid.

[8] Actual number as of December 2005; International Security Assistance Force, "Media Frequently Asked Questions," ISAF Fact Sheet, 30 December 2005, www.afnorth.nato.int/ISAF/Update/media_faq.htm.

[9] As of September 2005; International Security Assistance Force, "ISAF Structure," ISAF Fact Sheet, 5 September 2005, www.afnorth.nato.int/ISAF/structure/structure_structure.htm.

[10] Permanent Mission of Slovenia to the UN, "Operation Alba," 1998, www.un.int/slovenia/pk-alba.html.

[11] Ettore Greco, "Delegated Peacekeeping: The Case of Operation Alba," *Insituto Affari Internazionali*, 1998, www.ciaonet.org/wps/gre01/.

[12] Selected resolutions relate to the UNPROFOR mandate, troop strength, humanitarian relief escorts, no-fly zone, safe areas, and exclusion zones. For an extensive list of UN Security Council Resolutions related to UNPROFOR, IFOR and SFOR, see NATO SFOR Security Council Resolutions online: www.nato.int/ifor/un/un-resol.htm.

[13] UN Department of Public Information, "Former Yugoslavia – UNPROFOR: United Nations Protection Force Profile," 31 August 1996, www.un.org/Depts/dpko/dpko/co_mission/unprof_p.htm.

[14] UN Department of Public Information, "United Nations Protection Force: Background," September 1996, www.un.org/Depts/DPKO/Missions/unprof_b.htm.

[15] "The Balkan Conflict: Implementation Force (IFOR), Chronology of Events," 24 August 2004, http://home.wanadoo.nl/tcc/balkan/ifor_chron.html.

[16] "The Balkan Conflict: Stabilization Force (SFOR), Chronology of Events," 3 February 2001, http://home.wanadoo.nl/tcc/balkan/sfor_chron_1b.html.

[17] "The Balkan Conflict: Force Structure," 20 September 1996, http://home.wanadoo.nl/tcc/balkan/ifor_org.html.

[18] The International Institute for Security Studies, *The Military Balance 1997/1998* (London: Oxford University Press, 1997), and The International Institute for Security Studies, *The Military Balance 2000/2001* (London: Oxford University Press, 2000).

[19] Henri Boshoff, "Burundi: The African Union's First Mission," Institute for Security Studies, African Security Analysis Programme Situation Report, 10 June 2003, www.iss.co.za/AF/current/burundijun03.pdf.

[20] UN Department of Public Information, "African and UN Peace Missions," *Africa Recovery*, 17 October 2003, www.un.org/ecosocdev/geninfo/afrec/vol17no3/map_p17.pdf.

[21] Boshoff, "Burundi," 1.

22 There was also a provision for 114 international civilian staff, 111 local staff and 13 United Nations Volunteers. Additional short-term and medium-term United Nations observers were deployed during the legislative (November/December 1998) and presidential (September 1999) elections.

23 UN Department of Public Information, "Republic of the Congo – ONUC: Facts and Figures," www.un.org/depts/DPKO/Missions/onucF.html.

24 Ibid.

25 GlobalSecurity.org, "Operation Uphold Democracy," 2 March 2004, www.globalsecurity.org/military/ops/uphold_democracy.htm.

26 Ibid.

27 Jim Garamone, "Haiti Interim Force Rises to 3,300; Confiscates Arms," *American Forces Press Service*, 23 March 2004, www.dod.gov/news/Mar2004/n03232004_200403233.html.

28 Ibid.

29 Center for Defense Information, "U.S. Military Deployments/Engagements 1975-1997," http://cicg.free.fr/diremp/depl7597.htm.

30 GlobalSecurity.org, "Operation Provide Comfort," 28 November 2003, www.globalsecurity.org/military/ops/provide_comfort.htm.

31 Kosovo Force: Official Website of the Kosovo Force, "Background to the Conflict," www.nato.int/kfor/kfor/intro.htm.

32 Kosovo Force: Official Website of the Kosovo Force, "Nations Contributing to KFOR," www.nato.int/kfor/kfor/nations/default.htm.

33 US Department of State, "Background Note: Liberia," November 2004, www.state.gov/r/pa/ei/bgn/6618.htm.

34 UN Mission in Liberia, "All ECOMIL Contingents to Be Rehatted on 1 October 2003," UNMIL Press Release, 28 September 2003.

35 In February 1995, the authorized strength of the civilian police was increased to 120. Authorized troop levels for UNAMIR varied significantly over the course of the mission. For a timeline of UNAMIR's various troop levels, see "UNAMIR Facts and figures," Department of Peacekeeping Operations, www.un.org/depts/dpko/dpko/co_mission/unamirF.htm.

36 Sophie Haspeslagh, "Safe Havens in Rwanda: Operation Turquoise," www.beyondintractability.org/iweb/docs/Safe_Havens-Rwanda.pdf.

37 Ibid.

38 GlobalSecurity.org, "Operation Restore Hope," 10 October 2002, www.globalsecurity.org/military/ops/restore_hope.htm.

39 UN Department of Public Information, "Somalia – UNOSOM I: Mission Backgrounder," 21 March 1997, www.un.org/Depts/DPKO/Missions/unosomi.htm.

40 United Nations, "Somalia – UNOSOM II: Mandate," Department of Peacekeeping Operations, United Nations, www.un.org/depts/dpko/dpko/co_mission/unosom2mandate.html.

41 Irish Defense Forces, "Background to the East Timor INTERFET Mission," Press Release, 12 March 2000, www.military.ie/pr/12-03-2000.htm.

42 Steve Ayling and Sarah Guise, "UNTAC and INTERFET: A Comparative Analysis," National Defense University, www.ndu.edu/inss/symposia/pacific2001/aylingpaper.htm.

SELECTED BIBLIOGRAPHY

African Union. "Policy Framework for the Establishment of the African Standby Force and the Military Staff Committee, Part I (Exp/ASF-MSC/2)." Adopted by the African Chiefs of Defence Staff. Addis Ababa: African Union, 15-16 May 2003.

--------. "Protocol Relating to the Establishment of the Peace and Security Council of the African Union." Durban: African Union, July 2002.

--------. "The Constitutive Act of the African Union." Lomé: African Union, 11 July 2000.

--------. Peace and Security Council. "Communiqué of the 17th Ordinary Session." PSC/PR/Comm. (XVII). 20 October 2004.

--------. Peace and Security Council. "Communiqué of the 46th Ordinary Session." 10 March 2006.

Amnesty International. "Haiti: Disarmament Delayed, Justice Denied." AMR 36/005/2005. London: Amnesty International, 28 July 2005.

--------. *The Human Rights Crisis in Ituri.* web.amnesty.org/pages/cod-040803-background_2-eng.

--------. *Ituri: A Need for Protection, a Thirst for Justice.* New York: Amnesty International USA, 21 October 2003.

--------. "Sudan: UN Security Council Must Meet 'Responsibility to Protect' Civilians." Press Release. 25 May 2006.

Ayling, Steve and Sarah Guise. "UNTAC and INTERFET: A Comparative Analysis." National Defense University, 2001. www.ndu.edu/inss/symposia/pacific2001/aylingpaper.htm.

Ayoob, Mohammed. "Humanitarian Intervention and International Society." *Global Governance* 7:3 (July-September 2001).

Bagshaw, Simon and Diane Paul. *Protect or Neglect? Toward a More Effective United Nations Approach to the Protection of Internally Displaced Persons.* Washington, DC: The Brookings-SAIS Project on Internal Displacement and the UN Office for the Coordination of Humanitarian Affairs, November 2004.

Baldo, Suliman and Peter Bouckaert. *War Crimes in Kisangani: The Response of Rwandan-Backed Rebels to the May 2002 Mutiny.* No. 6(A). Human Rights Watch, August 2002.

Bankus, Lt. Col. Brent. "Training the Military for Peace Operations: A Past, Present, and Future View." In *Peaceworks 43: Training for Peace and Humanitarian Relief Operations*, Robert M. Schoenhaus, ed. Washington, DC: United States Institute of Peace, April 2002.

Beardsley, Major Brent. "Lessons Learned or Not Learned from the Rwandan Genocide." 7th Annual Graduate Student Symposium. Royal Military College of Canada, 29-30 October 2004.

Bellamy, Alex J., Paul Williams, and Stuart Griffin. *Understanding Peacekeeping.* Cambridge: Polity Press, 2004.

Berger, Major Joseph B. III, Major Derek Grimes, and Major Eric T. Jensen, eds. *Operational Law Handbook.* JA 422. Charlottesville, Virginia: International and Operational Law Department of the Judge Advocate General's Legal Center and School, United States Army, 2004.

Bernath, Clifford and Anne Edgerton. *MONUC: Flawed Mandate Limits Success.* Washington, DC: Refugees International, May 2003.

Bernath, Clifford and David C. Gompert. *"The Power to Protect": Using New Military Capabilities to Stop Mass Killings.* Washington, DC: Refugees International, July 2003.

Bhatia, Pooja and Benjamin S. Litman. *Keeping the Peace in Haiti? An Assessment of the UN Stabilization Mission in Haiti Using Compliance with its Prescribed Mandate as a Barometer for Success.* Harvard Law Student Advocates for Human Rights and Centro de Justica Global, March 2005.

Boshoff, Henri. "Burundi: The African Union's First Mission." African Security Analysis Programme Situation Report. Pretoria: Institute for Security Studies, 10 June 2003. www.iss.co.za/AF/current/burundijun03.pdf.

--------. "Overview of MONUC's Military Strategy and Concept of Operations." In *Challenges of Peace Implementation: The UN Mission in the Democratic Republic of the Congo.* Mark Malan and Joao Gomes Porto, eds. Pretoria: Institute for Security Studies, 2004.

Caverzaslo, Sylvie Giossi. *Strengthening Protection in War – A Search for Professional Standards. Summary of Discussions Among Human Rights and Humanitarian Organizations.* Geneva: International Committee of the Red Cross, 2001.

Center on International Cooperation. *Annual Review of Global Peace Operations 2006.* Ian Johnstone, ed. Boulder: Lynne Rienner, 2006.

Center of Excellence in Disaster Management and Humanitarian Assistance. *Cobra Gold 2005 – Thailand.* coe-dmha.org/cobragold.htm.

The Challenges Project. *Challenges of Peace Operations: Into the 21st Century, Concluding Report, 1997-2002.* Stockholm: Elanders Gotab, 2002.

Chandler, David. From *Kosovo to Kabul: Human Rights and International Intervention.* London: Pluto Press, 2002.

Chatterjee, Deen K. and Don E. Scheid, eds. *Ethics and Foreign Intervention.* Cambridge: Cambridge University Press, 2003.

Chesterman, Simon. *Just War or Just Peace? Humanitarian Intervention and International Law.* Oxford: Oxford University Press, 2001.

Chief of Defense Staff, Canadian Forces. *Peace Support Operations.* Joint Doctrine Manual B-GJ-005-307/FP-030. Canada: National Defense, November 2002.

Chief of Joint Operations, Permanent Joint Headquarters. *Peace Support Operations,* Joint Warfare Publication 3-50 (JWP 3-50). United Kingdom: As Directed by the Chiefs of Staff, 1998.

Chin, Sally and Jonathan Morgenstein. *No Power to Protect: The African Union Mission in Sudan.* Refugees International, November 2005.

Cilliers, Jakkie and Mark Malan. *Progress with the African Standby Force.* Occasional Paper No. 98. Pretoria: Institute for Security Studies, May 2005.

Clough, Michael. "Darfur: Whose Responsibility to Protect?" In *World Report 2005.* New York: Human Rights Watch, 2005.

Coghlan, Benjamin, Richard J. Brennan, Pascal Ngoy, David Dofara, Brad Otto, Mark Clements, and Tony Stewart. "Mortality in the Democratic Republic of Congo: A Nationwide Survey." *The Lancet* 367:9504 (7 January 2006).

Cohen, Roberta and Francis M. Deng. "Exodus Within Borders: The Uprooted Who Never Left Home." *Foreign Affairs* 77:4 (July/August 1998).

--------. *Masses in Flight: The Global Crisis of Internal Displacement.* Washington, DC: The Brookings Institution, 1998.

Crane, Conrad. *Landpower and Crises: Army Roles and Missions in Smaller-Scale Contingencies During the 1990s.* Carlisle, PA: Strategic Studies Institute, US Army War College, January 2001.

Dallaire, Roméo A. and Brent Beardsley. *Shake Hands with the Devil: The Failure of Humanity in Rwanda.* Toronto: Random House, 2003.

Darcy, James. *Human Rights and International Standards: What Relief Workers Need to Know.* Network Paper 19. London: Humanitarian Practice Network, February 1997.

Defense Science Board. *2004 Summer Study on Transition to and From Hostilities.* Washington, DC: US Department of Defense Office of the Undersecretary of Defense for Acquisition, Technology, and Linguistics, September 2004.

Dell'Amico, Michael. "STM 3 Humanitarian Assistance: Challenges and Opportunities in an Integrated Mission Context." UNHCR Geneva, presented in Abuja, 12-22 April 2005.

Deng, Francis M. *Protecting the Dispossessed: A Challenge for the International Community*. Washington, DC: The Brookings Institution, 1993.

Denning, Mike. "A Prayer for Marie? Creating an Effective African Standby Force." *Parameters* 34:4 (2004/2005).

Durch, William J., ed. *UN Peacekeeping, American Politics, and the Uncivil Wars of the 1990s*. Washington, DC: The Henry L. Stimson Center, 1996.

Durch, William J. and Tobias C. Berkman. *Who Should Keep the Peace?: Providing Security for Twenty-first Century Peace Operations*. Washington, DC: The Henry L. Stimson Center, forthcoming.

--------. "Restoring and Maintaining Peace: What We Know So Far." In *21st Century Peace Operations*. William J. Durch, ed. Washington, DC: United States Institute of Peace, forthcoming.

Durch, William J., Victoria K. Holt, Caroline R. Earle, and Moira K. Shanahan. *The Brahimi Report and the Future of UN Peace Operations*. Washington, DC: The Henry L. Stimson Center, December 2003.

Economic Community of West African States. *Protocol Relating to the Mechanism for Conflict Prevention, Management, Resolution, Peacekeeping, and Security*. Lomé: ECOWAS, 10 December 1999.

Egeland, Jan. "Statement by Under-Secretary Jan Egeland to the Security Council on the Protection of Civilians in Armed Conflict." United Nations Department of Public Information, 21 June 2005.

Elliott, Lorraine and Graeme Cheeseman, eds. *Forces for Good? Cosmopolitan Militaries in the Twenty-First Century*. Manchester and New York: Manchester University Press, 2005.

État-Major des Armées. *The French Force Commitment Concept*. No. 827/DEF/EMA/EMP.1/NP. État-Major des Armées, 23 July 1997.

Falk, Richard, Mary Kaldor, Carl Tham, Samantha Power, Mahmood Mamdani, David Rieff, Eric Rouleau, Zia Mian, Ronald Steel, Stephen Holmes, Ramesh Thakur, Stephen Zunes. "Humanitarian Intervention: A Forum." *The Nation* 277:2 (14 July 2003).

Feil, Col. Scott R. *Could 5,000 Peacekeepers have Saved 500,000 Rwandans? Early Intervention Reconsidered*. ISD Report 3:2. Washington, DC: Institute for the Study of Diplomacy, Georgetown University, April 1997.

Findlay, Trevor. *The Use of Force in UN Peace Operations*. Oxford: Oxford University Press for the Stockholm International Peace Research Institute, 2002.

Flavin, Col. William. *Civil Military Operations: Afghanistan Observations on Civil Military Operations During the First Year of Operation Enduring Freedom.* Carlisle, PA: United States Army Peacekeeping and Stability Operations Institute, Army War College, 23 March 2004.

Flournoy, Michèle, Julianne Smith, Guy Ben-Ari, Kathleen McInnis, and David Scruggs. *European Defense Integration: Bridging the Gap Between Strategies and Capabilities.* Washington, DC: Center for Strategic and International Studies, 2005.

Forum for Early Warning and Early Response (FEWER). *Ituri: Stakes, Actors, Dynamics.* London: FEWER Secretariat, October 2003.

Frohardt, Mark, Diane Paul, and Larry Minear. *Protecting Human Rights: The Challenge to Humanitarian Organizations.* Occasional Papers 35. Providence, RI: The Watson Institute, 1999.

Gompert, David C., Courtney Richardson, Richard L. Kugler, and Clifford H. Bernath. *Learning from Darfur: Building a Net-Capable African Force to Stop Mass Killing.* Defense and Technology Paper 15. Washington, DC: Center for Technology and National Security Policy, National Defense University, July 2005.

Gregoire, Joseph P. "The Bases of French Peace Operations Doctrine." Carlisle Papers in Security Strategy Series 4. Carlisle, PA: US Army War College, Strategic Studies Institute, September 2004.

Grevi, Giovanni, Dov Lynch, and Antonio Missiroli. "ESDP Operations." European Institute for Security Studies. www.iss-eu.org/esdp/09-dvl-am.pdf.

Guéhenno, Jean-Marie. "Opening Remarks of Mr. Jean-Marie Guéhenno, Under-Secretary-General for Peacekeeping Operations to the Special Committee on Peacekeeping Operations." *UN News Center*, 31 January 2005.

--------. "Present-day Peacekeeping Demands Exceed Capacity of Any Single Organization." Presentation to the UN Fourth Committee, 25 October 2004.

Guha-Sapir, Debarati and Olivier Degomme with Mark Phelan. *Darfur: Counting the Deaths, Mortality Estimates for Multiple Survey Data.* Brussels: The Centre for Research on the Epidemiology of Disasters, University of Louvain, School of Public Health, 2005.

Hayes, Margaret Daly and Rear Admiral Gary Wealty, eds. *Interagency and Political-Military Dimensions of Peace Operations: Haiti – A Case Study.* Washington, DC: Institute for National Strategic Studies, National Defense University, 1996.

Henkin, Louis. "Kosovo and the Law of 'Humanitarian Intervention.'" *The American Journal of International Law* 93:4 (October 1999).

Henkin, Louis, Ruth Wedgwood, Jonathan I. Charney, Christine M. Chinkin, Richard A. Falk, Thomas M. Franck, and W. Michael Reisman. "Editorial Comments: NATO's Kosovo Intervention." *The American Journal of International Law* 93:4 (October 1999).

Henricks, SFC Richard. "COBs: The Civilian Element." *Soldiers Online* (April 1999). www.army.mil/Soldiers/apr1999/features/cob.html.

Herrly, Peter F. *The Impact of Peacekeeping and Stability Operations on the Armed Forces.* Conference Report, 17-18 June 2005, No. 915. Washington, DC: The Heritage Foundation, 2005.

Holt, Victoria K. *The Responsibility to Protect: Considering the Operational Capacity for Civilian Protection.* Pre-publication draft. Washington, DC: The Henry L. Stimson Center, January 2005. www.stimson.org/fopo/pdf/Stimson_CivPro_pre-pubdraftFeb04.pdf.

--------. *The Military and Civilian Protection: Developing Roles and Capacities.* HPG Report 22. London: Humanitarian Policy Group, Overseas Development Institute, March 2006.

Holt, Victoria K. with Moira Shanahan. *African Capacity-Building for Peace Operations: UN Collaboration with the African Union and ECOWAS.* Washington, DC: The Henry L. Stimson Center, 2005.

Holzgrefe, J. L. and Robert O. Keohane, eds. *Humanitarian Intervention: Ethical, Legal, and Political Dilemmas.* Cambridge: Cambridge University Press, 2003.

House of Commons International Development Committee. *Darfur, Sudan: The Responsibility to Protect.* Fifth Report of the Session 2004-2005, Vol. 1. London: House of Commons, 30 March 2005.

Human Rights Watch. "DR Congo: War Crimes in Bukavu." Briefing Paper. New York: Human Rights Watch, June 2004.

--------. *Uganda in Eastern DRC: Fueling Political and Ethnic Strife.* New York: Human Rights Watch, March 2001.

--------. *World Report 2005.* New York: Human Rights Watch, 2005.

--------. *World Report 2006.* New York: Human Rights Watch, 2006.

Igiri, Cheryl O. and Princeton N. Lyman. *Giving Meaning to "Never Again": Seeking an Effective Response to the Crisis in Darfur and Beyond.* Council Special Report No. 5. Washington, DC: The Council on Foreign Relations, September 2004.

Indian Army. *Indian Army Doctrine.* Shimla, India: Headquarters Army Training Command, 18 October 2004. indianarmy.nic.in/indianarmydoctrine.htm.

Inter-Agency Standing Committee. *Growing the Sheltering Tree: Protecting Rights through Humanitarian Action.* UNICEF, 2005.

International Commission on Intervention and State Sovereignty. *The Responsibility to Protect: Report of the International Commission on Intervention and State Sovereignty.* Ottawa: International Development Research Centre, 2001.

International Committee of the Red Cross. *Workshop on Protection for Human Rights and Humanitarian Organizations: Doing Something About it and Doing it Well.* Geneva: International Committee of the Red Cross, 1999.

International Crisis Group. *The Agreement on a Cease-Fire in the Democratic Republic of the Congo: An Analysis of the Agreement and Prospects for Peace.* Brussels: International Crisis Group, 20 August 1999.

--------. *Congo Crisis: Military Interventions in Ituri.* New York: International Crisis Group, 13 June 2003.

--------. *The Congo's Transition is Failing: Crisis in the Kivus.* Africa Report No. 91. Washington, DC: International Crisis Group, 30 March 2005.

--------. *Darfur: The Failure to Protect.* Africa Report No. 89. Washington, DC: International Crisis Group, 8 March 2005.

International Institute for Security Studies. *The Military Balance 1997/1998.* London: Oxford University Press, 1997.

--------. *The Military Balance 2000/2001.* London: Oxford University Press, 2000.

International Regional Information Network. "DRC: Six Killed as Fighting Erupts During Protest in Bunia." *International Regional Information Network*, 16 September 2003.

--------. "DRC: UN Troops Killed 50 Militiamen in Self-Defence, Annan Says." 4 March 2005.

--------. "EU Calls Artemis Operation 'A Big Success.'" 17 September 2003.

International Rescue Committee. "The Lancet Publishes IRC Mortality Study from DR Congo; 3.9 Million Have Died, 38,000 Die per Month." Press Release. International Rescue Committee, 2 January 2006.

Kassa, Michael. "Humanitarian Assistance in the DRC." In *Challenges of Peace Implementation: The UN Mission in the Democratic Republic of the Congo.* Mark Malan and Joao Gomes Porto, eds. Pretoria: Institute for Security Studies, 2004.

Kissinger, Henry. *Does America Need a Foreign Policy? Toward a Diplomacy for the 21st Century.* New York: Simon and Schuster, 2001.

Kuperman, Alan J. "Humanitarian Hazard." *Harvard International Review* 26:1 (Spring 2004).

Lang, Anthony F. *Agency and Ethics: The Politics of Military Intervention.* New York: State University of New York University Press, 2002.

Mace, Catriona. "Operation Artemis: Mission Improbable?" *European Security Review* 18 (July 2003).

MacFarlane, Neil S., Carolin Thielking, and Thomas G. Weiss. "The Responsibility to Protect: Is Anyone Interested in Humanitarian Intervention?" *Third World Quarterly* 25:5 (2004).

Malan, Mark. *Developing the ECOWAS Civilian Peace Support Operations Structure.* Report of an Experts' Workshop convened at the Kofi Annan International Peacekeeping Training Centre, 9-10 February 2006. Accra, Ghana: KAIPTC, 23 February 2006.

Malan, Mark and Joao Gomes Porto, eds. *Challenges of Peace Implementation: The UN Mission in the Democratic Republic of the Congo.* Pretoria: Institute for Security Studies, 2004.

Malone, David M., ed. *The UN Security Council: From the Cold War to the 21st Century.* Boulder: Lynn Reinner, 2004.

Martin, Sarah, Peter Gantz, and Braun Jones. "Haitian Voices: Response to the Brazilian Peacekeepers." Washington, DC: Refugees International, 4 March 2005.

Médecins sans Frontières. *Nothing New in Ituri: The Violence Continues.* Médecins sans Frontières, August 2005.

Mitchell, John. "Preface." In *Protection: An ALNAP Guide for Humanitarian Agencies,* Hugo Slim and Andrew Bonwick, eds. London: Overseas Development Institute, August 2005.

NATO. "Improving Capabilities to Meet New Threats." Briefing. December 2004. www.nato.int/docu/briefing/capabilities/html_en/capabilities01.

--------. *Istanbul Reader's Guide.* Brussels: North Atlantic Treaty Organization, October 2004.

--------. *NATO Glossary of Terms and Definitions.* AAP-6(V). August 2000. www.dtic.mil/doctrine/jel/other_pubs/aap_6v.pdf.

--------. *Peace Support Operations* (AJP 3.4.1). Brussels: North Atlantic Treaty Organization, 2001. www.carlisle.army.mil/usacsl/new_site/divisions/pki/Military/Doctrine&Concepts/AJP341Rat.PDF.

--------. *Peace Support Operations Techniques and Procedures* (AJP 3.4.1.1) Brussels: North Atlantic Treaty Organization, 28 May 2003.

O'Brien, LCDR William, ed. *Operational Law Handbook.* Charlottesville, Virginia: International and Operational Law Department of the Judge Advocate General's School, 2003.

O'Hanlon, Michael E. *Expanding Global Military Capacity for Humanitarian Intervention.* Washington, DC: Brookings Institution Press, 2003.

--------. *Saving Lives with Force: Military Criteria for Humanitarian Intervention.* Washington, DC: Brookings Institution Press, 1997.

O'Hanlon, Michael E. and Peter W. Singer. "The Humanitarian Transformation: Expanding Global Intervention Capacity." *Survival* 46:1 (Spring 2004).

O'Neill, William G. *A New Challenge for Peacekeepers: The Internally Displaced.* The Brookings Institution-Johns Hopkins School of Advanced International Studies Project on Internal Displacement, April 2004.

O'Neill, William G. and Violette Cassis. *Protecting Two Million Internally Displaced: The Successes and Shortcomings of the African Union in Darfur.* Occasional Paper. Washington, DC: Brookings Institution, 2005.

Oxfam International. "Protection into Practice." Oxford: Oxfam International, 2005.

--------. "Ugandan Government Must Fulfill Its Responsibility to Protect Civilians in War-torn North." Press Release. 27 October 2005.

Plumer, Bradford. "Do Something... But What?" *Mother Jones*, 4 May 2005.

Powell, Kristiana. *Opportunities and Challenges for Delivering on the Responsibility to Protect: The African Union's Emerging Peace and Security Regime.* Monograph No. 119. Ottawa: The North-South Institute, May 2005.

Power, Samantha. *A Problem from Hell: America in the Age of Genocide.* New York: Basic Books, 2002.

Refugees International. "Brazilian Troops in MINUSTAH Must Intervene to Stop Violence." Bulletin. Refugees International, 17 March 2005.

Ricci, Roberto. "Human rights challenges in the DRC: A View from MONUC's Human Rights Section." In *Challenges of Peace Implementation: The UN Mission in the Democratic Republic of the Congo.* Mark Malan and Joao Gomes Porto, eds. Pretoria: Institute for Security Studies, 2004.

Rieff, David. *At the Point of a Gun: Democratic Dreams and Armed Intervention.* New York: Simon and Schuster, 2005.

Roessler, Philip and John Prendergast. "The Democratic Republic of the Congo: The Case of the United Nations Organization Mission in the Democratic Republic of the Congo (MONUC)." In *21st Century Peace Operations.* William J. Durch, ed. Washington, DC: United States Institute of Peace, forthcoming.

Royal Netherlands Army. *Peace Operations: Army Doctrine Publication III.* Netherlands: Royal Netherlands Army, 29 June 1999.

Rynning, Steve. *Changing Military Doctrine: Presidents and Military Power in Fifth Republic France.* Westport, CT: Praeger, 2001.

Sabella, Joelle. *Operation Night Flash: Hope is Born Again in Kanyola*. United Nations Mission in the Democratic Republic of Congo (MONUC), 15 April 2005.

Samuels, Kirsti, rapporteur. *Use of Force in United Nations Peacekeeping Operations*. Report of International Peace Academy/UN Department of Peacekeeping Operations workshop. New York: International Peace Academy, 6 February 2004.

Schoenhaus, Robert M, ed. *Peaceworks 43: Training for Peace and Humanitarian Relief Operations*. Washington, DC: United States Institute of Peace, April 2002.

Security Council Report. "Update Report No. 7: Protection of Civilians in Armed Conflict." 20 April 2006. www.securitycouncilreport.org/site/c.glKWLeMTIsG/b.1563699/k.B611/Update_re port_No_7brprotection_of_civilians_in_armed_conflictbr20_April_2006.htm.

Seybolt, Taylor B. *Humanitarian Military Intervention: The Conditions for Success and Failure*. Oxford: Oxford University Press, forthcoming 2007.

Slim, Hugo. "Military Intervention to Protect Human Rights: The Humanitarian Agency Perspective." *Journal of Humanitarian Assistance*. (March 2002).

--------. "Why Protect Civilians? Innocence, Immunity and Enmity in War." *International Affairs* 79: 3 (2003): 481-501.

--------. *With or Against? Humanitarian Agencies and Coalition Counter-insurgency*. Geneva: Center for Humanitarian Dialogue, July 2004.

Slim, Hugo and Andrew Bonwick. *Protection: An ALNAP Guide for Humanitarians*. London: Overseas Development Institute, August 2005.

Smith, Joshua. "The Responsibility to Reflect: Learning Lessons from Past Humanitarian Military Interventions." *Journal of Humanitarian Assistance*. (March 2006). www.reliefweb.int/rw/lib.nsf/db900SID/AMMF-6NJFRX?OpenDocument.

Smith, Lawrence. "MONUC's Military Involvement in the Eastern Congo (Maniema and the Kivus)." In *Challenges of Peace Implementation: The UN Mission in the Democratic Republic of the Congo*. Mark Malan and Joao Gomes Porto, eds. Pretoria: Institute for Security Studies, 2004.

Solana, Javier. *A Secure Europe in a Better World: European Security Strategy*. Brussels: European Union, adopted by the Heads of State and Government, EU Council, 12 December 2003. ue.eu.int/uedocs/cmsUpload/78367.pdf.

Sow, Alpha. "Achievements of the Interim Emergency Multinational Force and Future Scenarios." In *Challenges of Peace Implementation: The UN Mission in the Democratic Republic of the Congo*. Mark Malan and Joao Gomes Porto, eds. Pretoria: Institute for Security Studies, 2004.

Sow, Ndeye, Annie Bukaraba, Vénantie Bisimwa, and Jeanne d'Arc Chakupewa. "Report on the Causes and Consequences of Sexual Violence Against Women and Girls in South Kivu, Democratic Republic of Congo." International Alert, 12 March 2004.

www.wilsoncenter.org/index.cfm?topic_id=1417&fuseaction=topics.documents&do
c_id=91796&group_id=44656.

Stedman, Stephen John. "Spoiler Problems in Peace Processes." *International Security*
22:2 (1 January 1997).

Swarbrick, Peter. "DDRRR: Political dynamics and linkages." In *Challenges of Peace
Implementation: The UN Mission in the Democratic Republic of the Congo*. Mark
Malan and Joao Gomes Porto, eds. Pretoria: Institute for Security Studies, 2004.

Swing, William Lacy. "The role of MONUC and the international community in support
of the DRC transition." In *Challenges of Peace Implementation: The UN Mission in
the Democratic Republic of the Congo*. Mark Malan and Joao Gomes Porto, eds.
Pretoria: Institute for Security Studies, 2004.

Taft, Patricia with Jason Ladiner. *Realizing 'Never Again': Regional Capacities to
Protect Civilians in Violent Conflicts*. Washington, DC: The Fund for Peace,
January 2006.

Tardy, Thierry. "French Policy Toward Peace Support Operations." *International
Peacekeeping* 6:1 (Spring 1999).

Task Force on the United Nations. *American Interests and UN Reform*. Washington, DC:
United States Institute of Peace, 2005.

Tower, Wells. "Under the God Gun: Battling a Fake Insurgency in the Army's Imitation
Iraq." *Harper's Magazine*, 1 January 2006.

Traub, James. "The Congo Case." *The New York Times Magazine*, 3 July 2005.

United Kingdom Ministry of Defence Joint Doctrine and Concepts Centre. *The Military
Contribution to Peace Support Operations*. Joint Warfare Publication 3-50.
Swindon, UK: Development Concepts and Doctrine Centre, 2004 (2nd Edition).

United Nations General Assembly. *2005 World Summit Outcome* (A/RES/60/1). 24
October 2005.

--------. *A More Secure World: Our Shared Responsibility. Report of the Secretary-
General's High-level Panel on Threats, Challenges and Change* (A/59/565). 2
December 2004.

--------. *Implementation of the recommendations of the Special Committee on
Peacekeeping. Report of the Secretary-General* (A/60/640). 29 December 2005.

--------. *In Larger Freedom: Towards Development, Security and Human Rights for All.*
Report of the Secretary-General (A/59/2005). 21 March 2005.

--------. *Report of the Secretary-General Pursuant to General Assembly Resolution 53/35:
The Fall of Srebrenica* (A/54/549). 15 November 1999.

--------. Special Committee on Peacekeeping Operations. *Report of the Special Committee on Peacekeeping Operations and its Working Group at the 2006 Substantive Session* (A/60/19). 22 March 2006.

--------. Special Committee on Peacekeeping Operations. "UN Faces Major Challenge With 'Almost Unprecedented' Surge In Creation, Expansion Of Peacekeeping Missions, Special Committee Told." Press Release. (GA/PK/180). 29 March 2004.

--------. "Special Committee on Peacekeeping Operations Concludes Current Session." Press Release. (GA/PK/189). 20 March 2006.

--------. *"We the Peoples": The Role of the United Nations in the 21st Century.* Millenium Report of the Secretary-General of the United Nations (A/54/2000). 27 March 2000.

United Nations General Assembly and Security Council. *A Comprehensive Strategy to Eliminate Future Sexual Exploitation and Abuse in United Nations Peacekeeping Operations* (A/59/710). 25 March 2005.

--------. *An Agenda for Peace: Preventative Diplomacy, Peacemaking, and Peacekeeping* (A/24/277-S/2411). 17 June 1992.

--------. *Report of the Panel on United Nations Peace Operations* (A/55/305-S/2000/809). 21 August 2000.

--------. *Supplement to An Agenda for Peace: Position Paper of the Secretary-General on the Occasion of the Fiftieth Anniversary of the United Nations* (A/50/60-S/1995/1). 25 January 1995.

United Nations. Department of Peacekeeping Operations. "Glossary of UN Peacekeeping Terms." September 1998. www.un.org/Depts/dpko/glossary/.

--------. Department of Peacekeeping Operations. *Guidelines for the Development of ROE for UNPKO, Provisional Sample ROE.* Attachment 1 to FGS/0220.001. United Nations, April 2002.

--------. Department of Peacekeeping Operations. "Non-paper: Employment of EU Battle Groups Concept in Support of UN Peacekeeping Operations." United Nations, 4 June 2004.

--------. Department of Peacekeeping Operations. "Standardized Generic Training Modules." Integrated Training Service/Military Division, DPKO. www.un.org/depts/dpko/training/sgtm/sgtm.htm.

--------. Department of Peacekeeping Operations. Integrated Training Service. "Protection of Human Rights for Military Personnel of Peace Operations." Module 3 of "Human Rights for Military Personnel of Peace Operations," STM 2-1 *United Nations Officers Common Training*, DPKO, as updated February 2006.

--------. Department of Peacekeeping Operations. Peacekeeping Best Practices Unit. *Handbook on United Nations Multidimensional Peacekeeping Operations.* United Nations, December 2003.

--------. Department of Peacekeeping Operations. Peacekeeping Best Practices Unit. *MONUC and the Bukavu Crisis 2004*. United Nations, March 2005.

--------. Department of Peacekeeping Operations. Peacekeeping Best Practices Unit. *Operation Artemis: Lessons of the Interim Emergency Multinational Force*. United Nations, October 2004.

--------. Office for the Coordination of Humanitarian Affairs. "General Guidance for Interaction between United Nations Personnel and Military and Other Representatives of the Belligerent Parties in the Context of the Crisis in Iraq." White Paper 2.0. United Nations, updated version, 9 April 2003.

--------. Office for the Coordination of Humanitarian Affairs. "Institutional History of Protection of Civilians in Armed Conflict." OCHA Online. ochaonline.un.org/webpage.asp?Page=780.

--------. Office for the Coordination of Humanitarian Affairs. "Protection of Civilians in Armed Conflict." OCHA Online. ochaonline.un.org/webpage.asp?Site=civilians.

United Nations Security Council. *Eleventh Report of the Secretary-General on the United Nations Organization Mission in the Democratic Republic of the Congo* (S/2002/621). 5 June 2002.

--------. *Fifteenth Report of the Secretary-General on MONUC* (S/2004/251). 25 March 2004.

--------. "Letter Dated 15 December 1999 From the Members of the Independent Inquiry Into the Actions of the United Nations During the 1994 Genocide in Rwanda Addressed to the Secretary-General" (S/1999/1257). 16 December 1999.

--------. *Report of the Panel of Experts on the Illegal Exploitation of Natural Resources and Other Forms of Wealth of the Democratic Republic of the Congo* (S/2001/357). 12 April 2001.

--------. *Report of the Secretary-General to the Security Council on the Protection of Civilians in Armed Conflict* (S/1999/957). 8 September 1999.

--------. *Report of the Secretary-General to the Security Council on the Protection of Civilians in Armed Conflict* (S/2001/331). 30 March 2001.

--------. *Report of the Secretary-General to the Security Council on the Protection of Civilians in Armed Conflict* (S/2004/431). 28 May 2004.

--------. *Report of the Secretary-General to the Security Council on the Protection of Civilians in Armed Conflict* (S/2005/740). 28 November 2005.

--------. *Seventh report of the Secretary-General on the United Nations Organization Mission in the Democratic Republic of the Congo* (S/2001/373). 17 April 2001.

--------. *Special Report of the Secretary-General on the United Nations Organization Mission in the Democratic Republic of the Congo* (S/2002/1005). 10 September 2002.

--------. *The Causes of Conflict and the Promotion of Durable Peace and Sustainable Development in Africa* (S/1998/318). 13 April 1998.

--------. *Third Special Report of the Secretary-General on MONUC* (S/2004/650). 16 August 2004.

--------. Resolution 713 (S/RES/713), 25 September 1991.
S/RES/757, 30 May 1992.
S/RES/787, 16 November 1992.
S/RES/816, 31 March 1993.
S/RES/836, 4 June 1993.
S/RES/918, 17 May 1994.
S/RES/1258, 6 August 1999.
S/RES/1264, 15 September 1999.
S/RES/1265, 17 September 1999.
S/RES/1270, 22 October 1999.
S/RES/1291, 24 February 2000.
S/RES/1296, 19 April 2000.
S/RES/1464, 4 February 2003.
S/RES/1484, 30 May 2003.
S/RES/1493, 28 July 2003.
S/RES/1528, 27 February 2004.
S/RES/1529, 29 February 2004.
S/RES/1542, 30 April 2004.
S/RES/1545, 21 May 2004.
S/RES/1565, 1 October 2004.
S/RES/1590, 24 March 2005.
S/RES/1592, 30 March 2005.
S/RES/1674, 28 April 2006.
S/RES/1678, 15 May 2006.

United States Department of Defense. *Universal Joint Task List: Chairman of the Joint Chiefs of Staff Manual 3500.04B*. Washington, DC: United States Department of Defense, 1 October 1999.

--------. *Department of Defense Dictionary of Military and Associated Terms*. Joint Publication 1-02, as amended through 31 August 2005. Washington DC: United States Department of Defense, 31 August 2005.

--------. "Military Support for Stability, Security, Transition, and Reconstruction (SSTR) Operations." Directive 3000.05. Washington, DC: United States Department of Defense, 28 November 2005.

--------. *Quadrennial Defense Review Report*. Washington, DC: United States Department of Defense, 6 February 2006.

--------. *The Joint Training System: A Primer for Senior Leaders*. Washington, DC: United States Department of Defense, 1998.

--------. Joint Chiefs of Staff. *Joint Tactics, Techniques, and Procedures for Foreign Internal Defense*. Joint Publication 3-07.1. Defense Technical Information Center, 30 April 2004. www.dtic.mil/doctrine/jel/new_pubs/jp3_07_1.pdf.

United States Department of the Army. *African Crisis Response Initiative Program of Instruction May 1998*. Fort Bragg: United States Department of the Army, Headquarters, 3rd Special Forces Group, 12 May 1998.

--------. *Military Police Internment/Resettlement Operations*, Field Manual No. FM 3-19.40. Washington, DC: Headquarters, Department of the Army, 1 August 2001.

--------. *Operation Restore Hope*. TF Mountain OPLAN 93-2, TC-7-98-1. US Army Stability and Support Operations Training Circular. Undated.

--------. *Stability Operations and Support Operations* (FM 3-07). Washington, DC: Headquarters, United States Department of the Army, February 2003.

--------. *Stability and Support Operations Training Support Package*. Training Circular 7-98-1. Washington, DC: Headquarters, United States Department of the Army, 5 June 1997.

United States Marine Corps. *Expeditionary Operations* (MCDP 3). Washington, DC: United States Department of the Navy, 16 April 1998.

--------. *Marine Corps Operations (MCDP 1-0)*. Washington, DC: United States Marine Corps Headquarters, United States Department of the Navy, 27 September 2001.

--------. *Small Wars Manual, 1940*. Washington, DC: US Government Printing Office, declassified 1972; Manhattan, Kansas: Sunflower University Press, 1996.

United States National Security Council. "The National Security Strategy of the United States of America, September 2002." White House, 2002. www.whitehouse.gov/nsc/nss/2002/.

--------. "The National Security Strategy of the United States of America, March 2006." White House, 2006. www.whitehouse.gov/nsc/nss/2006/.

Van Woudenberg, Anneke. "Ethnically targeted violence in Ituri." In *Challenges of Peace Implementation: The UN Mission in the Democratic Republic of the Congo*. Mark Malan and Joao Gomes Porto, eds. Pretoria: Institute for Security Studies, 2004.

Von Flue, Carlo and Jacques de Maio. *Third Workshop on Protection for Human Rights and Humanitarian Organizations: A Report of the Workshop Held at the International Committee of the Red Cross*, 18-20 January 1999. Geneva: International Committee of the Red Cross, 1999.

Waldman, Ronald. "Public Health in War: Pursuing the Impossible." *Harvard International Review* 27:1 (Spring 2005).

Wallenstein, Peter and Patrik Johansson. "Security Council Decisions in Perspective." In *The UN Security Council: From the Cold War to the 21st Century*. David M. Malone, ed. Boulder: Lynn Reinner, 2004.

Walzer, Michael. "The Argument About Humanitarian Intervention." *Dissent* (Winter 2002).

Weiss, Thomas G. "The Humanitarian Impulse." In *The UN Security Council: From the Cold War to the 21st Century*. David M. Malone, ed. Boulder: Lynn Reinner, 2004.

--------. "The Sunset of Humanitarian Intervention? The Responsibility to Protect in a Unipolar Era." *Security Dialogue* 35:2 (June 2004).

Weiss, Thomas G. and Don Hubert. *The Responsibility to Protect: Research, Bibliography, and Background*. Supplementary Volume to the Report of the International Commission on Intervention and State Sovereignty. Ottawa: International Development Research Centre, December 2001.

Welsh, Jennifer M. *Humanitarian Intervention and International Relations*. Oxford: Oxford University Press, 2004.

Western European Union Council of Ministers. *Petersburg Declaration.* Bonn: Western European Union Council of Ministers, 1992.

Wheeler, Nicholas J. *Saving Strangers: Humanitarian Intervention in International Society*. New York: Oxford University Press, 2000.

Wheeler, Victoria and Adele Harmer, eds. *Resetting the Rules of Engagement: Trends and Issues in Military-Humanitarian Relations*. HPG Report 21. London: Humanitarian Policy Group, Overseas Development Institute, March 2006.

Williams, Paul D. "Military Response to Mass Killing: The African Union Mission in Sudan." *International Peacekeeping* 13:2 (June 2006).

Williamson, Roger. "*Protection of Civilians: Bridging the Protection Gap*." Report on Wilton Park Conference 766. West Sussex, United Kingdom: Wilton Park, 2005.

World Federalist Movement of Canada Peace Operations Working Group and Canadian Peacebuilding Coordinating Committee. *The Responsibility to Protect and Canada's Defence Effort*. Report from NGO-Government Roundtable. Ottawa: World Federalist Movement of Canada, 22 September 2003. www.worldfederalistscanada.org/R2Ppapers.htm.

Zenko, Micah. "Saving Lives with Speed: Using Rapidly Deployable Forces for Genocide Prevention." *Defense and Security Analysis* 20:1 (March 2004).

ABOUT THE AUTHORS

Victoria K. Holt is a Senior Associate at the Henry L. Stimson Center, where she co-directs the *Future of Peace Operations* program. She has written on a range of issues, including the protection of civilians, UN peacekeeping and reforms, US policies, regional capacities in Africa for peace operations, and tools for international rule of law. Victoria Holt joined the Center in 2001, bringing policy and political expertise from her professional experience within the State Department, Congress, and the NGO field. She served as Senior Policy Advisor at the State Department (Legislative Affairs), focusing on peacekeeping and UN issues. Earlier she directed a bipartisan coalition of leading statesmen and non-governmental organizations on US policy toward the United Nations, and worked on Capitol Hill as a senior Congressional staffer for seven years, focusing on defense and foreign policy issues. She has held positions with other Washington-based policy institutes on international affairs. A graduate of the Naval War College, Holt also holds a BA with honors from Wesleyan University. Holt is a board member of Women in International Security (WIIS).

Tobias C. Berkman is a Zuckerman Fellow and joint degree candidate in law and public policy at Harvard Law School and the Kennedy School of Government. He is focusing his studies on international human rights, conflict resolution, public international law, and post-conflict rule of law. Toby Berkman was a Research Associate and Herbert Scoville, Jr. Peace Fellow in the *Future of Peace Operations* program at The Henry L. Stimson Center from January 2004 to June 2006. His experiences abroad include teaching in Casablanca, Morocco, and working for coexistence among Palestinians and Israelis at *Seeds of Peace* in Jerusalem.